Kate Figes is the author of *Because of Her Sex – The Myth of Equality for Woman in Britain* (1994); *The Terrible Teens – What Every Parent Needs to Know* (2002); and *The Big Fat Bitch Book* (2007). She has also written two novels, *What About Me?* and *What About Me, Too?* She is an established journalist and Books Editor for *You* magazine.

LIFE AFTER BIRTH

Kate Figes

virago

VIRAGO

First published in Great Britain in 1998 by Viking
First published in paperback in 2000 by Penguin Books
This revised and updated edition published in 2008 by Virago Press

Copyright © Kate Figes 1998, 2008

The moral right of the author has been asserted.

A CIP catalogue record for this book is
available from the British Library.

Grateful acknowledgement is made to Faber and Faber Ltd
for permission to quote from 'Morning Song', from
Sylvia Plath's *Collected Poems*.

ISBN 978-1-84408-466-1

Typeset in Garamond by M Rules
Printed and bound in Great Britain by
Clays Ltd, St Ives plc

Virago Press
An imprint of
Little, Brown Book Group
100 Victoria Embankment
London EC4Y 0DY

An Hachette Livre UK Company
www.hachettelivre.co.uk

www.virago.co.uk

Contents

Preface

When *Life After Birth* was first published in the spring of 1998, it received glowing reviews and provoked discussion throughout the media. The book was passed around covertly at antenatal groups, and countless women have told me how helpful they found it when they had their first child.

I spent the best part of three years on a quest. I read my way through the literature in the Royal College of Midwives library (the Royal College of Obstetricians and Gynaecologists wouldn't let me in as I wasn't a doctor) and interviewed over a hundred new mothers in order to navigate the radical physical, emotional, psychological and social changes of new motherhood. Essentially, I wanted to write a book that would tell me what had happened to me as a woman when I became a mother, because nothing like that existed in the bookshops. There were dozens of handbooks on pregnancy and childbirth and even more books on childcare and child development. But the literature seemed to hurdle over the mother as if she didn't exist or wasn't crucial to bringing up a happy, healthy child. Do not be fooled by the absence of line drawings and bullet points: *Life After Birth* is essentially a handbook, a hybrid handbook as one journalist put it, full of all the factual and anecdotal evidence a new mother needs to realize that she is entirely normal. For there is a period of upheaval and transition after the birth of a baby and we are not bad mothers when we find that period hard.

It has been such a pleasure and a privilege to have been given the opportunity to update and revise this book. Even though it was originally published ten years ago, its message is as relevant and topical as ever. The turmoil of new motherhood is increasingly talked about and I am proud of the part I have played in triggering the debate. But what also struck me as I re-read this book several times was how little has actually changed in a decade. The small amount of research that has been conducted into the health and wellbeing of mothers does not indicate much of an improvement. Statutory maternity and paternity leave and benefits are much better than they were ten years ago, but that's just about it. Conditions in labour wards have deteriorated, exacerbating postnatal health problems. Women want to feel safe when they give birth and most still choose to go to hospital, but many wards are dirty and the first case of a baby contracting MRSA was announced earlier this year.

The birth rate has risen rapidly but we haven't seen an accompanying growth of resources and we have a chronic midwife shortage. An edition of *Panorama* screened in May 2007 sent an undercover reporter into two hospitals. She found resources severely overstretched, with a lack of equipment such as ultrasound monitors and too few midwives left in charge of dozens of labouring women without enough support staff. The health of women and their babies was at risk because of delays in diagnoses and thoroughly negligent postnatal care. 'You can kill a baby and push it under the carpet,' commented one midwife. But it is going to take a sharp rise in maternal deaths before the government backs its pledge, made in 2004, to give every woman in labour a dedicated midwife 100 per cent of the time.

The experience of childbirth profoundly effects the first precious weeks and months of motherhood and the welfare of babies. The National Patient Safety Agency examined 60,000 maternity ward errors between November 2003 and June 2006 and found that nearly 18,000 labouring women had been injured unnecessarily; a thousand of these injuries were serious. Bad experiences of childbirth can trigger postnatal depression, lasting perineal pain, urinary and faecal incontinence, disillusionment and unhappiness. With greater investment and support so many more of these experiences could be less traumatic and painful, and therefore happier. The Caesarean rate has risen rapidly too in the past ten years, with consequent health problems. Some women now voluntarily opt for Caesareans, which was unheard of when I first began work on this book, and we have growing numbers of older women giving birth for the first time. But Caesarean rates have also risen because there is a lack of support for and supervision of junior doctors on the wards; they lack expertise to interpret electronic foetal monitoring and they fear litigation.

When it comes to work-life balance little has changed in ten years. While the fact that many mothers want and need to continue working may be more accepted and talked about, practical support for this principle is thin on the ground. Few families can manage now without both parents earning a living. But it is mothers who still bear the brunt of that stress, not fathers. It is mothers who usually pay for childcare – when they can find it – and mothers who take primary responsibility for their children's welfare, not fathers. Most would not want to have it any other way. They love being mothers to their children. But their expectations are still shaped by stereotypical notions of how 'good' mothers ought to behave and they strive to be perfect in both roles, which in turn takes its toll on their sense of self and well-being.

Adequate preparation helps to ensure smoother adjustment to any major life change. No book can completely prepare you for motherhood. And each of us hopes to be exemplary as a mother. Some have better times in those first few months and years than others, but every woman will identify with some aspect of this book. Motherhood is a magnificent rollercoaster of emotional highs and lows. It changes the way we think and feel about life, love, family and friends. It changes our priorities radically and permanently. This book puts new mothers centre stage and talks openly about those high and lows. Read it, realize that you're doing much better as a new mother than you thought, and then pass it on to another woman who is doing a good job of pretending she can cope.

Kate Figes

2008

Acknowledgements

It is customary for authors to thank their family last in their list of acknowledgements. However, in this case, my husband Christoph and my daughters Eleanor and Grace must come first. They deserve thanks for living with me during the writing, but, more important, they have inspired it. This book is dedicated to them as a small and inadequate way of saying, 'Thank you, for everything.'

Thanks go to the librarians at the Royal College of Midwives, Susan Bewley, Director of Obstetrics at St Thomas's Hospital, and Christine MacArthur at the Department of Public Health and Epidemiology at the University of Birmingham for help with medical background. Cassia Kidron and Clair Goodwin helped me with interviewing and I am deeply grateful to them both. Thanks, too, to all of the hundreds of women who were interviewed for this book for being so honest and generous with their time. I have changed their names in order to protect their anonymity.

Sarah Lutyens and Felicity Rubinstein have been guardian angels as agents as well as good friends throughout. Fanny Blake's brilliant editing has made this a much, much better book than it once was, and thanks go to Penguin for publishing this book in its original form and to Lennie Goodings and Virago for publishing this updated edition.

Lastly, two dear friends deserve special thanks for years of conversations about motherhood, work, creativity and writing. Helen Simpson and Beeban Kidron – thank you both for your encouragement, and for being such good friends. You have both inspired me more than you will ever know.

1

Childbirth: Just the Beginning

Now that my children are older and I have grown used to being their mother, I can honestly say that motherhood is the best thing that has ever happened to me. I now live for and through my children. I stand humbled daily by the way I have to put their needs first, and marvel at their growth. I find it hard to believe that two such vibrant, different individuals were once tiny foetuses inside me. I always loved children, but I never realized how much more I would love my own. Now, other children never quite seem as special as mine. I can see only their faces in a crowded room, and I love them so much that it hurts. They have added so much to life that it would now seem pointless and incomplete without them. They have changed me, brought out the best and the worst in me, altered my priorities and destroyed my emotional defences. Now that I am used to the changes that motherhood brings, I love the rich turmoil of daily life unconditionally and relish the way that my children will continue to force my life to change. But it wasn't always that way.

There were weeks and months after childbirth which were riddled with confusion, exhaustion and unhappiness. When my first child was born, I was unprepared for the great landslide of physical, sensory, emotional and psychological upheaval that motherhood brings and I had never seen, let alone held or looked after a newborn baby before. Antenatal classes, handbooks, friends and family focused on the birth, but no one mentioned the aftermath other than in the vaguest terms. I considered childbirth to be the grand finale and the greatest hurdle to the physical process of reproduction, after which life would quickly settle back to normal. I didn't realize that the birth of a child brings with it a whole new definition of normal.

I was convinced during my first pregnancy that I would carry on working, thinking, feeling and behaving socially as I had always done; and then I felt incompetent and inadequate as a mother and as a woman when I couldn't because of my new child. Childbirth is just the beginning of a process and not the end. The birth of a child can provoke profound change in a woman. Life turns upside down for a while and every mother enters a period of transition with a new child when she has to get used to life as it is now. Some women adjust in a matter of weeks, others take far longer, but no woman can adjust overnight to every aspect and new demand of motherhood. But I didn't know this. This book is about how women make that transition from childlessness to motherhood. This is the book that I so badly needed to read in the weeks and months after I gave birth to my first child.

My closest friends were still childless and therefore unable to understand my predicament. New acquaintances with babies roughly the same age were too competitive and guarded to confide in. My family had brought up their children in a different era, with different pressures, and in any case now lived too far away to be able to help in any constructive way. And the books I read at that time were of little use. They were either inadequate, impersonal or patronizing. They spoke in glowing terms about the joys of motherhood without touching on the darker, more frightening areas – the shock of childbirth and sudden responsibility for a helpless child; the rush of undiluted emotions of love, anxiety, fear, resentment and sometimes hate; the way that relationships with friends, family and the father of the child can change so quickly and so radically; the way that the exhaustion of new motherhood rocks you to the core. They didn't answer the questions that I had about managing *me* and *my life* rather than baby care. They seemed to me to be discussing the most important thing that had ever happened to me in the style of a do-it-yourself manual.

We talk more openly now about pregnancy and the fact that childbirth hurts, but few talk of the aftermath. It is almost as if there is a conspiracy of silence surrounding the transition to motherhood. Friends who are a stage further along the road of parenthood with small children are reluctant to mention it in case it should put you off, and those with older children forget what it was like to live through the fog of those early weeks and months.

Silence about the whirlwind of change inherent to new motherhood seems unnecessarily cautious. Research shows that people cope better with stressful events when they feel adequately informed and supported. I hope that this book will fill in some of the gaps left by existing literature. I needed to know that I was not alone in finding aspects of motherhood hard, that my problems were normal and that in time I would find more fulfilment from my children than I had ever dreamed possible. I have interviewed more than a hundred women from different social backgrounds and described some of my own personal experiences to show just how common it is for new mothers to face a period of upheaval. I have drawn on historical material to show how the experience of motherhood has changed, for many of the problems of adjustment that women experience today are influenced by modern pressures. And while not a medic, I have trawled existing medical literature and research wherever possible in order to give the intelligent, educated, modern mother as much information as possible so that she might be better able to make informed decisions about her own health and welfare.

Motherhood is a great leveller. The most privileged mother has far more in common with a socially and financially deprived mother than with a childless woman from the same social background. As I searched for differences amongst mothers I became acutely aware of the fact that the experiences of mothers felt uncannily similar. Money, education and expectations inevitably affect the way that women manage motherhood, but the essence of the experience is essentially the same. The experience of childbirth differs from woman to woman depending on her physical make-up, her state of mind, the position and size of the baby, and the environment she gives birth in, but the physical rite of passage of giving birth is the same for every woman. It is an extraordinarily powerful event which can be enjoyable or nightmarish, but either way it is a landmark memory.

Every new mother shares a sense of wonder at the miracle of procreation as she stares down at the wriggling limbs of her newborn, the tiny fingers clasped around her own giant thumb. Every new mother cannot help but wonder whether she is up to the task of raising it. She may not love it yet, for love grows as the shock and physical distress of childbirth fades and as confidence in her ability to care for her baby grows. But as that love grows, it is greater than anything a woman has ever known before. Every mother I interviewed expressed amazement at the intensity of her emotions, 'aware of the horror and beauty of my mortality while I shiver at *theirs*'.[1]

Every working mother from whatever background finds it difficult to marry the conflicting demands of work and motherhood. Money makes it easier to buy high-quality childcare that women feel more able to trust, but that does not eliminate the guilt that many mothers feel about leaving their children to go to work, even when they love their job.

The mind and body of a woman take a battering through pregnancy and childbirth and it takes time to recover, time that few women these days feel that they can legitimately allow themselves. Large numbers of women suffer from lingering physical problems such as backache, incontinence and exhaustion. Better living standards do, however, aid recovery, while damp, over-crowded housing, poor diet and poverty inevitably exacerbate the symptoms of ill health after childbirth.

All new mothers get tired because of the physical drain of pregnancy and childbirth, broken sleep and the demands of a new baby. But women whose health is also being undermined by poverty find it even harder to recover their equilibrium or buy time away from their baby to rest.

All new mothers find that their adult relationships change, often in ways which are impossible to predict – relationships with friends and family, but particularly with the father of their baby. Men change as well when they become fathers and they too enter a transition period. With both partners affected by their new responsibilities, it takes time for them to arrive at a new equilibrium. This is not a book about fatherhood, but a book for men to read in order to understand what happens to women and their relationships when they become mothers. Men can grow to love their children just as passionately as women, and they share the same concerns for their children's welfare. But they do not live through the same physical and psychological changes – they carry on living and working in the world in much the same way as they have always done, while women suddenly have cultural expectations of motherhood to live up to. 'For women, conflicts concerning motherhood, often expressed as the tensions between independence and dependence, between self-assertion and self-abnegation and between love and hate, can be a central reason for seeking therapy,' writes Rozsika Parker in *Torn in Two*. 'I do not think the same is yet true for men in relation to father-hood.'[2]

In spite of all of the above, or perhaps because of it, women find new reserves of strength and tenacity as mothers which they never knew they had. Mortality levels during pregnancy and the year after birth are between four and five times lower than mortality in women without a recent pregnancy.[3] When women become mothers their priorities shift radically. This book attempts to describe these radical changes so that new mothers might feel reassured and less alone as they grapple with the revolutionary uncertainties triggered by childbirth. For practical reasons I have divided the book into chapters by subject, but in many ways such divisions are false because the subjects dealt with overlap and are inextricably linked. Thus, health problems after childbirth may be exacerbated or even triggered by the psychological upheaval of early motherhood. The flood of new emotions after childbirth can make it harder to return to work or to focus even the slightest emotional attention on one's partner, and of course it is deeply draining to feel such extremes of emotion daily. The tiredness that comes from sleepless nights and breastfeeding on top of the phenomenal creative energy required to manufacture another human being and then push them out into the world affects everything – our health and ability to recover physically; our state of mind; our ability to work; our relationships and sex drive; our social life. But as time passes and the child's demands change, the problems women face in adapting to motherhood fade and are forgotten as they give way to others. Joy in the child takes over and life becomes indescribably rich and worthwhile.

'The change' is a term which is regularly used to describe the end of a woman's reproductive life during the menopause, but it is having a baby which changes a woman's way of life more than anything else. The birth of a child forces sudden and irrevocable physical, psychological and emotional changes on a woman. 'Motherhood changes you because it literally alters a woman's *brain* – structurally, functionally and in many ways irreversibly,' writes Louann Brizendine in her book *The Female Brain*.[4] Babies change the nature of our relationships to relatives, friends and lovers, and they can change our attitudes and priorities in very profound ways. You cross a one-way bridge when you have your first child. You can look back to where you have been, but you can never go back there. This book describes the voyage across that bridge from pregnancy, labour and those early months and years until some sort of resolution is reached – acceptance with few regrets of life as it now is as a mother.

2

Health After Birth

With the benefit of hindsight, I am staggered by my own naivety about the timescale of recovery from pregnancy and labour. I assumed that after birth, my body would quickly revert to what it had once been. I didn't realize that pregnancy and childbirth place immense strain on a great deal more than just the abdomen and genitals. A woman's entire physiology and metabolism is altered radically by the process of reproduction. I had my beautiful baby, but I little realized how difficult it would be even to walk in the days after giving birth. Months after labour I still had next to no energy. When so many other new mothers appeared to be able to leap about, with stomachs as flat as a pancake, I was obviously to blame and inadequate. Now that I have interviewed other women and read the medical research, I know that there were very good reasons for my innocence and that I was typical and not abnormal.

We hope, even expect, to feel great immediately after birth and to be able to squeeze straight back into our jeans, but actually most of us feel as if we have just been run over by a bus. And that stomach just keeps on hanging around. 'Oh, but my stomach, she is like a waterbed covered with flannel now,' writes Anne Lamott in her journal of the first year of motherhood, *Operating Instructions.*[1] 'When I lie on my side in bed, my stomach lies politely like a puppy.'

Caitlin is twenty-nine and worked as a teacher before she had her first child three years ago. She had her second child just eighteen months later, felt physically fine during both her pregnancies and found labour less difficult than she imagined it would be. 'Although that's easy for me to say now that it's over, but I did think that all of my inside bits would go back to normal quite quickly and they didn't. I couldn't run and I'm still not as physically fit as I was before I was pregnant. I definitely feel older somehow.' Jill at thirty-seven has a five-month-old son and has just gone back to work as a nurse in Manchester. 'I haven't got my shape back and I don't feel physically recovered yet. Walking to the bus stop two weeks after he was born felt like walking a hundred miles. I was completely shattered. I was trying to run before I could walk, not realizing how much I'd been knocked sideways. My strength's still not as good as it was.'

We expect to be able to bounce back quickly from childbirth because the modern emphasis on the naturalness and the healthiness of pregnancy and childbirth disregards the physical toll on the body. Pregnancy places every cell and every organ of the body under great strain. The lungs and heart increase in size to cope with the extra blood flow and ventilation. Huge quantities of hormones flood through the body, hijacking nutrients so that the foetus can feed and grow. Iron stores are depleted and between 100 and 150 mg of calcium per kilogram of foetal body weight must be transferred from the mother to the foetus every day.[2] This severely drains the mother's calcium stores and if the consequent lack cannot be met from her diet, then it is mobilized from her bones. There is as yet no medical evidence for the old saying that women 'lose a tooth for every child', but women are more likely to need fillings during the latter half of pregnancy and it can take several months for a woman's bones and ligaments to regain their pre-pregnancy strength.

Pregnancy is natural, and pregnant women are not technically ill, but it is capable of exacerbating existing or setting off latent conditions such as herpes or food allergies. Pregnancy has been known to trigger more serious conditions such as ME and multiple sclerosis in previously healthy women. Many new mothers find that they have lingering symptoms undermining their health, and have lowered resistance to infection in the months after childbirth. Susan Bewley, Director of Obstetrics at St Thomas's Hospital in London, compares having a baby to running a marathon or climbing a mountain. 'If you do these things, those who are more unhealthy may end up having a heart attack, or very exhausted, even though they are exhilarated because of their achievement. It's completely natural to go for a run, but things can go wrong if you do.'

Great improvements in medical knowledge and practice, together with confidence in the fact that in developed countries it is rare for women not to survive childbirth, all contribute to the diminishing of the damaging consequences of pregnancy and childbirth. In the past, childbirth often either killed women or left them with lasting health problems which were far worse than anything that we in the modern Western industrialized countries suffer today as a result of labour. In general, women were far less healthy because of poor diet, exposure to crippling diseases, hard physical labour and the toll of repeated pregnancies. Rickets distorted the spines and pelvises of many women, making natural delivery of a healthy child impossible. A woman might die through prolonged labour; if she encountered difficulties, the child had to be killed and dismembered in the womb, inflicting lasting damage on the mother. If women tried to abort an unwanted child through abortifacients, knitting needles or back-street surgery they risked death or long-term health damage. If women survived week-long, complicated and brutal deliveries, the chances that their health would never be the same again were high indeed. 'It has been calculated by competent authorities that 75 per cent of the diseases peculiar to women owe their origin to impregnation,' wrote C. Berkeley in

1929 in a report on maternal morbidity.[3] In 1931, W. Blair Bell, the first president of the British College of Obstetricians and Gynaecologists, estimated that roughly 10 per cent of all mothers in England and Wales were 'more or less crippled as the result of childbearing', and studies during the 1930s found that up to 70 per cent of all new mothers had lesions from childbirth and that for 35–40 per cent of these women the lesions were disabling.[4]

If women were lucky enough to survive childbed fever contracted through the open wounds left by labour, the infection left lifelong health problems. 'It is the rare exception to examine a multiparous female pelvis without finding some traces of a previous cellulitis or peritonitis,' commented a gynaecological textbook of the 1880s. These traces were likely to have been abscesses, adhesions or persistent tubal infections which may well have damaged other internal organs as well as producing buckets of pus. For working-class women, half-starved through poverty and living in damp, overcrowded slum dwellings where diseases such as TB, scarlet fever, diphtheria and pneumonia spread quickly, life was a daily struggle to keep a family healthy as well as fed, clean and warm. The life expectancy of a working-class woman aged twenty in 1900 was forty-six, and she could expect to spend roughly a third of that time either pregnant or nursing infants.[5]

The sheer toll of such fecundity is revealed in *Maternity*, a collection of letters from working-class women at the turn of the century.

I have had nine children. I was two years between my first three babies. I suffered least from these three . . . my last two confinements I was not able to come downstairs for about three or four months – no strength to walk, no appetite, and with being so much torn had then to come downstairs for a long time on my hips (slide down, as it were). When able to get about, could scarcely walk owing to my condition.

My little girl was born, strong and healthy, although for nine months I was unable to walk or do my housework . . . I never recovered my usual health, as I could not afford to rest after my confinement, as I had to work to help pay the debt incurred through my long illness.[6]

Margery Spring Rice's' study, *Working Class Wives*, which surveyed 1,250 women in the 1930s, also reveals high levels of ill health after childbirth.[7] Working men during the 1930s had access to free medical treatment under the National Insurance Acts, but, until the establishment of the National Health Service in 1948, women did not unless they were pregnant or had recently given birth.[8] Unsurprisingly, working-class mothers were reluctant to run up doctors' bills, instead putting up with physical disabilities that would today be considered unacceptable. One 38-year-old woman in Cardiff with eight children said that she felt fit, but also admitted to decayed teeth, bronchitis every winter, and a prolapsed uterus since her second pregnancy; she had sought no treatment. 'Another in Battersea,' writes Margery Spring Rice, 'says she feels pretty well, but suffers from "internal trouble" which has lasted from the birth of her first child who is ten years old: she is thirty-one and has had four children. She has "severe pains in the inside", but has not consulted anyone and takes no remedy. Such cases can be multiplied by the dozen.'[9]

Her survey found many women suffering from anaemia, headaches, constipation, rheumatism, gynaecological problems, toothache, varicose veins, ulcerated legs, asthma, bronchitis, kidney and bladder trouble, and gallstones. Those few women who had sought medical treatment soon gave it up when repeated visits to the doctor cranked up the expense. Poor living conditions in damp, dark, bug-ridden basements or in overcrowded tenements with a daily domestic workload that few of us now could tolerate exacerbated their symptoms, while rest was out of the question unless they literally couldn't get out of bed.

Medical progress has substantially altered our attitude to childbirth, illness and death. Women used to fear giving birth because of the high chance of death or serious injury. Childbirth was a leading cause of death, second to TB for women of child-bearing age until the early part of this century. 'Risks of this magnitude create a collective sense of fearfulness.'[10] Women were likely to have either known or known of someone who had died in childbirth; health problems after childbirth were just something to put up with. Now we expect childbirth to be safe, we aspire to natural childbirth without medical intervention and feel hard done by if we have had so much as an episiotomy. The notion of what is normal in childbirth has shifted dramatically. 'The modern portrayal of birth is that everyone who goes into pregnancy will come out unscathed,' says Christina McKenzie, Director of Midwifery at St Thomas's Hospital in London. 'The media and health-care professionals are a lot to blame. Women expect to come out the same as they went in and we can't match their expectations.'

When so many women died or suffered greatly through childbirth, medical and midwifery attention was inevitably focused on the welfare of the mother more than that of the child. Such an attitude extended up to the Second World War, when maternal mortality at last began to drop, and is well illustrated by an anecdote from Professor James Waller of Dundee at the end of the 1930s. 'I remember delivering a woman of a baby in the middle of the night and getting a baby with a broken collar bone, a breech. And the next morning my chief said to me, "I hear you did a breech in the middle of the night. How is the mother?" I said, "She's fine." Two hours later he said, "Oh, by the way, how did the baby do in that case?"'[11]

Now that women rarely die in childbirth and our babies are so precious and chosen rather than a whim of God, it is hard to imagine doctors being quite so casual. For, as maternal mortality dropped, medical attention shifted from the mother to the baby, striving to improve aspects of antenatal and neonatal care to produce healthier, more perfect babies. There was great concern at the beginning of this century in Britain that we might be committing national suicide because of the high levels of infant mortality, and mothers quickly became the focus of attention as the funnel for rectifying this and raising the quality of infant care. Infant welfare centres and health visitors were established all over the country and legislation was introduced to protect the health and welfare of children. Once, very sickly or disabled babies were taken away by midwives and doctors to die. Now they are rushed into Special Care Baby Units for resuscitation and every conceivable care.

The shift from mother to baby was so swift that maternal health and welfare were overlooked. 'Overall issues have been improved, but the emphasis has been more on perinatal outcome rather than maternal,' according to Clive Spence Jones, Consultant Obstetrician at the Whittington Hospital in London. 'The other thing is that there is still so much maternal death in the world. In some African countries one in every forty women dies, so when you compare women's welfare in the West with that of women globally there is still this attitude of "Well, what do you expect when you have a baby?" However, I do think that maternal health has been largely overlooked.'

Few research papers have focused on the health and welfare of the mother after childbirth since the Second World War, and the evidence available is largely anecdotal. One large survey of new mothers, conducted in Britain in 1987, found that 47 per cent had at least one health problem, such as backache, frequent headaches and migraine or bladder problems six weeks after childbirth, and that at least two-thirds of these women still had health problems at the time of questioning for the survey, thirteen months to nine years after giving birth.[12] A study of all women who gave birth in 1998 in the South East Thames region confirms these findings. Six to twelve months after delivery many women were still experiencing symptoms. Obstetric intervention exacerbated health problems but even in normal births women complained of health problems.[13] Yet, officially, women are discharged at their six-week postnatal check-up and are not asked specific questions in relation to their health. Their haemo-globin levels are not always checked, even though it can take months for an anaemic woman to recover her former strength.

'Women don't complain and the focus is always on the baby,' says Christine MacArthur, author of the research quoted above.

> There's this huge change in your life, yet many women feel guilty about even thinking about themselves. The health visitor tends to focus on the baby and I think mothers are often quite loath to say how they really are. They feel that they should be talking about the baby and not about themselves. Tiredness must also affect a mother's motivation to go to the doctor and report backache or haemorrhoids. You just haven't got the energy to go and by the time you have, you've had whatever it is for ages and you've talked to your friend and realized that she's got it as well. Then you think it's normal so you don't go at all. And then when I talk to GPs they say that they knew that women suffered ill health after childbirth but that they had no idea how frequently until we conducted our survey because women never reported it.

A woman at the pinnacle of physical fitness, with no concerns about coping with ordinary domestic life or work, or the emotional demands of other members of her family, who has had an easy labour without any form of obstetric intervention or perineal tear, and who enjoys a great deal of support at home as well as three nourishing meals a day cooked by somebody else, may well feel fit again at the six-week cut-off point which doctors define as the end of the puerperium, or recovery period. But for most of the rest of us, the six-week postnatal check is mere routine and we struggle on feeling under par and tired just as we did before. The most important requirements of recuperation, such as rest, sleep, silence and solitude, are usually denied to us and furthermore we have additional concerns about caring for our newborn baby to hamper recovery.

Daily visits from the midwife last for just ten days after giving birth. Society now expects women to recover quickly from pregnancy and childbirth. A new mother is considered to be not ill, but 'a healthy, intelligent individual who has just achieved a memorable event' according to *Fundamentals of Obstetrics and Gynaecology*, the definitive, modern medical textbook.'[14] She is encouraged to get up and move around as soon as possible in order to prevent blood clots and she is left by midwives, family and friends to care for her baby alone even though she may feel physically and emotionally shaken by the experience of childbirth.

In the past, new mothers were considered to be ill. In seventeenth- and eighteenth-century England, women had to 'lie in' in the room that they had given birth in for up to three weeks afterwards without daylight or fresh air, in order to recover while the 'gossips' (local women) took care of the household chores. New mothers were considered to be in an altered spiritual and social state, needing to be sealed from the outside world to prevent infection from evil spirits. After three weeks they could receive visitors and breathe fresh air, but they were still considered to be in social and physical transition and therefore not allowed out of the house. Gradually from the mid-eighteenth century onwards, the 'lying-in' time reduced with upper-middle-class women spending seven to fourteen days in bed while working-class women had to get up much sooner. People believed in the principle of bed-rest for new mothers even if many were unable to adhere to it.

Midwives were not engaged in the factory-like hospital production of childbirth as they are today, where few have the time to show mothers how to bath a baby or help them overcome difficulties in breastfeeding. They were once able to offer a much more personal and extensive range of services to the new mother. In the early nineteenth century in the village of Oppin, for example, the local midwife had 'in addition to delivering the mother, to stay up all night with her until the infant was baptized, to wash out the diapers and swaddling clothes, to invite the guests to the baptismal feast, and to change the infant daily, until the mother's churching, at least three weeks'.[15] The only way that new mothers can obtain any of these services these days is by engaging a maternity nurse at great expense.

We have few traditions and rituals these days, other than the sending of flowers and cards, to mark the arrival of a baby and honour new mothers with respect or respite from daily chores and burdens. Far too many Third World women still die in childbirth and many of those who survive have long-lasting health problems similar to those experienced by European women in the past due to difficult labours, poor obstetric intervention and the effects of poverty. But they do still consider the puerperium as a time of cleansing, rest and recuperation, with specific rituals governing the weeks after childbirth, while we feel inadequate if we are not up and about smiling cheerfully within days.

Women in Malay villages are allowed forty days before a ritual rejoining of mother and baby to the community. During these weeks she is given hot baths infused with 'hot' and fragrant leaves because it is believed necessary to add heat to restore health and balance to a new mother. A paste of ginger, garlic, tamarind and lime is rubbed into her abdomen to help the uterus to shrink, after which a long sash is wound tightly around her waist. She is then massaged from head to toe and her breasts are massaged to encourage the milk to flow.[16] New mothers in the mountains of Ecuador are secluded for up to forty days, during which time they are fed special nourishing food cooked by the other women in the family.[17] New mothers of the Ibo people in south-eastern Nigeria are cleaned with very hot water at least three times a day, from day four after delivery. A new mother sleeps with her baby by a fire made specially for her and does no domestic work for at least twenty-eight days. From the 1960s onwards, when Ibo women began to have their babies in hospital, their husbands would accompany them, but as soon as they returned home, the women of the family would take up postnatal care as they had always done.[18]

Modern China is extremely dictatorial over women and their fertility, allowing them only one child each and forcing abortion on a woman if she gets pregnant a second time. But the traditional practice of 'doing the month' lives on in both countryside and city with only slight modifications. Like many other cultures, traditional Chinese medicine maintains that a woman's 'hotness', her Yang, has been depleted by the growing foetus and must be restored by following specific rules during the month of recuperation. If she ignores these rules, it is believed that she will suffer long-term health problems such as asthma, arthritis and general aches and pains. She must eat nourishing foods such as chicken soup and the livers and kidneys of other animals in order to strengthen her own liver and kidneys. Ideally she should eat five or six times a day and consume plenty of foods that will help flush out the dirty blood, such as fermented rice with egg and infusions of ginger and rice wine. She should eat foods that will help her milk production, and sweet foods to reduce her desire for salt, because it is believed that too much salt at this time will cause future aches, particularly in the lower back, as well as kidney ailments.

New mothers are thought to need to spend as much time as possible in bed during 'the month' in order to straighten the spine from the curves and strains of pregnancy, while too much walking will encourage the stomach to sag. A new mother's joints are still open from childbirth and therefore she should avoid exposure to any outside wind or breeze to prevent rheumatism in the future. Other rituals of 'doing the month', such as avoiding reading, crying or washing, are harder for the modern Chinese woman to adhere to but have been modified individually in such a way that women feel they are conforming to traditional as well as modern principles of Chinese health.[19]

It has to be said that many of the ritual taboos surrounding the segregation of a new mother stem from a deep male fear of the female anatomy and horror of contagion as well as from the recognition that a new mother needs special care and protection.

Laws governing the ritual purification of women following childbirth in Judaism, Islam and Catholicism state that a man must not come into contact with her cooking, or her bodily fluids in case her magical powers should debilitate him.[20] But whether or not these rituals work or why they came into being is perhaps less important than the fact that they give new mothers a feeling of being pampered and cared for at an acutely vulnerable time, which inevitably enhances recovery. She is not left feeling weak, alone and inadequate with her brand-new baby. And such rituals publicly acknowledge that pregnancy and labour are profound drains on the physiology of a woman and that she needs time to recover well.

Western medicine and childbirth experts define a newly delivered mother as healthy even though her physical and mental state can be greatly out of sorts. Chinese medical theory defines anybody as ill when the vital forces of Yin and Yang are out of balance. Pregnancy and childbirth throw everything off balance for a while, and while the Chinese language has a common term for the period immediately after childbirth, we have only the medical 'puerperium', which is not in common usage and is barely pronounceable.

Fewer children and vast improvements in general health and in medical care and knowledge have meant that new mothers have never been healthier. But choosing to have children in the modern world creates specific additional pressures for mothers. Often women feel that they cannot complain about feeling ill because things could have been so much worse. Feminism has succeeded in persuading many women that they can and should work as well as have children, and many women now view the admission of health problems after childbirth as a sign of weakness which will be misinterpreted, by men especially, and particularly at work. Principles of equality mean that a woman should not be allowed any form of special pleading even if she has just had a baby.

But the fact of the matter is that it takes time to recover from the physical upheaval of pregnancy and childbirth, far longer than we like to allow ourselves. Specific health problems triggered by complications in childbirth are covered in more detail in Appendix I, but even normal, textbook, trouble-free pregnancies and labour place great stress on a woman's body and we still know little about the long-term effects. How, for instance, does the trigger of such vast quantities of hormones during pregnancy change women? And how much of that change is irrevocable? Doctors say that the high hormonal levels drop substantially seven to ten days after labour and maintain that women recover quickly from the hormonal chaos. But anecdotal evidence from women suggests otherwise. Abdul Sultan is a Senior Registrar in Obstetrics who has undertaken research on postpartum health. 'When you talk to new mothers, most of them will say that they do not feel the same, or as well after delivery as they did before. Whether that's due to pregnancy and delivery or the stress of looking after children is hard to tell, but either way childbirth changes your life completely.'

The research currently available indicates that pregnancy can place the organs of the body under considerable stress. Oestrogen, for example, has a mildly cholestatic effect which puts more than usual pressure on the mother's liver and gall-bladder. The liver functions less effectively – the mother's skin may become itchy as bile salts are deposited under the skin rather than broken down and excreted. Progesterone slows down the contractions of the gall-bladder and cholesterol crystals may well be left behind when the gall-bladder fails to empty itself completely in late pregnancy: 75 per cent of gall-bladders examined during Caesarean sections were found to be large and tense with thick viscid bile. Ultrasound studies have also found impaired contraction in the enlarged gall-bladder during pregnancy, which perhaps gives some credence to the saying that 'fat, female and fertile' can lay the foundations for gallstones.[21]

Near the end of pregnancy, oestrogen levels are up to one

thousand times higher than in non-pregnant women. The uterus is an involuntary muscle that contracts all of the time, like the heart or the gut, and it is the pregnancy hormones which prevent the uterus from expelling its contents. As the uterus grows bigger, hormonal levels have to increase in order to prevent premature delivery. By late pregnancy the stress hormone levels in a woman's brain are as high as they would be during strenuous exercise.[22] These huge quantities of hormones may not be present in the bloodstream a week to ten days after delivery, but their effect on a woman's body is still obvious months later. Pregnancy hormones thicken a woman's hair and make her skin look warmer and flushed. Her hands become redder and clammy, there may be darker patches called chloasma on her cheeks and large quantities of fat are laid down on her stomach, thighs and breasts. These physical manifestations do not disappear overnight, but slowly diminish over time, time that few women allow themselves. 'Women do this amazing thing and then they expect to carry on as if nothing has happened,' remarked Susan Bewley. 'I had one recently who said that she had to recover quickly because she was going to be acting in a pantomime in December and I thought, "Oh dear, what am I going to say to this woman?" She had no idea what it's like to have a small baby. It's definitely underappreciated. New mothers should be cherished and recognized as special.'

Having a baby may be natural and healthy but it can also provoke profound physiological upheaval bordering on trauma. If women deny that fundamental truth and refuse to allow themselves time to recover well, they may be creating additional and unnecessary hurdles for themselves psychologically. The upheaval is that much greater if surgery is involved. A woman who has time to investigate the reasons for obstetric intervention or a Caesarean section has time to come to terms with it, and her physical wounds will heal faster than a woman who still feels distressed by what she perceives as failure to give birth naturally.

Every woman who gives birth needs an extensive period of

adjustment to come to terms with the irrevocable changes to her body so that she can more easily accept her new role as a mother. There are billions of tiny lights glowing inside each one of us, and it can feel as if the effort it takes to produce each child is so great that it extinguishes a few of those lights for ever. We can live perfectly well without them, but that does not mean that we do not need time to mourn their loss.

There has to be a healthier compromise, a balance between the rigid disciplines of Western stoicism with its neglect of maternal health, and Eastern religious strictures which view the new mother as untouchable. Christina McKenzie believes that 'the way back to the middle ground is to be absolutely honest with women about the outcomes. Women get bombarded with glowing views of motherhood. There's a great fear of scaring women and putting them off, but it's patronizing to assume that they can't cope with the full facts. I still hear discussions where people say that if you give women that much information, then you'll just confuse them.'

Nature gives us time to recover in those early days. Babies can sleep for up to twenty hours in the first few weeks of life just so that the mother can lie around in a stupor, sleeping for three or four hours at a time around the clock and waking only to eat, breastfeed, bath and change the baby's nappy. But as babies get bigger they sleep less and less during the day, forcing their mothers to do more and more for them. If nature had given a newborn baby the ability to make the same demands as a child twelve months older, the mother would be devastated and levels of infanticide would probably soar. Babies give their mothers up to a year's grace in which to recover their physical and mental faculties before they really tax her by walking and throwing themselves into life-threatening situations. Women who can make the time to rest and recuperate in those early weeks are building a better basis for the future and may be better able to cope with some of the other problems adjusting to motherhood discussed elsewhere in this book.

Lydia gave up work as a teacher to look after her four boys aged five to twelve. Each experience of childbirth was short but very intense, and she didn't feel too tired and debilitated. 'I've always felt that the best eight weeks of my whole life were the first two weeks of each of their lives. It was magical, with vivid, vivid memories even though obviously there was discomfort as well. I always made sure that I had someone around to look after the other ones and me, and I remember the best time was when a friend came and cooked nice food for me at lunchtime. I'd stay in bed as much as I could, get loads of magazines and treats and just wallow in it. I wonder if that makes a difference to how you then cope with the whole of motherhood? Even if you've had an easy birth, the physical upheaval needs as much rest as possible, just to get the milk going.'

Motherhood is intensely physical, and the older a child gets the more physically challenging it can become. Pushing a buggy or carrying it up steps gets harder as the baby grows heavier. A baby who cannot walk does not tax the biceps of a mother as does a toddler who needs to be repeatedly lifted up and down steps, away from danger, or comforted after the intense frustration and humiliation of a fall. Children force us to get fit again by kicking balls, climbing frames and always running in the opposite direction from the way that you want them to go. It helps to be one step ahead of them. It's far easier to cram a recalcitrant two-year-old into his coat and then into his buggy, or to hold his writhing body down as you change his nappy if you've got the muscles to do it with. It's more fun racing with your four-year-old in the park if you know that you can win.

Certain bits of the body never quite regain their former shape. Nipples can become darker and larger and breasts either drop and change shape after breastfeeding or disappear completely. The muscles of the abdomen wall do eventually come back into line with the rest of the body but will never be concave unless you spend the best part of every day doing stomach curls – and who can be bothered with that? And as for the vagina, well, no one puts it better than Caroline, who works for a charity and has an eight-month-old daughter: 'I feel very different now, so open. I get into the bath and half the water disappears.'

When a woman has a baby, she moves up a generation and loses the feeling that her body is physically intact and undamaged as is the privilege of the childless. She can despise her new shape and work to change it through physical exercise, or decide to love its defects as evidence of the fact that she is a mother. Rare is the mother without a single permanent physical change or scar gained through having a baby. Forensic scientists can tell just by looking at the outside of a female corpse whether or not she has had a baby. They are our stripes, reminders of the fact that we have lived through a profound, extraordinary, exhilarating and debilitating experience, and that babies take physically from their mothers, sometimes for good. It may only be a matter of weeks – though it is more likely to take months stretching into years – but eventually the body does settle down into a new state of equilibrium where mourning for the loss of one's physical youth changes into a new and confident acceptance of the temple that your small child worships.

3

Adjusting to Motherhood

Any woman who says that she never felt shocked or over-whelmed by the anarchy of new motherhood is probably lying. 'Normal' mothers find that life is dominated by chaos and confusion after childbirth because so much happens all at the same time. Suddenly the day is consumed by the minutiae of baby care and the urgency of a newborn's needs. A woman's own needs are subsumed by her child's – there never seems to be time for a bath or the shortest daydream. Everything five feet away from the baby seems to be in a mess and women chastise themselves for not knowing instinctively how to mother or for feeling unable to accomplish the simplest household chore.

Then there's the physical discomfort, for childbirth can leave a legacy of complaints. Plummeting hormonal levels and the dramatic drop in blood volume spin everything out of control for a while, and sleep deprivation drives the final nail into the coffin. On top of all that, there's the shock of having given birth, the extraordinary video of the event which runs repeatedly minute by munute, through our minds. All these things happen at the same time, a time of sensory and psychological overload, a time of great stress as well as great joy, so it is hardly surprising that 'even psychologically well-adjusted women, who have desired to become mothers, may experience considerable psychological upheavals during pregnancy and the adjustment to a new baby'.[1]

Giving birth can produce great unhappiness – perhaps the hardest thing to cope with, especially when we feel that we ought to know only joy. We think of postnatal depression as an unfortunate affliction, an illness which blights the lives of a small number of new mothers rather than a syndrome which affects us all to a greater or lesser extent because we live through so much change in such a short space of time. The medically defined symptoms of postnatal depression are all-encompassing: tearfulness, irritability, feelings of despondency and inadequacy, self-reproach, excessive anxiety and sleep disturbances.[2] It is hard to find a new mother who does not suffer from some or all of these. Pregnancy, childbirth and new motherhood are inherently stressful and any stressful event can produce these symptoms, as well as physical ones, such as headaches, stomach upsets, a reduction in resistance to infection and a slowing-down in the healing of wounds. One definition I read even included 'an inability to cope'.[3] The inherent assumption is that 'normal' mothers can cope. Queen Victoria was more in touch with reality when she wrote to one of her daughters who had just given birth: 'Occasional lowness and tendency to cry you must expect. You of all people will be inclined to this . . . for it is what every lady suffers with more or less and what I during my first two confinements suffered dreadfully with.'[4]

Motherhood is riddled with contradictions. We can relish the domesticity one minute and feel trapped the next. A mother is never alone with her child, yet she can feel deeply lonely. She has gained a new identity, yet paradoxically there is also a sense of loss of her former life. She needs to learn how to play again and relish the anarchy of childhood, yet she is now also the authoritative, responsible figure who structures the day.

These contradictions do not necessarily diminish as our children get older, we just get used to them. But in the days and weeks after childbirth, when we sit alone at home, feeling out of control of our lives and of the tiny, wailing, wriggling baby that is now permanently by our side, we can feel terrifyingly close to madness. Clare works in publishing, lives in London and has two children. 'You get so used to organizing and controlling things and then here's something that's completely out of control and controlling you and you're thrown. I think to begin with my feelings of misery far outweighed my feelings of pleasure. I just kept longing for him to go away so that I could feel better and be able to cope with him. I kept searching for a pattern and it's only now that I have two children that I know that there is no pattern.'

The realization that you've jumped the divide, and a generation, that you're a parent now and have to be responsible can be deeply shocking, for parents are by definition uncool, sensible figures of authority. The future suddenly seems mapped out and boxed by feeds, nappy changes and phases of child development. Normal time transmutes into 'mother time' when you put your child's needs first, and 'male time' when you are relieved of your mothering responsibilities by someone else and can concentrate on yourself.

These are natural aspects of every woman's adjustment to motherhood. But, if in addition to all of this, a woman develops problems breastfeeding, has a screaming colicky baby or suffers unduly from some of the other potential difficulties of new motherhood (described elsewhere in this book), such as marital difficulties or chronic fatigue, then her defences can easily give way.

Women on low incomes find that many of their problems of adjustment to motherhood are exacerbated by poor housing and anxiety over money. If new mothers are living in tower blocks where the lifts are regularly out of service, then getting out to pursue normal activities becomes even harder to achieve with a small baby, and even more tiring. One new mother I met in hospital the day after she had given birth was anxious to get the council to transfer her to another estate because there were rats in her flat. Another was technically homeless, living in a cramped single room in bed-and-breakfast accommodation with her two-year-old son without access to a kitchen where she could prepare her baby's feeds.

Irene was brought up in a working-class household in the north of England and worked in a number of jobs, ranging from cleaning to research work in television, before she had her first child at the age of thirty-two. 'You're controlling your destiny, you make something happen to you by getting pregnant and then when it does happen it's the biggest shock of your life. Life goes upside down for a while. Suddenly you're on a rollercoaster of unpredictability without much confidence. For me it took ten months, and I know almost to the minute when I began to feel in control of what was happening to me. Every time I went out I'd either forgotten my keys or nappies, and I couldn't predict what was going to happen from hour to hour. Then one day I was walking along Church Street, the baby was ten months old and I remember thinking, I've got everything with me, the baby's OK and this is my life! Suddenly it didn't feel like my chaotic new life, but as if this was everyday life.'

These feelings of loss of control begin to some extent with pregnancy. We can feel taken over by the foetus and lose control over the shape of our body. We become more and more aware of the fact that we can only guess at what motherhood may be like, we cannot shape it. A mother has only limited means at her disposal for ensuring the health and welfare of her baby – through diet, exercise and giving up smoking and alcohol – for unknown hereditary or environmental factors could be influencing the development of her foetus. Childbirth is the ultimate involuntary act. We have no choice but to surrender our bodies. We hope to be able to stay in control and keep an eye on what the medics are doing, but we lose it as we rock and moan and shout and scream obscenities. We lose all sense of perspective and time as contractions whittle away our reserves of energy and resistance. We drift in and out of consciousness with the pain or the effect of drugs. We lose all sense of reason during the remarkable sensations of transition and find it hard to obey the midwife and resist the urge to push when that is all our bodies want to do.

Some women find this loss of control exciting, like riding a horse that could bolt at any moment. Anne is a literary agent living in London with two children, who enjoyed two drug-free 'natural' experiences of childbirth. 'I didn't feel in control, but I did feel that I was part of something extraordinary that was about to happen. There's something wonderful about not being in control, when you spend most of your life in control.' But other women find this and the inability to determine the course of their labour in the way that they would like deeply distressing, even shocking. Labour can be prepared for but it can never be predicted, and no two experiences of labour are the same, even in the same woman. Pregnancy handbooks and antenatal classes focus on the stages of childbirth with little room for explanation of the millions of different ways that each individual labour can progress. The seventeenth-century male midwife, Percivall Willughby, was one of the first to record extensive case histories. 'Every delivery hath taught me something, or, at the least, hath confirmed my practice. For although much practice enlighteneth the understanding, yet . . . all bodies be not alike, and . . . some unexpected newness, or casualty, may happen in the mother, or in the child, or in the labour, or in the most of them, the which I have sometimes seen.'[5]

Giving birth can be unbelievably difficult for human beings, because we are bipeds and have offspring with large heads. Numerous other species produce litters annually in order to ensure the survival of at least one or two into adulthood, but, when given the choice with contraception, human beings are not prepared to go through the experience too often. 'Our data suggests that some degree of difficulty [in labour] is at least statistically "normal",' conclude the American researchers of *Pregnancy, Birth and Parenthood*.[6] Bats probably have an easier time of it, giving birth hanging upside down from the roof of a cave and catching the baby with their tail in order to prevent it from splattering to the ground.

The shock of childbirth can also exacerbate problems adjusting to motherhood, for it is always a dramatic, landmark memory for women. Any woman who has given birth can describe her labour minute by minute months after the event, and few women forget the experience while their children are young. Some women genuinely enjoy the experience. But others, the majority of new mothers, find themselves frightened by the intensity of pain or shocked by the sensation of splitting in two during the second stage. Those women who have never been in hospital before can feel alienated from their surroundings and frightened by the acute drama of the situation. Small things can and do go wrong all of the time, because women in labour depend completely on the skill and judgement of the professionals around them, professionals involved in the factory-like production of different dramas of other women in labour at the same time. There are countless ways that the reality of labour can differ from the theory, because each woman responds differently to the stress of labour according to her physical condition, psychological make-up, upbringing and previous experience.

Every woman I interviewed had a story to tell which she perceived as negative or detrimental to her experience of labour. There were those who had been left to labour alone because women are considered not to be technically in labour until they are three centimetres dilated. Others tell of induction drips that never worked or made the labour too intense too quickly, of contractions that seemed to have no end, middle or beginning, let alone regular spacing between them, of anaesthetists' repeatedly failed attempts to insert an epidural, of cut-happy doctors, inconsiderate midwives, and of excruciating pain. Others found the quality of postnatal care lamentable, with nobody around to show them how to breastfeed or bath a baby and no opportunity for rest and recuperation because other people's babies were always crying.

Whether a new mother's experience of childbirth is good or bad, it is always extraordinary and something which mothers readily admit no book or class could have prepared them for. You have to live through childbirth to understand its physical and emotional intensity and then to marvel at the birth of your own child.

Jean Ball's extensive research, in *Reactions to Motherhood*, found that the type of postnatal care a new mother receives can be far more detrimental to her subsequent wellbeing than her experience of labour. Once the birth is over, women can more easily understand the reasons for a Caesarean or a forceps delivery and look back on the event more positively if they feel supported and encouraged by the medical staff around them. But lack of understanding and poor conditions can blacken the entire experience.[7]

Caesareans can prompt specific psychological problems such as feelings of failure or inadequacy, and some women worry about the effect that the absence of vaginal birth may have on their child's future development. The psychologist Joan Raphael Leff maintains that it is not uncommon for a woman who has given birth by Caesarean 'to feel so guilt-ridden at having deprived her baby of birth-canal stimulation and spontaneous birth that she may believe that she has pre-determined his/her personality to bypass conflict, avoid work process and/or seek premature gratification'.[8] But many women can understand and accept the medical reasons for their Caesareans provided that the little morale they have left isn't annihilated by the isolation and sense of disability felt on the average maternity ward. 'I was transferred to the maternity ward and lay in bed, immobile, a drip in my arm, a catheter in place and a tube draining blood from my scar into a bottle by my bed. It was the antithesis of all my visions of motherhood,' writes Sarah Clement, author of the *Caesarean Experience*, in a magazine article. 'It was hard to watch the non-Caesarean mothers playing with their babies, changing them and handling them with great confidence, while I, by contrast, could not stand up without assistance, let alone pick up Joe, during those first few days.'[9]

Most women recover quickly from the psychological upheavals of childbirth in the months that follow it. But often women report violent and terrifying dreams in the subsequent weeks, and many find that they are left with a lasting sense of shock even when they have achieved the joyful, textbook birth experience they had hoped for. Gemma works in television and has a keen interest in health and fitness. She decided to get into physical and psychological training for labour by attending yoga classes, and found most of her labour exhilarating, without pain relief or any form of medical intervention. But even so she found the physical sensation of splitting in two during the second stage and the tearing deeply traumatic.

'I think it was the sheer knowledge that the skin was tearing that was so shocking. What I find astonishing is that the urge to push is somehow greater than the pain of splitting, that your body tears itself apart with this urge to push. How come the body doesn't say "Whoa! You're splitting!" It's beyond your control and it's happening. For weeks I couldn't sit down properly. It was like sitting on barbed wire. I had to lie down to breastfeed her and the terror of having a crap! I flashbacked to the birth, it was exactly like watching a home movie running in my head and it was as vivid as watching a real film. I couldn't seem to turn this projector off that was beaming in my brain because even though it was a good experience, it was nevertheless a shock. You physically shake after you have given birth and there's a reason for that – it's physically shocking.'

Giving birth can be as devastating as living through an accident where the body sustains major injury, and often women find that they are nursing that trauma long after their physical wounds have healed. 'Giving birth is like having a near-fatal car crash where you just manage to crawl out of the wreckage,' remarked Grace, a Nigerian single mother who had a twelve-hour labour without complications. 'The shock that I was still alive was so great that I cried for half an hour.' Childbirth reminds a woman of her own mortality. Many women feel close to death in labour, and some even beg the midwife to kill them rather than give birth.

Post-traumatic stress disorder is now recognized as a medical condition requiring treatment. It can follow anything such as a car crash, violent crime, an experience of war or an earthquake, when a person feels threatened by death or serious injury, extreme pain and a sense of loss of control. Symptoms include nightmares, insomnia, excessive irritability, anxiety and flashbacks. Sufferers may also blank out all memory of the experience or go to extraordinary lengths to avoid any possibility of repeating it and become deeply distressed at times when they are reminded of what happened. Many women have similar symptoms after giving birth. An ability to recount every moment, movement or comment from the medical staff are common, as well as insomnia, irritability and anxiety. Childbirth can retrigger previous traumas such as rape and traumas of human origin can be far more damaging psychologically than natural disasters. Yet specialists in trauma rarely include labouring women in their research because childbirth is considered a natural, joyful event.

Rachel is a lesbian single mother who had her first baby at thirty-seven. She found herself flashing back not only to the birth seven months earlier, but also to a serious car crash when she was nineteen. 'It brought it back quite strongly and I felt quite similar. I just wanted to go to bed without the baby. I know that it is a physical trauma and from having the car crash I know that it takes time to recover.' A woman's sense of her own parameters and physical wholeness gives way in childbirth, and her defences against death and injury are broken down in much the same way as survivors of road accidents. The fact that you prepare for labour in pregnancy and know that it is going to happen will lessen the impact of childbirth slightly, but only slightly, given that no woman can really know what to expect until the time comes. Women are known to recover more quickly physically and psychologically from the birth of their second baby simply because of their previous experience.

One of the first sudies of post-traumatic stress disorder in women who had given birth in 1993 found that one fifth of them felt their experience of labour to be 'very distressing' or 'terrifying', and when these women were followed up, thirty were found to be suffering from post-traumatic stress disorder, with scores similar to those of eighty-nine Vietnam War veterans who had completed the same questionnaire.[10] A study of 500 women conducted in 2000 found that one third had suffered traumatic births and that 28 met the criteria for acute post-traumatic stress disorder.[11] A study from St George's Hospital in London estimates that 10,000 new cases of PTS Disorder are created every year.[12] In all cases the trauma is associated with high levels of obstetric intervention and inadequate levels of care during labour and therefore could often be avoided.

The effects can be long term. Some women subsequently avoid smear tests or further pregnancies. For others, childbirth invokes earlier experiences of sexual abuse or rape or seek elective Caesareans. A small handful of women find vaginal delivery so traumatic that they literally dissociate themselves from the bottom half of their bodies and undergo sexual difficulties or incontinence. 'They just don't want to think about it,' says Dr Abdul Sultan, who is researching postpartum faecal incontinence. 'They may end up needing bio-feedback – we ask them to squeeze their bottom muscles and they can't. They need retraining to get over the trauma. They've shut out the whole area because they've had an instrumental delivery, or great pain or tears. I think women can be permanently damaged psychologically from a traumatic labour.'

Childbirth is too significant a rite of passage to forget easily. If these images of labour are not fading, if they seem to impinge on your daily life or hamper your relationship with the baby or other family members, then you do need to find somebody to talk to. Post traumatic stress disorder is not the same as postnatal depression. Ask for your case notes and go through them with your GP of midwife. Some hospitals have a Birth Afterthoughts service where women can go back and discuss their labours with those who helped them deliver. Ask your GP to refer you for cognitive therapy. Homoeopathic remedies such as arnica in the right doses can be particularly good for shock.

Both my daughters were delivered by Caesarean section after prolonged, difficult labours. I recovered far quicker after the second, even though it was far worse than the first, and memories of hours of pain and turning forceps receded quickly. But the eighteen months after the delivery of my first child were plagued with a painful scar that didn't seem to heal and with powerful flashbacks to an event which I had found deeply shocking. I went to see a homoeopath because I just didn't feel well, and as I recounted my experience of childbirth I burst into tears, for it felt so real, as if it had happened yesterday. She could tell that I was still in a state of shock and believed that the morphine I had been given through the epidural had frozen that shock moments after birth in a sort of time warp. She gave me homoeopathic opium and within days I felt much better. The memories of childbirth began to fade and the scar healed quickly. Many women are now routinely given morphine after Caesareans in Britain to help relieve post-operative pain and consequently feel blissfully happy for a while. But if you find yourself unable to recover psychologically then it may well be because of the opiates given as painkillers.

Some women find that writing down their experiences helps to exorcize the trauma. Others just need to talk and talk. Maintaining links with women from your antenatal class will give you a forum for these discussions. Seek out medical help if you need it and don't allow others to dismiss your symptoms as part and parcel of new motherhood. Countless women in the past had no choice but to live with the psychological trauma of child-birth. We now have the science of psychology at our disposal, which we should use after labour to help us recover and feel able to look after our babies. But one psychological change is perma-nent: giving birth, however we do it, forces us to be more mature and accepting of our own mortality and vulnerability as well as our strengths.

It came as a complete shock to me that once I had delivered my baby into the world I would have to look after it, all of the time and on my own. I could barely walk because of the Caesarean, let alone get out of bed, and beside me lay this bundle of miracle that slept and fed and cried. Generous paternity leave from the BBC meant that my husband was there to help, but he too was exhausted, stunned and shaken by the experience of childbirth and becoming a father. So together we stumbled through those early days, stared anxiously at our precious newborn, wondering whether she was all right and how on earth we were going to look after her.

When he went back to work I was left alone. Visits from the midwife had stopped. We had just moved into the area and hadn't had time to make friends of our neighbours. My family tried to be supportive down the telephone but lived too far away to be of any real use. I still couldn't walk very well because of the scar. I couldn't get out of the house to shop or live a normal life with the baby because she had to be in a pram and I couldn't lift it up the stairs to our house. She slept most of the day and I tried to rest, but most of the time I just felt inadequate, an invalid, because I couldn't think straight, work or be useful, and I couldn't soothe or satisfy my baby other than with my breasts, which were sore and one of which was infected with mastitis.

When she cried inconsolably, her wails sounded so accusing, so tormented and so loud that I used to be convinced something was seriously wrong with her and feel rising anger and shame at my inability to calm her. I would pace the floor with a racing heart and knotted stomach, shushing her ceaselessly while I rubbed her back. 'I hope Buonaparte may have a sick child,' wrote Melisina Trench (1768–1837), who lost four of her nine children, 'as I think the cry of an infant, whose pain we cannot know or assuage, would make him feel his want of power, though nothing else has done it.'[13]

The stresses of normal new motherhood are enough to drive the strongest woman insane for a while. 'It's either a pit or a nest,' says Wendy, who is a university lecturer with two children aged six and three. 'I just remember becoming very irrational about some things over feeding. I felt that if I gave her a bottle, that would be it, the beginning of a slippery slope, so as well as waking up two or three times in the night to feed, I'd be up for hours using the breast pump. Really nutty stuff. That's the bad bit, the pit. But the cosy bit is where you just find all of your satisfaction in a tiny baby. I can't quite see now what we used to do with all of that time, just me and the baby. It's very satisfying and moreish and isolating.'

The fact that one can feel so positive and negative about the same experience is perhaps the most surprising contradiction of all. Babies can give us such a strong sense of purpose, of belonging to someone important, of being needed, of nurturing, of warmth. But through this remarkable gain we also lose all sense of ourselves as separate, integral beings for a while. The myth is that the presence of the baby makes everything worthwhile. They undoubtedly offset the losses, but babies can never compensate for them completely. They are two entirely separate nuggets of being and one can feel immense joy or satisfaction from one source as well as deep unhappiness about other things, such as a radical change of identity, at the same time. 'I sometimes wonder whether I lived enough before I had Joe,' Rachel said sadly when I asked her whether she had any regrets, even though she clearly adored her seven-month-old son and loved being with him. Pursuing former pleasures seemed impossible to her now.

'Your sense of self becomes non-existent,' says Suzanne, who works in a shoe shop in Chippenham and has two girls. 'You go from this strong sense of who you are and then it took me a year to get used to being a mum. What am I supposed to act like? Who am I supposed to be?' Motherhood is so common that it is hard for a woman to feel special or unique. If everybody is doing it, then it ought to be easy. 'And yet it is so weird and difficult and demanding and relentless and so incredible that you can't believe that you are the same as anybody else. There's this dichotomy between how special it is and how demanding it is. It changes you in more ways than you could possibly imagine. And there's the normality of it which I find difficult – it means that you can't admit that there are difficulties.'

'The eleven weeks after the birth of my first baby really was one of the worst times in my life,' says Imogen, a writer and journalist who had her first baby at the age of thirty-seven. 'I think I had really high expectations and then found I was deeply shocked, because people lied to me. For years I asked people, "Is there life after babies?" and they said, "Yes, you take them here, you take them there." But nobody said, "It'll be a total fucking nightmare for a while but it'll be all right because you'll come out of it." I couldn't believe the amount of co-dependency, that you couldn't do anything without this baby, and I felt completely incompetent. The night after she was born and we were still in hospital, I remember feeling completely detached from her when she woke up. I thought, What's this got to do with me? *I've* got to deal with it? I couldn't cope with the responsibility. I'd been a carefree person and all I'd had to do was look after myself and suddenly this responsibility felt completely overwhelming. I felt that I couldn't put her down and that I had to give her everything and at the same time I was very scared of handling her. But I also knew that it was only by handling her, by being with my daughter, that I'd gain confidence and come through. I looked at other people who seemed to be able to cope with it and I felt ashamed. I felt that my life was over and I was furious that no one had told me and I looked at women walking down the street with several children and couldn't believe that anybody could volunteer to have more than one child.' But of course, like most of the rest of us, she did eventually have another child and now considers motherhood to be the best thing that ever happened to her. Imogen's problems were typical, experienced to a greater or lesser

degree by most women in the period after childbirth, a time of
major adjustment and transition to new life as a mother.

Postnatal depression has been defined throughout history as a
psychiatric illness, an aberration that other, more unfortunate
women suffer from rather than a condition that all new mothers
are vulnerable to. Women have always been thought to be particularly prone to madness because they have wombs.
Hippocrates first described postnatal mental illness in *The Third
Book of Epidemics* in the fourth century BC. He believed that
'when blood collects at the breasts of a woman it indicates madness'. In 1600 Sennert blamed depressions after childbirth on
vapours rising from the uterus to the brain. Women were thought
to be controlled by their gynaecology rather than their brains, and
removal of the ovaries was regularly recommended by doctors in
the middle of the nineteenth century as a cure for troublesome
women.

Nowadays, severe cases of postnatal depression are still
treated in psychiatric hospitals with strong drugs and ECT where
the staff's primary concern is to prevent the mother damaging
herself or her child, rather than providing more intense and therapeutic care that many heavily depressed new mothers say they
need. Fiona Shaw voluntarily admitted herself to a mother-and-
baby unit in a psychiatric hospital after the birth of her second
child. 'I wanted women to put their arms around me, to hold me
in the briefest gesture of reassurance. But the nurses never
touched me, unless it was to prevent something,' she writes in her
memoir, *Out of Me*.[14] She was treated with psychotropic drugs
and sixteen sessions of ECT which temporarily killed her short-
term memory and turned her into a pale zombie. They didn't
cure her, merely froze her so that she could just about cope until
the depression passed. 'ECT seemed to be its own kind of break-
down. My sense of identity was so bombarded that it was
impossible for me to have any continuous sense of myself at all.'

The great biological and hormonal changes of pregnancy and

childbirth may well trigger postnatal depression in some women, but a conclusive link has never been found in spite of a substantial body of research into the most likely cause. Some doctors and researchers such as Katharina Dalton believe that it is the sharp drop in the level of hormones, particularly progesterone, which can trigger postnatal depression in those who are more sensitive to hormonal change. Others such as John Studd, Consultant Gynaecologist at the Chelsea and Westminster Hospital in London, believe that it is oestrogen, because oestrogen is a mood elevator while progesterone is a tranquillizer. Both Dalton and Studd have found that women with postnatal depression have responded positively to their individual trials. Other researchers have found a connection between high levels of prolactin or cortisol and depression in women after childbirth.'[15]

The thyroid gland has also been linked by research to postnatal depression. During pregnancy the thyroid and pituitary glands increase in size, but in the weeks after childbirth the level of thyroid production slowly decreases and can drop to a level *lower* than it was pre-pregnancy and stay that low for a year or more. The symptoms of low thyroid include feeling mentally slow and lethargic, melancholia, headaches, sensitivity to the cold, slow speech, feeling highly emotional, no periods and hair loss. Treatment with thyroxine appears to quickly lift a woman's mood as well as clear the physical symptoms.

Postnatal depression can affect any woman after the birth of her first, second or third child, although new mothers are known to be at greater risk.[16] Antenatal depression, particularly, in the last trimester is as common as postnatal depression but rarely recognized. Evidence suggests that approximately two thirds of women with postnatal depression were also depressed while pregnant.[17] There is no conclusive evidence to suggest that education or social background, financial status, age, marital status or obstetrical and gynaecological factors have any bearing on the incidence of postnatal depression. Research into depression after childbirth has been so focused on the substantial physiological and hormonal stress of pregnancy and childbirth that surprisingly few researchers have taken the trouble to ask new mothers themselves *why* they feel depressed. When asked, their answers point to the nexus of sudden physical, emotional and environmental upheaval that motherhood brings, a time when women are least likely to have the strength to cope with the sudden new range of demands being made of them. They feel isolated, bored and unsupported. They never knew that it was possible to be this tired, and their physical health is under par. They feel they do not have enough time to themselves, and often worry about their financial security, their housing or going back to work.

There are numerous good reasons why women should feel depressed or generally unhappy after childbirth. It is very common, an essential natural defence, perhaps, against feeling too much emotion at a time when a woman has no choice but to learn how to let go of a great deal of her former life. The deepest wells of depression are a time of mourning and not necessarily an illness requiring treatment, although the symptoms can be alleviated medically. If we think of it as a period of stasis or gestation, or, as Louise Erdrich writes,[18] 'a time enclosed, a secluded lightlessness in which, unknown and unforced, we grow', then it becomes easier to see postnatal depression in a more positive, productive light.

'Depression is about anger, it is about anxiety, it is about character and heredity,' writes Tim Lott in *The Scent of Dried Roses*. 'But it is also about something that is in its way quite unique. It is the illness of *identity*, it is the illness of those who do not know where they fit, who lose faith in the myths they have so painstakingly created for themselves.' Women are probably more vulnerable to a crisis of identity when they become mothers than at any other lifestage.

It is an attempted defence against the terror of losing your invented sense: who you believe yourself to be and the way in which you think the world operates. It is fear of annihilation,

of doubt, of insignificance. It is a reaction to a very particular
kind of stress, the kind that brings into question the world that
you, being human, have to imagine and re-imagine, maintain
and defend every moment of the day, in order to keep chaos
at bay.[19]

'I felt like I'd had a molecular rearrangement,' says Judith, who
was a successful editor and journalist in New York before she
had her two children. 'I'd been really interested in public things,
in literary things and being out there getting work, and then I
changed. I used to think of myself as a unitary thing moving
through the world with very clear edges and I lost that because
you don't know where you end and the baby begins – in a very
profound way. It wasn't just professional, it was as if all of the
windows had been opened and my boundaries had become very
porous and so it was much, much harder to go out into the
world.'

Judith gave up work and immersed herself in her son and rel-
ished the intimacy of their relationship. It was only when she
gave up breastfeeding when he was twenty months old that she
found herself depressed and in need of Prozac. 'I think it was
because I'd left this old identity which didn't sustain me enough
through having a child and I'd given myself up to this baby, happily, and now the baby didn't need me so much any more and I
felt like I had nothing left. There was a way in which having that
first baby shook everything down for me – the bits of me that
weren't central started flying off in all directions, and then you're
left with this question of what is there left in the middle and what
am I really about, to which I still don't have the answer.'

Judith's depression lasted for about a year and lifted when she
moved back to London, which seemed more like home, and
when she renegotiated the terms of her marriage so that she
felt less dependent on her husband. She realized she was
depressed, accepted it and then did something about it by taking
anti-depressants and changing the terms and conditions of her

new life. But numerous women still struggle unsupported through the fog of new motherhood, afraid of being pigeonholed as 'ill' or 'inadequate'.

The statistics say that roughly 20 per cent of women suffer from some form of depression in the year after giving birth, but the true incidence is probably far higher, for postnatal depression is often missed or misdiagnosed since it can be provoked or compounded by unavoidable aspects of motherhood such as exhaustion, poor health and changes in marital relations. Women are often reluctant or simply too tired to consult doctors. Sometimes they do not know that they are depressed until they emerge from the fog and look back on those grey days.

Postnatal depression is not something that happens to a small group of unfortunate women at the very end of the spectrum who cannot cope. It is a sliding scale, starting with the 'baby blues' affecting 80 per cent of women, and ending with puerperal psychosis, which affects approximately one in every 500 women. The majority of women sit somewhere on this scale, and the extent to which a woman suffers depends on her individual psychology, her ability to tolerate stress and the amount of emotional support she enjoys.

Women with the 'baby blues' can be highly sensitive, feel tired, have poor concentration and can be suddenly overwhelmed by feelings of helplessness and uncontrollable weeping. They may feel irritable and hostile towards the hospital, the doctor or the father of their child, or all three. Often this is just an essential release of tension after the ordeal of labour, for women who have operations are just as likely to experience the blues as women who have given birth, and doctors and nurses know well that all patients are likely to become tearful a few days after surgery. Other studies have found that people who have lived through periods of extreme stress such as intensive paratroop training suffer similar symptoms to those of the baby blues, and men who have been present at their wives' deliveries often develop a blues-type reaction.[20]

It is also likely that conditions on postnatal wards in hospitals contribute. If women are in pain, shaken by the experience of labour and in need of deep sleep, then hospital is often the worst place to be. Postnatal wards are usually intolerably hot and noisy. If you're not being woken by somebody else's baby, it's the tea trolley at 6.30 a.m. just as you've finally dropped off after feeding your own baby. There is little privacy in hospital, unappetizing food, and women can feel trapped within a hospital routine where they often receive inadequate care and the nearest loo seems 100 miles down the corridor. New mothers are separated from the comforts of their own home and from the father of their baby at a time when they most need to be together. Such circumstances are hardly an ideal way to welcome women to motherhood and can add insult to the injury of birth.

The symptoms of puerperal psychosis at the other end of the scale are far more severe. They usually occur suddenly after an interval of well being within four weeks of delivery and include hallucinations, delusions, suicidal impulses, disorientation and/or impulses to hurt the baby, or a belief that there is something wrong with the baby. Between 15 and 20 per cent of women who become psychotic after childbirth have had a previous psychotic episode.[21] Fiona Shaw saw how varied the manifestations of extreme postnatal depression can be in the mother-and-baby unit of a psychiatric hospital.

> Some had experienced extraordinary delusions, seeing ghouls and goblins, monsters and angels. They remembered shaping the world into bizarre forms, animating ordinary objects like beds, crockery, pills and food, or imbuing them with far-fetched profundity. Others, more like me, had been struck with appalling self-contempt and the wish to flee their own lives.[22]

Women who have just given birth are extremely sensitive to any form of danger that could harm their child. Newborn babies seem so small, weak and vulnerable that they send us all a little mad with the responsibility of keeping them safe. When each of my babies was just weeks old, I saw dangers everywhere: a kitchen knife could so easily be plunged into her stomach, too great a squeeze could break her neck, or a pillow could so easily smother her. I knew that I would never kill my babies, but the images were so vivid and frequent that they were frightening and felt uncomfortably close to madness at times, for I had no control over them and couldn't prevent them from coming. A psychiatrist might interpret this as suppressed anger and a longing for release from the constant demands of a small baby, but I know that there is also a deeper, maternal reason for such powerful imagery. Every sense had to be tuned to potential dangers. Nothing could ever be allowed to harm my babies, and the urge to protect them was so strong that I could only be aware of each potential danger by imagining it and so prevent it from happening.

Postnatal depression hovers in the huge chasm between these two extremes of mild 'baby blues' and psychosis. It can be live-able with or debilitating, and when women are strongly affected the feelings of self-blame are often the worst aspect. When Lady Tebbit was interviewed by Sue Lawley on *Desert Island Discs*, she said that her experience of postnatal depression was far harder to live with than the injuries she sustained when the IRA blew up the hotel she was staying in at Brighton during the Conservative Party conference.

'No matter how severe the pain is, it is always possible to separate ourselves from the pain and put ourselves mentally elsewhere,' writes Dorothy Rowe, a clinical psychologist and expert on depression, in her bestselling book, *Depression*. 'But when we are depressed there's no way we can separate ourselves from our misery.' Friends and family can comfort us when we are in physical pain but when we are depressed, no one can reach us and we persecute rather than comfort ourselves.

'I have no social problems, no financial problems, my partner is fantastic and yet I still find it difficult.' Catherine is a psychiatric social worker who had her first child at the age of thirty. I, too, found it hard to reconcile the fact that I now had so much after the birth of each child, but felt so worn out and negative. Looking back on those times, I realize that I was suffering from what could be clinically categorized as postnatal depression after my first child, but that after the second I was just basically tired and down, not depressed. Yet I thought I ought to be the happiest woman in the world. My children were healthy, beautiful, intelligent. Money was tight but I didn't have to get up at the crack of dawn to clean office toilets to make ends meet or worry about whether I had enough cash in my purse to pay for food at the supermarket. The father of my children didn't abuse me or abandon me, and he doesn't expect me to do anything for him when he comes home from work although I expect plenty from him. The knowledge that I had no cause for complaint didn't make me feel better, it made me feel worse, for it made me think that I of all people ought to be able to snap out of it.

Hormonal treatment, such as wearing an oestrogen patch can help counteract the rapid drop after chilbirth. Anti-depressants can also be effective and alleviate the symptoms of postnatal depression. Therapy can be helpful too. Women who have been depressed after having a child emphasize how important it is to get out of the house at least once a day and to find someone to talk to. Fiona Shaw found that being at home alone was a major trigger to depression, 'not because of what I might do to them, or they to me, but because then I could not escape from the knowledge that this was my life now, and there was no getting away from it'.

Maintaining contact with other new mothers from an NCT class can be an essential lifeline for women in the months after giving birth. These women may not be like you and they may not turn into lifelong buddies, but you may be able to share aspects of motherhood with them and they may help buffer the hours of isolation. Babies root their parents within a neighbourhood.

Pushing a pram along the street will elicit comments and conversation from passers-by, shopkeepers and neighbours, and encourage you to talk to people you may never have noticed before. As babies grow older, they need more stimulation from the outside world, they force you out to playgrounds and mother-and-toddler groups and if you find a friend there with a slightly older baby, then she will have the added knowledge of how the strains of new motherhood lift as the child grows and its needs change.

Women also say that taking just a short time off from mothering helps to relieve the pressure. Just an hour away from the baby to go for a walk alone or a swim, or to read a book without fear of interruption, can make the rest of the day feel manageable and more enjoyable. If you find that the general chaos of your home or the garden is getting you down, then clear it up. 'All of this advice that you're given, to let the whole thing go for a while and concentrate on your baby, is a nonsense, because if you feel as if you're in chaos internally, the last thing you want is chaos externally,' says Imogen. 'I desperately needed to feel as if I could impose some sense of order on my environment, so when my baby was eleven weeks old I got a dishwasher and that changed my life.' Paying someone to clean up may help, but some women find that feeling able to do it for themselves is more therapeutic. If you work to improve your immediate environment, you feel better about yourself and more in control.

Imposing order on a situation is one of the more positive ways in which people cope with stress. A mother who imposes a rigid regime on her baby's day is 'attacking' the source of stress before it can overwhelm her. But if people feel unable to control or extricate themselves from a stressful situation (and nothing feels more irreversible than new motherhood), they may quickly sink into a form of apathy called 'learned helplessness' by psychologists. Fay Weldon put it brilliantly when she said, 'When men find themselves in a hole, they get out of it. When women find themselves in a hole, they grow flowers in it.'

One of the more stressful aspects of new motherhood is that there seem to be so many more things to do in a day, every day, that there is never a sense of accomplishment. 'If you find yourself rushing from one thing to the next, stop, let the thinking you say to your body stop and your body will stop,' says midwife Betty Parsons. 'Finish one job before you move on to the next. Nothing is more soul-destroying or fatiguing than leaving half-finished jobs at the end of the day. In labour women have to learn how to deal with one contraction at a time – if you look ahead, to how many more there may be to come, a woman quickly loses confidence. The same is true of life.' Women also discover as their children grow that they are expected to be good at or enjoy every aspect. But if you try to be all things to your children – a stimulating cook, an expert in arts and crafts, a brilliant sports and pastimes initiator as well as good at the voices in *Winnie the Pooh*, you're possibly well along the road to burn-out. 'You've got to work to your strengths and not your weaknesses,' says Charlotte, mother of three children. 'If you try to do everything, you're crap at all of it.'

Because of the lack of historical research, we have no way of knowing whether rates of postnatal depression and the problems women face adjusting to motherhood have changed over time. We can only presume that certain aspects of modern life may make the transition to motherhood harder. If women have work and interests which they enjoy, they have more to lose when they become mothers. That loss is temporary for most women, but it feels sudden and permanent at the time and amplifies feelings of sacrifice and subservience. The absence of an extended family nearby to help hold the baby exacerbates the isolation a new mother can feel and makes it harder for her to find time for herself. Our mothers' experience of motherhood was very different and may only be marginally helpful, while modern expectations of mothers are more demanding than ever. Conflicting advice from handbooks, health visitors and friends doesn't help create confidence in a mother, and the absence of postpartum rituals in much of the Western world leaves the rite of passage to motherhood unfinished. Women are encouraged to get back to 'normal' too soon, when 'normal' involves a whole new set of rules. Third World rituals, where women are encouraged to enter a period of seclusion while chores are taken over by other female members of the family, may well help a woman to adjust to her new way of life. This seclusion is then followed by feasting and celebration when a woman is more able to enjoy it.

But perhaps it is the modern, misguided belief that we can now control and direct our lives, without pain or unnecessary misfortune and without the all-embracing force of a wider religious power determining our course, which makes adjusting to motherhood so much harder to accept. Life is, as John Lennon put it, what happens to us while we are making other plans. Accepting motherhood means accepting the random chaotic nature of daily life. It means accepting the healthy organic change that children bring into our lives.

You can never reclaim completely what you have lost through having children, but you can learn how to grow with the gains. 'One morning I was washing the encrusted orange juice out of the bottom of Benjamin's bottle and thinking of freedom,' writes Jane Lazarre in *The Mother Knot*.[23] The ordinary idea of freedom was becoming less and less seductive to me. For freedom to do as I please meant doing without Benjamin. And that was very simply a tormenting thought.'

Sue had her first baby at thirty-five and left a successful career in newspaper publishing before she became pregnant so that she could focus entirely on motherhood. She is now two stones heavier than she was before pregnancy and has lost all confidence in the way she looks and in her sexuality, but is surprised by how much more positive she feels about the world out there. 'I used to be very cynical about the world. I've lived here for twelve years and all I saw was the grimy smoke outside the door. Now I really appreciate the small things in life and take things far more slowly. Now when we go out we have to push up the lock and then there might be a crisp packet or two that has to be picked up and thrown away and then we have to rattle the gate and then there's probably a big red bus! This first year of motherhood has been the happiest, most fulfilling year of my life.'

When we find aspects of motherhood hard to cope with, it helps to think of it as a series of phases and we do not necessarily have to like each bit. When you feel that your wailing, teething baby is pushing you uncomfortably close to psychosis, the briefest thought that this is just a phase which will pass and never return can offer momentary relief. 'I remember when Polly was three months old and had colic,' says Anne. 'All those sleepless nights and that dreadful feeling that the world had now become 100 yards from your front door and I thought, It doesn't really matter because I've spent twenty years going to the opera and parties and this is going to be over soon. There was a fantastic feeling of this is just a phase and soon it's going to be over.'

Some women find tiny babies uninteresting, others love them and cope admirably with their care, but then find life difficult and feel inadequate when their eighteen-month-old child cannot be contained in buggies, high chairs or supermarket trolleys, or by reason. The crying of a newborn baby sounds as threatening as a sheep bleating when compared to the screams of a two-year-old having a tantrum or a three-year-old being left at nursery school. Children soon learn to cry when they want things and we soon have to learn how to find the strength to say no.

Other women loathe the chaos and mess of the under-fives and long for the independent seven-year-old friend. But the mess increases with the child's age. It doesn't diminish – we just get used to it and accept our children's belongings as we accept them. 'If I went into a home that wasn't all messed up now, I would feel that it was arid and strange,' says Anne, 'even though the mess that children make drives me utterly insane. At first I'd think, How wonderful! This flat is always going to be like this unless they move something. But actually it's very healthy because otherwise everything you decide is for yourself. Children decide things for you, like going to the same place on holiday.'

Children drive us madder as they grow older. When you are constantly in their presence they can obliterate all intelligent thought and concentration with regular interruptions and questions which need thought before answering. The noise increases as children grow older, and when you have more than one they fight each other and you for your dwindling reserves of attention and resources. 'I never feel I hate them, but I do often feel as if they are driving me mad – the sound of a chair scraping across the floor will make me flip.' Maggie works for a local authority part-time and has two children, aged two and three. 'You can feel your voice droning on. You're always saying "Do this" or "Don't do that", and I think, This isn't what a nice loving mother is all about. I'm supposed to be "Hello, darling" and "Isn't that lovely!"'

When I am not searching the house for a headband, the hair-brush, sellotape or a pencil sharpener or retrieving bits of lost toys from under the sofa, I am thinking of ways to construct an Ancient Egyptian watering device for homework or coaxing a recalcitrant younger child to eat with spoons of food which turn into helicopters or cows, or, madder still, T-shirts and doors. When I ask her how a T-shirt goes, she can tell me. But the moment you know that you have really flipped your lid is when you start cutting the crusts off toast for adult guests, or when you are the only one in the car singing along to the remix of 'The Animals Went in Two by Two' while the children stare mindlessly out of the window.

Gradually a new sense of self with new priorities does emerge, and then the life we had before we had children becomes more distant, integral to who we are but less important somehow. 'I thought I knew myself before, but now I realize that I don't. It's such a lifestage, a massive milestone that there's a distance now from the life that was and you can now look back on it and analyse it,' according to Maggie.

The personal gains of motherhood can be enormous. Sue feels that now she has been brave enough to have a child and succumb to the 'ultimate no-control action. I'm stronger about everything else. It's not that I'll never be frightened again, it's just that I won't be frightened in the same way of taking on something new.' She has decided to start sculpture, a lifelong passion which she was always too frightened to attempt in case she should fail. 'Now I feel more able to stand in a studio and make things, get things wrong, try. Perhaps when people feel that they are mature, motherhood makes them feel as if they are being prevented from doing what they want to do, but for me motherhood has opened up the whole new possibility of developing in new directions.'

Kate worked as a lab technician and was incredibly shy before she had children. As the mother of two sons, one aged five, and the other just seven weeks, she said that having had to talk to other mothers she met while looking after her older son full-time enabled her to be far more confident about talking to other people. She thinks she is unlikely ever to return to her work as a radiologist, but has set up a weekly music group for small children in her own home, which she loves.

'While on the one hand there is this side of you which has to buy toilet rolls and all of the practical things and resents it,' says Charlotte, who suffered from postnatal depression after the birth of her third child, 'there's also this side that wants to walk on the walls behind the kids, or kick leaves or do all sorts of daft things. I care less and less about what other people think and there's far more spontaneity to my life even though paradoxically there's far more order.'

Clara is a historian with one daughter aged four, who feels that her attitudes have changed enormously through motherhood. 'I approach work with so much more confidence now and I no longer care what I look like when I go out the front door. My body image is better, which is weird when objectively speaking I'm not in as good shape as I was before pregnancy. I'm also not sure whether it's living through the pain and experience of child-birth or whether it's the raising of the child as well that has made me so much more tolerant. I'm amazed that more babies aren't thrown out of upper-storey windows – at least one a day I'd expect.'

Women who feel that they do not have a strong sense of place or status from their work can gain a sense of identity through motherhood, not lose it. Women who find their work dull and unstimulating can find the daily life of motherhood far more rewarding. But there are times when all mothers feel trapped and burdened by the responsibilities, however old their children are. These feelings are offset by our growing sense of confidence, pleasure and purpose. We become so integral to our children's way of life, their way of looking at the world, we are so important to the atmosphere we create at home, that it becomes impossible to imagine life without them, however much we may long for a Caribbean cruise alone when the going gets rough. But these contradictions, inherent to motherhood, are no longer distressing and guilt-making, for we know that it is possible to feel two such contrasting needs of belonging and separation at the same time.

Adjusting to motherhood takes time. It is often only with the arrival of a second baby that a woman really feels confident of her ability and relaxes enough to be able to enjoy those early weeks and months, as Kate found: 'I'm more relaxed this time in that I just do what I have to do without worrying about whether I'm doing it the right or the wrong way. With the first one, if he cried differently I'd be so worried. Now I've learnt that that's how babies are, so I ignore lots of things that I would have panicked about before. All of the things that overwhelm you with the first one are like an educational experience, but with the second one you are more in tune with yourself.'

The stress of pregnancy, labour and the life change of new motherhood can be immense. Louann Brizendine in her book *The Female Brain* believes that the hormonal changes of preg-nancy and childbirth are so great that they change brain function permanently. 'Mothers may have better spacial memory than females who haven't given birth, and they may be more flexible, adaptive and courageous', skills which women need to keep track of and protect their children. We need time to accept what has happened and adjust to life as it now is. If you feel that you have lost control over your life, you probably have, but you are not alone, and as the baby gets older life will slip into a new pattern. If you find it hard looking after your baby and feel your self-esteem plummeting, remember that motherhood is an acquired skill, that you are entitled to an apprenticeship and that no one expects you to turn professional overnight. And if you feel unhappiness bordering on despair at times, consider it integral to the radical change you are living through and know that it will pass when you are able to accept the new order. Imogen's post-natal depression was so severe after the birth of her first daughter that she seriously suggested to her partner that they give her up for adoption. 'I suppose it's a question of no pain, no gain. I've had such struggles coming to terms with being a mother, yet it's so wonderful, it's now the meaning of life for me. I needed to have children. I would have been so unhappy if I hadn't had them.'

4

Working and the 'Good' Mother

Throughout history mothers have worked. What was new to the twentieth century was the notion that they shouldn't, that the 'good' mother should stay at home rather than 'abandoning' her children to the assumed 'lesser' care of others. Work and motherhood are nowadays seen as opposing, contradictory forces. It is considered difficult, if not impossible, to do both well. Consequently, numerous women feel emotionally torn, demoralized and deeply guilty about going back to work when their children are young. But if we look to history we can perhaps find reassurance from the fact that this supposed contradiction between work and motherhood is a mirage, a modern cultural construct. Mothers of the past had little choice but to see their roles of mother and worker as interdependent rather than mutually exclusive. And when research shows so consistently that children gain far more from their mothers working than they lose, perhaps we should resist the needless self-indulgence of guilt and enjoy the fact that we can now succeed in both roles.

Mothers have always worked. Historically, upper-class and middle-class mothers did not need to, but their numbers were small compared to the vast numbers of women who had little

choice but to work. Domestic service was the largest area of
female employment until after the First World War. Large numbers of women have also always worked on farms tending
livestock, particularly chickens and pigs, digging potatoes and
beet, tending to bees, milking, preparing goods for sale, loading
them on packhorses and taking them to market. A farmer
expected his wife to carry on working after she had children.
'Throughout the period, whether in fifteenth-century York, six-
teenth-century Rome, seventeenth-century Amsterdam, Venice,
Seville, London or Paris, or the innumerable burgeoning towns of
the eighteenth century, women ran taverns, drink shops, *bettole*
(little stands in the streets selling refreshments), guinguettes (little
outdoor places selling drinks particularly on feast days), or they
provided pies and sausages and cooked meals,' writes Olwen
Huften in her magnificent book on women in Western Europe
from 1500 to 1800, *The Prospect Before Her.* Women worked in
industry too – lacemaking, straw-plaiting, needlework and embroidery – and of course large numbers of them were mothers.

These women didn't torture themselves with constant questioning about the morality of working when they also had
children to care for. Children came and went and women knew
that they had little control over the timing of either. Children
worked and contributed to the family budget as soon as possible.
Even when school became compulsory in Britain, in 1881, large
numbers of children continued to work, both during and after
school hours, selling newspapers, in factories doing work that
required small fingers such as sewing buttons on to cards, or
cleaning chimneys. No job was too dirty or too menial for the
poor. Even horse droppings were collected and sold as fertilizer.
At the turn of the century an estimated two and a quarter million
American children under fifteen were working full-time in coal
mines, glass factories, textile mills, canning factories, the cigar
industry and in the homes of the wealthy.[1]

Far more was expected of a child at an earlier age. 'Today a
four-year-old who can tie his or her own shoes is impressive. In

colonial times, four-year-old girls knitted stockings and mittens and could produce intricate embroidery; at age six they spun wool,' according to Barbara Ehrenreich and Deirdre English in their book, *For Her Own Good*.[2] While children were loved, they were not the cosseted, chosen individuals that we have today. Early integration into the adult world was considered normal and, consequently, the demands of motherhood and work were not mutually exclusive or in any way contradictory, but rather a fundamental fact of life, for work was all that kept such families alive. Work is as essential for millions of mothers today, yet we seem to have lost the ability to combine the two roles without guilt, largely because of the way that work environments are so unfamily friendly but also because of the way that motherhood and childhood have been culturally re-defined in little more than a hundred years.

Up until the middle of the nineteenth century responsibility for children lay within the household, an extended network of family members and servants, rather than solely with the mother and father. The intensity of the umbilical bond that we know today, where the natural mother exclusively provides every aspect of a child's care was not the way that the average child was raised, for children mixed with other adults soon after they were weaned and subsequent feeding, clothing or teaching could be done by any other woman of the household. Motherhood was linked to child-bearing rather than child-rearing, and so was episodic and part-time, even though child-bearing continued until menopause, with couples having an average of six children.

Some historians argue that it wasn't until the end of the eighteenth century that the concept of childhood, as distinct from adulthood, began to emerge. Paediatrics as a distinct medical speciality first emerged in the eighteenth century. Infant mortality began to decline and a new science of childcare developed, largely through the influence of Jean-Jacques Rousseau's book *Émile*, which was published in France in 1762. *Émile* was probably the most widely read child-rearing manual of the time amongst the upper-middle classes, and its influence swept through upper-middle-class England as well. Rousseau advocated breastfeeding by the mother rather than a wet-nurse, and the abandonment of the common practice of swaddling. The numbers of children sent away to boarding-school began to decline from an all-time high at the end of the eighteenth century and more and more mothers began to assume responsibility for their children's education. The function of the mother now extended beyond the biological to the moral, for her duty now was to raise a good Christian citizen.

Rousseau also introduced the concept that motherhood should be a source of joy and fulfilment for women. Women have always gained pleasure from their children, but what was new was the element of self-sacrifice that had to accompany the joy. 'The true mother, far from being a woman of the world, is as much a recluse in her home as the nun is in her cloister,' he wrote. A 'good' mother 'exhausts herself in her attempt to bring pleasure to her child', according to Balzac in *Memoirs of Two Young Married Women*. Rousseau's direct influence was limited to the upper-middle classes. The poor continued to struggle on as they always had. But he did succeed in introducing new imperatives for mothers which they felt they ought to obey. 'Women felt more and more responsible for their children,' writes Elizabeth Badinter in *The Myth of Motherhood*. 'When they could not assume their duties, they believed themselves guilty. In this sense Rousseau had won a very significant battle. Guilt had invaded women's hearts.'[3]

Growing numbers of middle-class women began to take up mothering as a full-time profession, and by the middle of the nineteenth century greater knowledge about health care, together with Darwinian theories of evolution, meant that there was far more for a mother to do. Children were now to be studied and moulded as 'science and religion had combined by then to make child-rearing a matter of continual nourishing and pruning, staking up and cutting back,' writes Christina Hardyment in her superb study of the history of childcare manuals, *Perfect Parents*. All over America at the end of the nineteenth century, groups of middle-class mothers gathered to study and discuss child-rearing as if it were a job. 'What profession in the world, then, needs so wide an outlook, so perfect a poise, so fine an individual development, such breadth and scope, such depths of comprehension, such fullness of philosophy as the lightly considered profession of motherhood?' asked one mother addressing the 1897 National Congress of Mothers Convention.[4]

Child-study associations and journals were founded in Europe and the United States, and their research provided childcare-manual writers for the first time with statistics which allowed them to establish 'norms' and guidelines for parents to follow. This meant that parents began to seek to fit their child within patterns of average behaviour. Then when the state began to intervene in the welfare of children, towards the end of the nineteenth century, motherhood became defined as an intense full-time activity for everyone, irrespective of class or social standing.

Living conditions and standards of health in the 1890s were so appalling that infant mortality rose. Fertility rates were plummeting, and there was concern that Britain might be committing 'national suicide', particularly after the great loss of life during the Boer War. Children were dying from bronchitis, pneumonia, whooping cough and diarrhoea, and the speedy spread of these diseases was largely linked to bad housing, overcrowding, inadequate diet, poor sanitation and contaminated water supplies rather than to poor mothering.

But as international tensions increased, it seemed increasingly important to politicians to raise the quality of the nation's children as future soldiers. So mothers were targeted as the main means of raising the nation's wellbeing. 'At the bottom of infant mortality, high or low, is good or bad motherhood,' said John Burns, President of the Local Government Board at the first National Conference on Infant Mortality in 1906. 'Give us good motherhood and good pre-natal conditions, and I have no despair for the future of this or any other country.'[5] A host of measures tried to instruct largely working-class mothers in the art and craft of motherhood. 'Mothercraft' welfare centres sprang up all over Britain. By the late 1930s there were more than 3,500 of them. Health visitors began to enter working-class homes to inspect and instruct, and the baby-care manuals that had previously only been read in upper-middle-class households were distributed to the poor. Advice columns on child-rearing began to appear in newspapers, and special magazines and books on child-rearing were successfully published. All child-rearing advice carried with it an implied threat: ignore this and you jeopardize your child's health. This element of preying on a mother's guilt in order to make her do more for her children is still used extensively to sell baby products to this day.

New legislation was introduced in the first ten years of the twentieth century to safeguard children's interests, ensuring the provision of school meals and regular medical examinations at school, and requiring all local authorities to report live births to the district medical officer within thirty-six hours. The Children Act of 1908 prohibited children from going into pubs, imposed fines or prison terms on parents whose children were killed owing to lack of fire-guards, for instance, or died as a direct or indirect result of the parent being under the influence of drink at the time. This legislation signalled a fundamental change in attitude towards children from the state. The state took on responsibility for safeguarding children's interests and parents were liable for neglect. A father could be imprisoned if he sent his son out to work rather than to school, as could a working mother if her children were not sufficiently cared for. During the 1930s the National Society for the Prevention of Cruelty to Children adopted a new role of chasing up families and threatening them with legal action if they did not follow the health clinic's prescriptions.

These measures may well have improved the overall health

and welfare of the nation's children, but so too did improving social conditions and medical knowledge through the twentieth century. They also had a specific impact on the way women mothered, undermining their confidence in their maternal instincts and giving them more to do. Regular measuring and weighing of babies established averages and set milestones of development which made many women competitive, prouder but often demoralized when their child fell short of the average. After all, an average is only a line with a huge number of children above or below it.

The new science of psychology introduced a whole new planet of influences which laid blame at the feet of mothers and led to greater feelings of guilt. In the 1920s the American psychologist John B. Watson introduced the theory of 'behaviourism', in which he maintained that children were like machines that could be programmed from birth, and that women's sentimentality clouded their judgement when it came to raising the hard, stoical individual now required in the modern industrial world (for 'individual', read 'man'). 'If you expect a dog to grow up and be useful as a watchdog, a bird-dog, a fox-hound, useful for anything except a lapdog, you wouldn't dare treat it the way you treat your child,' he wrote in his bestselling *Psychological Care of the Infant and Child*, published in 1928. 'When I hear a mother say "Bless its little heart" when it falls down, or stubs its toe, or suffers some other ill, I usually have to walk a block or two to let off steam.'

The child psychologist Bruno Bettelheim believed at one time that the cold and emotionally detached mother created autism in her child. Male homosexuality was considered to be a by-product of the emasculating or smothering mother, the mother who wanted a girl. The child 'expert' Dr Frederick Truby King influenced numerous mothers during the 1920s with his stern ethos of spaced feeding, not too much cuddling and a great deal of fresh air, advice which directly contradicted the methods which mothers had been using for centuries and made many women reluctant to trust their own instincts. Kathleen Davey brought up her two daughters, born in 1942 and 1944, using the Truby King regime. Her second baby caught pneumonia at eighteen months and had to be admitted to hospital as a direct result of being put outside for fresh air whatever the weather.

> She was in hospital for a fortnight and I wasn't allowed to see her. All you were allowed to do when you visited was to look at her through the glass doors. And she was crying her eyes out. I would have given anything to have gone in and comforted her but they wouldn't allow it, they said seeing the parents upset the children. As though she wasn't upset enough . . . I put it all down to the fact that she was allowed to go out in the cold and got pneumonia. I suppose if I'd been sensible and not been so conscientious I wouldn't have let her go out in the cold weather. But I felt guilty if I didn't. I used to think, 'She's got to go out once a day.' They said all babies should go out once a day. 'If you keep them indoors, then when they do go out they catch a cold.'[6]

This surge of interest in the welfare of the child at the turn of the century increased the demands on the mother. The part-time responsibilities of keeping a child alive, reasonably clean and educated, which were shared amongst servants and other family members or neighbours, were no longer enough. The profound influence of Freud meant a new understanding of psychological trauma beginning with birth itself and mothers quickly came to be seen as the prime influence on the child's psychic stability and responsible for the type of adult that child became. With the growth of the 'good' mother came the growth of the 'bad' mother, and direct evidence of that could be seen in the child – in babies who cried inconsolably, in withdrawn or destructive children, in the adult who steals, rapes or finds it hard to form lasting relationships. The psychoanalyst René Spitz (1887–1974) devoted a large section of *The First Year of Life* to diseases in the infant provoked by maternal attitudes: three-month colic was, he believed, caused by 'Primary Anxious Overpermissiveness'; 'Hostility in the Guise of Manifest Anxiety' caused eczema; and 'Oscillation between Pampering and Hostility' caused rocking in infants.[7]

The psychological influences of mothering and notions of being a 'good' or 'bad' parent are stronger today than they have ever been. The knowledge that sexual abuse and violence can be handed down through generations, that traumatic relationships with our own parents can be revisited on our own children, means that mothers are now highly sensitive to any negative influences or thoughts which may undermine their child's development. We cannot help but have our own traumas from childhood; some are more distressing than others; and when they have come from parental neglect or ignorance, or even from the most casual ill-natured comment which might have undermined our confidence in our own abilities, we know the power that parents have and the damage that they can do.

A smothering mother can stifle a child's curiosity, as can an apathetic mother. Unanswerable questions surface daily: if I make her eat her lunch, am I sowing the seeds of anorexia? How do I balance taking an interest in his life without squashing his individualism? How do I encourage her to be herself, to relish the profound differences between her and me without being accused of neglecting her needs, of not taking an interest or of not being there for her in later life? If I encourage him to be quiet and gentle, will he later be called a wimp by his classmates?

The result is agonizing doubt in one's instinctive ability to mother and an assumption that whatever one does has as many potentially bad effects on children as well as good. 'I would never be a good mother,' writes Jane Lazarre in *The Mother Knot*.

Hadn't I already caused him to be colicky with my own treacherous anxiety? The experts were right, I thought. Babies are born to be placid, contented creatures. It is only the bad mother repressing her unfair resentment, holding the baby too tightly, too loosely, too often, too rarely, letting him cry, picking him up too soon, feeding him too much, too little, suffocating him with her love or not loving him enough – it is only the bad mother who is to blame.[8]

'I think not only about what I have to do to guide them, but also about the sort of person that I have to be to be a role model.' Maggie is a part-time local authority worker with two children under five, who was born in Ireland and now lives in north London. 'I think that you grow up to respect your parents because of the people that they are and you learn by watching them rather than by what they tell you, so I think: I'll have to be a strong person, I have to be this and I have to be that, and it feels like a huge responsibility. Not only do you have to do the right thing for them, but you have to be the right sort of person all the time and while it is all right to make mistakes, you have to be able to acknowledge that you've made a mistake and start again.'

Like many mothers Maggie has realized that she is setting far too high a goal if she expects that she is always going to be able to do the right thing and be the quintessential 'good' mother. Accepting fallibility in mothering means accepting that all humans are fallible and that damage is done to children, sometimes irreparably. Our children have to grow up in the real world, where there is danger, stress and confusion, where mistakes are made by grown-ups as well as by children. All mothers can do is attempt to limit the damage caused to children so that it is not too harmful in the long run.

Sue, a confessed perfectionist who gave up a successful career in journalism so that she could be a dedicated, full-time mother, realized this on her son's first experience of Hallowe'en. Her neighbour's children came trick or treating and when she opened the door, holding her son on her hip, one of the children was wearing a devil mask. 'He shrieked in a way that I'd never heard before and went rigid. He was mortally terrified, I could feel it on my hip. I tried to make it better, I tried to think how I could repair it for him so that he knew that nice things come through that door as well as horrible things. My old self would say that was final, a stain on him, and therefore nothing was going to be the same again. Now, of course, that there have been days since then, I've learnt that he has dealt with it and that it's certainly not bothering him, that horrible things do happen and that some things are irreparable in people.'

With so much more for a mother to do in order to qualify as 'good', childcare books mushroomed to fill in the gaps in their knowledge. But history demonstrates that it is not necessarily wise to trust the 'expert' over and above one's own instinct, for theories of child-rearing go in and out of fashion. The Truby King austere orthodoxy was overturned after the Second World War and 'good' motherhood became more child-centred, intensifying the efforts required of mother. Truby King had encouraged mothers to leave their babies in a pram in the garden for hours on end so that they could get on with their household tasks while encouraging self-sufficiency in the child, for 'walks jarred its spine and worried its brain with too many uncensored impressions'.[9]

Then Dr Spock overturned this theory, believing such treatment to be both emotionally and intellectually damaging. Babies, he said, needed stimulation, encouragement and fun in order to grow bright and beautiful. Piaget's work on child development, Maria Montessori's theories of early education, as well as institutions such as The Better Baby Institute in Philadelphia, have shown that it is possible to sharpen a child's mind and improve his or her intellectual performance from a very early age. It wasn't enough for a toy to be distracting, it had to be instructive, and a vast industry of new educational toys became available for mothers to use in daily play with their children. Play is now not only considered a source of learning but a source of therapy, an opportunity for a child to air his or her anger or jealousies. Toys must suit the age of the child in order not to be frustrating.

Mothers now consider it important to play with or talk to their children whenever possible in order for them not to feel deprived. Occasionally we even worry that we may be overstimulating them with baby music groups and massage, television, toys, playgroups and playgrounds.

In the 1950s the American psychologist Carl Rogers introduced the idea that children need 'unconditional positive regard', which means that children must still feel valued even when they behave badly. A 'good' mother should make a child feel loved and cherished even when he has aroused such anger by his behaviour or attitude that she could give him away. This places difficult, if not impossible, demands on a parent when it comes to disciplining now that smacking is no longer a viable option. Sending a child into another room, or making him sit on a step until he has understood that his behaviour was unacceptable, is a direct rejection, a clear statement that the child is not wanted, and cannot be called 'unconditional positive regard' by any stretch of the imagination.

Psychologists such as Bruno Bettelheim have even impressed the need to make toddlers feel positive about their own excrement so that they do not grow up repulsed by their own bodies or anally retentive – but poo does smell awful even to a child and it can be hard to disguise one's disgust. Sexuality is to be encouraged rather than repressed even if the mother is being acutely embarrassed in front of Granny. The anthropologist Jean Liedloff, who has no children of her own, has written an influential book called *The Continuum Concept*, which is devoured by mothers who are keen to do the right thing.[10] In it she advocates that all the psychosocial ills of mankind are due to the fact that babies are not kept physically attached to their mothers until they positively struggle to get away, which means, for instance, carrying your sixteen-pound baby with you everywhere you go. Women accept that the theory makes sense, and then all too often find that it is physically and emotionally far too draining and then feel that they have failed themselves and their child by not doing what was best for them.

Modern understanding of psychology and principles of good child-rearing hold that the growth of happy, healthy children is down to considerate, tolerant and emotionally enriching parenting. More and more is required of women in order to qualify as 'good' or 'good enough' mothers. Motherhood is now such a full-time occupation that if a woman chooses to have a child, then she feels duty-bound to sacrifice everything in her own life for her child's welfare in order to be a 'good' mother. Co-existence and survival within a harsh and dangerous world are no longer enough. A 'good' modern mother is a teacher, occupational therapist, psychologist, nurse, cook and driver. She must raise well-rounded, socially responsible human beings without the wrath of God or the Rod. She should never show her depression or anger in case it should have a negative effect on her child. She must respect her child's rights, see things from a child's perspective and empathize with his feelings. She should always be careful to explain her actions or instructions in a way that a child can understand. 'This is all to the good, but it creates procedural problems,' writes Maureen Freely in her book on feminism and motherhood, *What About Us?*

> Children who are first-class citizens don't follow instructions, not even in an emergency. They stop in their tracks and ask why, and refuse to budge until they have accepted your request as reasonable . . . lecture an equal child for refusing to do his homework, and you'll hear what the suicide rate is amongst overworked pupils in Japan.[11]

Central heating and modern domestic appliances have liberated mothers from much of the more mundane, hard work of caring for children's basic physical needs. Contraception and fewer children have improved the overall health of mothers and the quality of daily life. But the growth of the 'good mother' theory through the twentieth century snatched away any sense of liberation that mothers may have got from such radical change and gave them more to do to occupy that spare time.

Without these new demands on a mother's time, women would undoubtedly have found it easier to marry their working and mothering needs. But one further 'expert' nailed the coffin of the working mother firmly shut. John Bowlby was brought up by a nanny in an upper-middle-class Cambridge home with five siblings, including a competitive older brother. He became a renowned psychiatrist and at the end of the Second World War was asked by the World Health Organization to study the mental health of orphans and children who had been separated from their parents during the war. His report, *Maternal Care and Mental Health*, was published in 1951 and its influence has been profound, even though his research methods were subsequently severely discredited. His 'attachment theory' maintained that children under three became severely distressed if they did not have the constant close presence of their mother and that this insecurity could affect their future development. He prescribed 'the provision of constant attention day and night, seven days a week and 365 in the year' in his report. He advised that mothers should not work outside the home and warned that 'there is a very strong case indeed for believing that prolonged separation of a child from its mother (or mother substitute) during the first five years of life stands foremost among the causes of delinquent character development'.[12]

Subsequent researchers have found that his samples were extremely small and that he studied atypical children who had been placed in institutions in which they were vulnerable to abuse, and who were separated completely and constantly from their entire families, rather than just from their mother for part of the day. His emphasis on the supreme importance of bonding with the mother excluded a child's other, just as important, needs such as play, stimulation, a variety of experience and a happy mother rather than a mother who is simply there. Research has also shown that small children can become securely attached to more than one person, not just the mother, and that it is the quality of care that a child receives that is more important than who he receives it from. The crucial factors to secure attachment in a young child when the mother works appear to be that the substitute is well known to the child, responsive to the child's needs and does not keep changing.

Bowlby later claimed to have been misrepresented by his critics, and said that he did not believe that it was only the mother who could satisfy a child's attachment needs. However, his findings were used extensively by writers of childcare manuals. They were timely, persuading women to vacate the jobs they had so enjoyed doing during the war and reinforcing the importance of family life and the family unit after the recent grief, child evacuations and social upheaval of war. Until that time, few children had enjoyed round-the-clock care from their mothers alone. Upper-middle-class children had been brought up by nannies, and childcare amongst working people was shared extensively throughout the family and local neighbourhood. It was easy to believe that more care and more mother love was the key to raising healthier, more balanced people when most women and men had never enjoyed that luxury as children. From now on only mother would do, yet more and more women were wanting to return to work due to economic necessity, rising educational standards and expectations, and growing fear of isolation within homes which no longer had servants and were without other family members. The result has been unparalleled levels of guilt and anxiety for mothers who work.

Some mothers who work full-time feel that they are failing to give their best to both their jobs and their children and find the adjustment between two such differing paces difficult. When mothers go back to work, they often feel confused about what they really want and can feel a strong emotional need to be with their child when at work and an overwhelming need to get to work when at home. We worry about the quality of care and emotional support that our children get from minders and nurseries. We torture ourselves with the thought that our children might love their nannies more than us and feel jealous of the time they spend together, even though we know that we would find aspects of full-time motherhood depressing. The working mother who feels confused about leaving her children is often unhappy with the childcare she has chosen. Nannies cannot by definition bring up our children as well as we like to think we could (only have never dared try), and we become obsessive about cleanliness or the amount of cheese that goes missing from the fridge in our absence. And all because we think that we do not spend enough time with our children, round-the-clock time, the time that 'good' mothers spend with their children. In fact mothers, including full-time working mothers, have never spent as much time with their children as they do today.

Death separated large numbers of children from their mothers. Before 1800, 1 to 1.5 per cent of all births ended in maternal death.[13] While this may seem like a low figure, women had an average of six children, which increased a woman's chances of dying from childbirth to a fearful 8 to 10 per cent throughout her reproductive life, and childbirth was a leading cause of death amongst women of child-bearing age. John Lister's discovery of antisepsis in the 1870s reduced maternal death from puerperal fever because doctors and midwives began to understand the nature of infection through the open wounds of a woman who had just given birth. But maternal death continued to be high in the early twentieth century. In 1918, one mother died for every 264 babies born alive.[14] Behind each cold statistic there is a child without a mother.

If a mother survived childbirth, poor general health meant that her life expectancy averaged at forty until 1900.[15] Children did not enjoy twenty years of continuous care, as many mothers expect to provide today. Mothers often died young, and if the children survived infancy they were farmed out at an early age. Wet-nursing was sufficiently common for Henry III to pass a law, in 1235, against Christian wet-nurses suckling Jews, and it continued until the end of the nineteenth century, with some families sending their babies away to nurse in the country for as long as two years. Wet-nursing was an essential way of nourishing a baby when the natural mother was unable to feed it and was for many poorer women an important source of income. In some rural areas, poor women would put their own child out to nurse so that they could take in a better-paying nurseling from elsewhere.

There has been a definite tradition throughout history of mothers allowing others to bring up their children. In France, children from poor families left at the age of seven or eight to work as domestic servants, shepherds, cowherds, or as apprentices to artisans until the mid-nineteenth century. In rural England, boys left at about the age of ten to work on farms, while daughters in the majority of poor homes went into service with richer households – or, if not richer, more genteel ones. Learning how to serve was considered crucial to a child's upbringing and it was easier to inculcate subservience in a house where other relationships had not been established, plus there was always the hope that a child's prospects could be furthered by their moving to a better-off household. Wealthier families packed their boys off to boarding-schools and many a daughter was incarcerated in a convent until she was of marriageable age. In Victorian Britain you were not considered middle-class unless you had at least a nursery maid, and the average nursery was a separate entity from the rest of the house, with parents having little day-to-day contact with their children. Mothers were remote and often idolized figures in a child's life.

Working women were in the past often separated from their children for many hours. In October 1843 a factory inspector's report on a large mill in Manchester mentioned women working from '5.30 a.m. till eight o'clock at night, with no cessation from work except a quarter of an hour for breakfast and three-quarters of an hour for dinner; so that these persons, having to be out of bed for 5 o'clock in the morning and not getting home till half-past eight o'clock at night may fairly be said to labour fifteen hours and a half out of the twenty-four.' Another factory inspector of 1844 reported women working from 6 a.m. to twelve at night with less than two hours off for meals. This meant 'half an hour to dress and suckle her infant and carry it out to nurse; one hour for household duties before leaving home . . .'[16]

These were not isolated incidents. Large numbers of working-class women had no choice but to work because their husbands were unemployed or unemployable, or because it was necessary to supplement the family income. In both cases working motherhood kept women and their children out of the workhouse. Over four million women were working in England and Wales according to the 1901 Census, and the overwhelming majority of these jobs were 'working class' in domestic service or agriculture or in the new industrial jobs, for the Industrial Revolution brought as many women as men into new types of work.'[17] Large numbers of these women continued working once they became mothers. According to a survey conducted by a Dr Robertson in a working-class area of Birmingham, out of 1,212 mothers who had given birth during 1908, 50 per cent had worked during that year; 70 per cent of these women worked in factories and workshops, which offered the highest wages; 20 per cent worked at home, and 9 per cent worked elsewhere ('elsewhere' isn't specified but is most likely to mean in other people's houses).[18]

With infant mortality still high – out of every 100 babies registered alive in England and Wales between 1865 and 1874, fourteen to sixteen died before they were twelve months old[19] – a mother's prime concern was for her youngest children. The psychological effects of working motherhood on growing children would not have worried mothers in the past when it was often their own earnings which prevented the children from starving. Lily Felstead was born in Cheshire in 1907, and when her husband became unemployed soon after they were married, she picked up whatever job she could in order to feed her four children.

> There was no money for coal, so we went cinder picking. You
> picked them, then you had to carry them half a mile back

again. You'd go to a second-hand shop for clothes, and I did
all my own knitting. I took in washing for two families and it
was a case of washing and ironing, probably for one and six-
pence, and then you'd go charring. You'd probably do a bit of
knitting for someone, a bit of sewing for someone, and for
two shillings, but that helped to pay for your bread. You were
the person that went hungry, never the children, because at
times you'd be too sick to want to eat – oh no, if there was two
pieces of bread that was divided in four, the kids had it.

Esther Peel was also born in 1907 and her three younger
brothers died of malnutrition when they were infants.

We were poverty-stricken. Really, my baby brothers starved to
death. I remember when my last brother died, the one I used
to look after. I think I looked on him as a doll, because I never
had a doll, I never had a toy. And one day they said he'd died.
When I went to bed that night he was in a coffin in my bedroom. My mother said, 'Say goodnight to him, won't you?' I
did.[20]

It is only now that we have the luxury of near certainty in our
children's survival, even though they seem so fragile when young,
that we are able to debate the morality and the theoretical notion
of damaging our children psychologically or emotionally by
working. It is only now that we have greater choice and control
over our fertility that the ubiquitous and disturbing question
'Why did she bother to have children at all if she doesn't want to
look after them?' threatens us daily.

At the turn of the century, as now, working motherhood
meant handing babies over to other women to care for them.
Surveys conducted in 1894 and in 1906 indicate that the vast
majority of these children were left with relatives and neighbours
and a small number were left in the care of older siblings, some
as young as seven, or daughters of other families paid to come in

to care for the younger ones.[21] Then, as now, cases of neglect were well publicized and therefore exaggerated by the upper-middle classes who had been influenced by the surge of childcare literature demanding greater input from the mother for the welfare of the child. Then, as now, such publicity sought to highlight the dangers of mothers working.

Reports from the Royal Commission on Labour in 1873 said that mothers working in the nail- and chain-making shops of the Midlands either left their babies in the care of little girls 'or else they are perched on a warm heap of fuel or dangled in an egg-box from the shop ceiling. When they are old enough to walk, they play in the gutter and thrust their arms into the holes which ventilate the drains.'[22] Several investigations were carried out into the death rates of children born to women working in the textile industry in the second half of the nineteenth century. They found that the death rate of children under twelve months with working mothers was higher than the general death rate, but the samples used were very small and the findings were similar to the death rates found in some rural areas. But these results were used by politicians and opinion formers to put forward the case that mothers should not work, despite the fact that it was not their working that caused children to suffer so much as the poor social and health conditions of the time.

Throughout history children have always been vulnerable to neglect from their carers. Wet-nursing severely reduced a baby's chance of survival, for 'the terrible poverty that had motivated the rural family to take on a nurseling in the first place created an environment that was in every way inhospitable to good mothering and even to physical survival,' writes the historian Edward Shorter in his book *The Making of the Modern Family*.[23] Housing was often overcrowded and filthy, babies were often weaned on to pap – a mixture of flour, water and sugar – at too early an age so that the nurse could take in another nurseling. Some wet-nurses fed their own children first, leaving little for their charges, and others were completely dry. Children of women factory workers during the second half of the nineteenth century were also liable to poor care – a diet of pap must have led to pain and fractious crying from the infant and often carers would give drugs to soothe a child to sleep, particularly if a nurse had several children in her care. Godfrey's Cordial, Atkinson's Royal Infants' Preservative and Mrs Wilkinson's Soothing Syrup were sold over the counter, and a narcotic – laudanum or morphia – was an ingredient in all of them.

Such treatment seems shocking to the modern mother, but has to be seen within the context of a generally high death rate and poor social conditions. 'That the children of the poor suffer from insufficient attention and care is not because the mother is lazy and indifferent to her children's well-being,' writes Maud Pember Reeves in her classic study of working-class family life in 1913.

It is because she has but one pair of hands and but one over-burdened brain. She can just get through her day if she does everything she has to do inefficiently. Give her six children, and between the bearing of them and the rearing of them she has little extra vitality left for scientific cooking, even if she could afford the necessary time and appliances.[24]

Wilful neglect from carers was undoubtedly exceptional rather than commonplace, just as it is today. Such examples are perhaps the historical equivalent of the childminder who smacks or the nursery that does not have a high enough regard for safety or allows the children to do what they like while the nursery workers chat and chainsmoke in the staff room. Vast improvements in health care, diet, living conditions and education, together with huge advances in the understanding of the psychological needs of growing children, have meant that our children are now largely left in prime care when we go out to work. Our worries are usually to do with them watching too much television or eating too many crisps while we are at work, rather than whether they are being fed at all.

Children have never had it so good, yet as mothers we still
punish ourselves for not doing more for them, for not being
there constantly to spoon-feed every mouthful of mashed
chicken breast or soothe every grazed knee. Our children are, in
the main, healthier and more stimulated than ever, because mothers now do so much more for their children. We now respect
childhood as distinct from adulthood and children are not forced
to work and behave like small adults from the age of ten. There
isn't an idyllic past where large numbers of women were kept by
men and spent every hour of their time looking after their children. Yet in spite of all this change, of all of the additional work
we do as mothers to bring up our children well, some of us still
feel that if we could only give up work we would be even better
mothers.

The concept of the 'good' mother, combined with modern
socioeconomic pressures on women to earn their own living
and compete head-on with men, has created a whole new range
of difficulties for women when they become mothers. Growing
numbers of women now expect to be able to work, pursue
their career aspirations and have children. But few of us are
prepared for the logistics of juggling the two responsibilities, or
for the way that our priorities and attitudes towards working
can change after the birth of a child. Like countless other
women, I presumed that I would be able to carry on working
much as I had done before. I would take the baby with me to
work and then, when she was old enough to be weaned from
me, I would take her to a childminder. I had no idea how hard
it would be to do either of these things in practice or how my
needs from work would change. I needed to get back to work to
feel attached to the real world again, the world that values professional status and career success so much more than
motherhood, but I found it almost impossible to leave my baby.
I felt more ambitious than ever before. I wanted to succeed for
my child rather than for myself, and saw no point in working at

something which would take me away from her, unless that work was worthwhile.

A woman faces three basic choices over work when she becomes a mother. She can return to work full-time provided that she can find affordable childcare that she trusts. If her partner earns enough to be able to support all three of them, she can leave work completely should she find that her career aspirations have evaporated with motherhood. Or she can try to have the best of both worlds by working part-time or becoming self-employed. Each choice has pros and cons.

Giving up work completely to mother full-time may still be many women's dream, but there are severe sacrifices to this option. It means complete financial dependence on the father of your child, which may alter the emotional balance in your relationship. It means you are losing out on contributory state benefits accrued through working, such as unemployment benefit and pension rights, which renders women more vulnerable to poverty, particularly in old age. And it is likely to be harder to go back into the labour market at the same level as you were pre-motherhood. Research shows that many women find themselves substantially demoted when they go back to work once their children have reached school age.

Increasingly, full-time professional women find that they have no choice but to return to work at the end of their maternity leave to retain their maternity pay. Gemma works for BBC Television. 'I was contractually obliged to go back to work, which is, I now realize, a two-edged sword. On one level I didn't have that terrible thing of thinking that nobody was ever going to employ me again, but I also had this clock ticking constantly, counting the number of days that I had left with my child. I thought the world divided into those who did go back to work and those who didn't. I never realized that it would be so difficult every day and that even women who have made the decision still find it hard, years later.' She feels guilty and inadequate on both fronts as a result, unable to give her best either to her children or to her job because she is tired and emotionally torn.

Other full-time working mothers feel guilty about the effect of a long working day on their child. Grace works as an administrator in a government health department. Her son Malcolm is six years old. 'I feel that he has such a long day. If he could get up at eight rather than at seven, to be bundled off to the childminder, and if I could be there at three thirty after school for him to help with his reading, then maybe it would be different. When he comes home from the childminder, he's so tired and I am too, I don't feel I have enough time for him, I don't listen. I just say, "OK, Malcolm, that's enough," and then I feel guilty. I don't think I'm doing very well as a mother. I'd give myself 3 out of 10.'

For mothers working full-time on low incomes, choices over work are often driven by economics. If too much of a woman's income is disappearing on childcare, then it makes sense to opt for one of the growing numbers of part-time jobs or flexible working, which can be fitted in around school hours or when other family members are around to look after the children free of charge. The overwhelming majority of part-time workers in Britain are women, and the majority of these are mothers. While this is often a conscious choice, made because women want to spend more time with their children, they lose out substantially in financial terms. Earnings are usually lower pro-rata for part-time workers and few part-time opportunities exist in management or the professions, which means that often women opt for demotion in order to qualify. Motherhood costs more than just meeting the immediate practical needs of a growing child. A woman's capacity to bring money into the home is severely compromised, at a time when it is most needed.

Research on working mothers damaging their children should always be taken with a pinch of salt. For every small sample showing that an even smaller number of children at nurseries are more aggressive there are at least five other studies showing no difference at all. What the research does show consistently is that childcare does not damage children provided that they are in good-quality consistent care, where they are nurtured emotionally and receive plenty of stimulation. If you take a child from a very poor household with few toys and a mother who is depressed by full-time motherhood and put him in a day nursery where there are plenty of stimulating toys and activities, other children and experts in child development who know how to encourage self-esteem and confidence in a child, he is far more likely to thrive than he would do cooped up in a flat at the top of a tower block, with no stimulus. The toddler of a working mother is more socially skilled, emotionally mature, self-sufficient and intellectually independent than children of mothers who do not work.[25]

Children need their mothers, but they do not need to be with them all of the time, even as babies. There is a tremendous arrogance in the assumption that only the mother of a child can best look after that child. Child psychologists know that children thrive in the presence of other children and learn through play. They get exposed to a wider world and to a variety of grown-ups and personalities if they go to nursery school, and if they have a consistent carer outside their immediate family they are privileged rather than deprived or confused. If a child has a loving mother, father and childminder or nanny, that child is likely to get better care and understanding, for, as Louise Erdrich writes:

> Women without children are also the best of mothers, often, with the patience, interest, and saving grace that the constant relationship with children cannot always sustain. I come to crave our talk and our daughters gain precious aunts. Women who are not mothering their own children have the clarity and focus to see deeply into the character of children webbed by family. A child is fortunate who feels witnessed as a person, outside relationships with parents, by another adult.[26]

The one possible cost of working motherhood appears to be a higher attachment disruption rate of up to 15 per cent over the attachment disruption rate of a family where the mother stays at home. Attachment disruption means that the child feels that his mother wants to respond sensitively, but doesn't genuinely understand his needs or preoccupations, and therefore feels less secure. Remember, though, that the child of a mother who stays at home can also feel misunderstood, particularly if that mother is depressed and inattentive, and that it is not an irreparable condition. There are ways in which a parent can inculcate the deep knowledge that 'Mummy and Daddy know and understand me' even if they are out at work. A child's mother is such a large and omnipotent force on a child that some child psychologists believe that mothers continue to exert that influence even when the mother is not there as an 'evoked companion'. Dr Daniel Stern of the Cornell Medical Center in New York believes that the image that a small child holds of its mother is so vivid that it is almost palpable, as if she is standing there holding his or her hand and that image is certainly enough to carry them through absences.[27]

According to Dr Sirgay Sanger, founder of the Parent/Child Interaction Program at St Luke's–Roosevelt Hospital in New York, parents can actively nurture a sense of attachment in very small children. A child who is given time and patience so that he or she can express his or her needs and desires automatically feels wanted and understood. One- and two-year-olds often find it distressing when their mother leaves in the morning because they still feel that their mother is part of themselves rather than a separate person. But if that child also has a strong relationship with his or her carer, then he or she will not be damaged by their mother's leaving. Mothers can build links between morning and night by starting a drawing or a book together which will be finished later that day. Transitional objects that go everywhere with a child, such as a bear or cloth, can give a child security, as will the bag that contains his or her nappies and spare clothes. Establishing tiny routines and rituals with the same song or lap game at feeding or bath time will give the smallest child landmarks and reassurance.

The agony and anxiety of leaving a screaming toddler can be extremely distressing, but it does end, and both of you do get used to it provided that you resist the urge to feel guilty and are completely honest about your motives. Like every other working mother, I have stood on the doorstep listening to my small child cry for me as I left for work. But the agony definitely waxes and wanes according to my own state of mind. On the days when we have had wonderful mornings together, I hear that screaming and resent every aspect of having to go to work. But on the days when I am suffering from broken sleep, when both children whine and tax my patience to the limit, any resistance to going to school or spending a day with their minder is quickly quashed with positive dismissal before I leave with a profound sense of liberation. On these days, if I linger on the doorstep, I soon hear the sobbing subside into laughter as the minder cracks a joke or announces plans for the day.

Even mothers who do not need to work do not want to be with their children all of the time. Feeling guilty about any separation will provoke or prolong any distress in the child because he will feel insecure by your reactions and vulnerable without you there. When leaving your child with a minder or at a nursery, research shows that he will make the smoothest adjustment if you treat it as a natural thing to do and approach childcare or nursery education as if you believe in it. Leave immediately after a positive and cheerful goodbye, preferably looking your child straight in the eye. Do not hover around or try to distract him with something before you sneak out, or feel the need to indulge in overlong explanations as to why you have to leave now, because that will only communicate your own confusion and distress to the child and give him something to worry about. Yet, when children get upset, don't ignore or dismiss their complaints. If your child senses that you understand how he or she feels, then you are automatically reassuring any insecurity.

Collectmg your child at the end of the day can also be fraught with difficulty when you are tired and on another intellectual wavelength. Gemma's daughters are four and one. 'For me, detaching myself from my work and attaching myself to my children is the hardest thing. There have been times when I've sat outside in the car on my own for ten minutes smoking a cigarette because I know that that's my time. There have been times when I've poured myself a drink before I go up to them shrieking in the bathroom because I need some energy from somewhere. Some people think it's a lovely way to unwind, to come home and put the children to bed, but I don't.'

Taking time to wind down to try to clear your mind before you actually resume contact with your child will help to make that meeting more joyful. If you then allow your child to dictate the pace for just ten to fifteen minutes so that he can show you his pictures and involve you in the world that you have told him matters because you have taken him there, then you are less likely to encounter conflict, resistance or further tears. You don't have to do anything special with your child, you don't have to stimulate him with a dozen different activities as soon as you come in the door in order to appease your guilt, because all a child wants you to do is concentrate on him for a while before you make a cup of tea or look through the morning's post. This will re-cement that bond with the child so he will forget that you have ever been away. Follow him rather than direct him with activities. It doesn't matter if he starts a book, then picks up another one and then shows you a toy, as long as you are there, responding to his attempts to communicate with you with smiles and encouragement. Small children go through phases daily with bursts of energy followed by periods of calm. Your return provokes a burst of energy.

Research by Dr Ellen Hock of Ohio State University has shown that if a woman's definition of good motherhood is broad enough to encompass the fact that a good mother can also work, then she is likely to worry far less about her child's welfare when she is at work.[28] But a working mother who feels confused and guilty about working transmits that confusion to the child, prolonging his or her distress at the prospect of separation. Being anxious will make the mother less receptive to her child's needs and make it more likely that her child will feel insecure. It is not working itself that can damage children, so much as the guilt that women feel about wanting or having to work.

Mothers spread a wide wing of love and care over the entirety of a child's life, not just over set hours of the day. We feel guilty and sad about missing breakthrough moments in a small child's life, but from the child's point of view it is not the first moment that some new skill is achieved that matters as much as when he first shows it to you, for your reaction validates it. The intimacy a child gets from his mother or father is irreplaceable and parents nurture a child's spirit in intangible, incomprehensible ways. This love is complemented by the affection and love of a nursery worker or nanny; it is never replaced. Mothers determine the wider culture of a child's life whether or not they are there.

'There is inherent in motherhood a continual giving up of self,' writes Anne Roiphe in her book, *Fruitful*, 'and few of us take to that without resentment, which itself creates a river of guilt.'[29] Self-sacrifice and self-denial seem integral to motherhood because a child's demands and needs are limitless. But we have to place limits on those demands. A baby sees his mother as an extension of himself, as an 'unusually busy limb', according to the psychologist Robin Skynner, until the mother fails to fulfil certain demands and he begins to see her as a separate being that isn't always controllable. This is essential to his development, to his understanding of his own boundaries. If mothers were perfect and able to respond to each and every demand made by a child at exactly the right time, their children would grow up with severe problems relating to a wider world where they can never be the most important aspect. If mothers were never separated from their children and followed every latest theory of 'good' motherhood, their children would never have space for spontaneity, imaginative play and healthy chaos. It isn't possible or wise to create a perfect, conflict-free world where our children's needs are always paramount, because they have to grow up and live in the real world, riddled with conflict where women work. Mothers have needs as people too and separation for part of the day from their children is now an integral aspect of modern life, something our children have to learn to live with.

Perhaps 'good' mothers have to find the generosity in their hearts to understand that their children are separate individuals who are entitled to as much love and variety of stimuli from different types of people as possible, rather than selfishly keep the child to themselves by not working. I know, now that my children are old enough to talk back with reason and intelligence far beyond their years, that they have gained a great deal and lost nothing by my working. They have gained physical confidence from a sporty nanny who encouraged them to climb and swim and ride a bike. They know more about Irish culture and karate than I do, and they have a trusted other confidante to turn to at difficult moments. The only person who has possibly lost anything is me, because as each day passes and my children grow and change I know that precious moments are slipping away.

If we have to work, but also want to do our best by our children, that means finding unprecedented levels of tolerance and generosity when it comes to employing someone to look after our small children during the day. It means accepting that your childminder or nanny has different but equally valuable attributes to give to your child because she is not you. It might mean tolerating a messy home if your child is happy; it means respecting that your child has a separate relationship with his or her carer rather than feeling jealous of it. Whenever I hear middle-class parents complaining about the difficulties of finding a good nanny, and almost boasting about how many disasters they have had in the past, I wonder what they must be like to work for. What did they do to drive her away? Nannies, childminders and nursery workers soon grow to love the children they care for and we must cherish that love because it protects and nurtures our children. The mother who punishes the nanny with unreasonable demands or expectations should look into her heart and ask herself why. A child's welfare and trust is of paramount importance, not whether or not the mother likes the carer or finds the quality of her washing-up intolerable. If we are to be responsible working mothers then we have to put our child's needs for continuity of care well above our own.

As each phase of childhood passes, mothers are reminded of the transient nature of motherhood, that it is just a phase which will one day pass out of one's life completely. Mothering my children is the most important part of my life now, but it is just a part of my life, and not its sole purpose. I have my own spirit which needs nurturing through work and adult company so that I can be a better mother and teach my children how to make their own way in the wider world. The phases of motherhood have focused my mind on life's stages, on the fact that one day they will not need me and I will need the satisfaction that comes from work more than ever. Motherhood has nurtured an ambition that I never knew I had. If I am to work, it has to be for something worthwhile; if I am to work, I now need to succeed for my children when I never previously needed to succeed for myself. Motherhood has made me more courageous at work and, like many other mothers and fathers, I have found that the ubiquitous, spiritual presence of one's own child diminishes the significance of office politics, hierarchy and the self-importance of people at work.

'I think it has something to do with seeing that there is more to life than strictly a professional career which makes one so much more productive and confident,' says Clara, an American historian living in London. 'Firstly I'm more productive in four hours than I used to be in three days because I now know that that is all I've got, but also my child's importance has overshadowed the importance of everything else. It puts everything into perspective, makes other things more enjoyable because I don't put nearly so much anxiety into them.'

Other women find that their children force a radical change of career, or they risk becoming self-employed because they want more control over their working hours. Sarah had a very high-powered job in advertising when she had her first child and was only the second woman at her level within that company to become a mother. She flung herself back into work for the next nine months and then realized that the values she now had were not those of the company she was being employed by. 'If I had an appraisal they said that I wasn't showing myself around the company enough, that it was profile that mattered, when I thought it was results, and mine were good. After nine months of this I thought, I'm not seeing enough of my baby, I'm exhausted. Yes, I'm earning money but where is it all going? I don't want to be Managing Director of this company and they don't value the way that I work.' So she left, had another child and set up her own consultancy.

Hannah also became self-employed, as a management consultant, after the birth of her daughter. 'She forced me to make a choice and take a risk. It's interesting how much risk comes into a woman's life once she has a child. I can't imagine doing anything for very long now because I'm used to a pattern of change. Having a baby means that everything is possible now, it doesn't mean that you'll actually do it but it creates a world of possibility.'

The idea that women have a choice about returning to work after they have a child is an increasingly outdated notion. Few families are able to maintain what is now considered to be a reasonable standard of living on one male salary and they need the valuable income that women provide. Increasing numbers of women find that they need to work for all of the same reasons that men do: for a sense of identity, achievement, gratification and the valuable friendships and social context gained from work as well as money. As a society we need the working input of women, and a commitment to equal opportunity must mean accepting that mothers work alongside fathers – yet women consistently find that they are compromised at work as mothers.

Some are dismissed outright for pregnancy, passed over for promotion or side-lined into lower-status, dead-end jobs if they opt for part-time work. Many women find it hard to get childcare that they trust or can afford and feel that their opportunities to strive at work are cramped by having to leave at set times to pick up children.

Isis is training to be a solicitor. She was clerking until she had her first child sixteen months ago and is now pregnant with a second. 'If I manage to get my law degree, then I might make it, but the course costs £8,000 and the idea of taking out an eight-grand debt in order to get my PGC and take articles seems unrealistic with two children. When you've just got yourself to think about, then you reason differently. But now with children, I've got to know that I can pay it back. Plus, solicitors' hours are hellish and there seems to be no point in having children if I'm not seeing them.'

For many women, combining the responsibilities of mothering with the responsibility of providing financially for their child means juggling low-paid part-time work. After she had her first child, Irene took up cleaning jobs where they would let her take her baby. 'I needed the money not for me but for her. You feel like you are falling into a hole where the only things that matter are: Can I feed them? Can I dress them? Can I keep them warm? If you're not earning, that's scary. I now know that I will do whatever it takes to get money for her and that makes me feel secure because I know that if my partner left us I could provide for her.'

Other women find any element of choice entirely compromised by the fact that their husbands are unemployed or unemployable. Kate works as an administrator in a hospital in London and had a stressful pregnancy. Her husband lost a well-paid job in the City and then she discovered that her contract was not to be renewed. She found a new job to go to but did not tell them she was pregnant because she was worried about miscarrying. Then an unexpected emergency Caesarean came as a severe blow to her self-esteem. Her husband looks after the baby while she is at work, but Kate feels that she has taken on a double burden. 'On top of the parental responsibilities, I now have the responsibility to maintain our son and John. I'm not saying that I don't value his contribution, but I do feel that if he was out earning the money, I would get a lot more done than he does.' Kate would love nothing more than to be at home with her son, but has little choice other than to work in order to provide for him. 'I imagined myself probably being like my mother who only went back to work when my father died when I was twelve. It is hard for me to accept this as the status quo, that I'll be working for X more years in order to bring my child up. It feels at times like being a single mother.'

Single mothers have even less choice, not having Kate's advantage of unpaid childcare. They either have to find a job which pays well enough for them to be able to sustain the costs of childcare as well as themselves or they have to live on state benefits. 'It's a struggle,' says twenty-year-old Kelly who lives on £50 per week income support in Essex with her three-year-old son. 'I'd like to get out to work every day. Sometimes I feel so cooped up at home. I was on YTS training to be a travel agent until I got pregnant. When Jason starts school I'd like to sort my career out, but until then I've got to stay put. I want to have more than just one child but I also want a career, so I may have to try and find a way of doing both at the same time rather than sort out one before the other, although I can't see how.'

Motherhood provokes change in a woman's working life. For many it brings a welcome breathing space to a boring job or an opportunity to give up work completely for a while. For others, motherhood raises intense and sometimes overwhelming feelings of inner conflict and phenomenal guilt about their working life. Many want to spend more time with their children and simply cannot for financial reasons. Others believe that they ought to be spending seven days of the week at home if they are to be 'good' mothers but cannot bear to give up work and a career that they love.

But there is no such thing as a 'good' mother, only a good-enough mother – one who does her best for her child, with love and respect for that child as an individual with individual needs, without denying her own needs totally in the process. 'Good-enough' mothering is about finding a compromise between the needs of both mother and child as an integral unit rather than subservient pandering to the needs of little emperors. We can only raise confident, independent, socially responsible children if we have those attributes ourselves, and putting ourselves in the wrong by assuming that only a 'bad' mother works is the wrong basis to start from. A mother who has confidence in the wider world breeds confidence in her children.

Working motherhood has always existed. It is not a new phenomenon. What is new is the concept that mothers should not work outside the home and that they should find unprecedented levels of joy and satisfaction from child-rearing alone. Huge cultural changes in the expectations of mothers and in the nature of the work mean that it is increasingly hard for women to feel as if they are 'good' mothers, when paradoxically they have probably never done a better job.

5

Emotions

We revisit the raw emotions of our own childhood when we have a child. We feel intense love, undiluted hate and anger, as well as extreme anxiety and fear, and can swing from one extreme emotion to another in a matter of minutes, just like a child. But unlike a child, we have to control our emotions, even though the sudden intensity of feeling can be overwhelming. When our children provoke unrecognizable depths of anger and hostility, we have to dig deep into our reserves of self-restraint in order not to be found guilty of manslaughter. If we reveal too much of our anxiety for their welfare, our children may grow up too fearful and inhibited by the world and its dangers. Even love, that great steaming cauldron which seems to drive everything we do for our children, can be a damaging force if we cannot learn how to love them enough in order to let them go. Clare works in publishing and has two children. 'One of the great things about family life that nobody tells you is how incredibly rich your life becomes, and how in the very balancing of all those things there is an immense many-stranded tapestry of emotion; it's so enjoyable having all of those feelings.'

Mother-love is considered absolute, a natural consequence of giving birth. The umbilical, hormonal and biological link between mother and child is presumed to be so strong, the effort of childbirth so all-engrossing, that women must fall deeply and immediately in love when they see their creation. But feelings of shock, grief, relief, disgust, amazement, joy and exhilaration are far more common than love after giving birth. A study of 120 new mothers in a London teaching hospital found that 40 per cent considered their first emotional reaction to holding their child after birth to be indifference.[1] 'Who gave birth to this child?' was the reaction of Nisa, in Marjorie Shostak's study of the !Kung people, as she stared down at the wriggling baby sucking her finger after she had given birth by herself beside a tree. 'I thought, a big thing like that, how could it possibly have come out from my genitals? I sat there and looked at her, looked and looked and looked.'[2]

I can remember vividly the first time I saw each of my daughters. Now that they have grown and memories of their birth have faded, first eye contact with each daughter has become the most important and lasting memory. After each birth I felt relief, wonder, amazement, contentment and fascination with my new baby's distinctive features, but whether these feelings add up to love, I cannot say. But as my babies have grown, I have grown to love them with a passion I never knew was possible. I couldn't love them more than I do, yet each day I seem to love them more. The pleasure gained from the love is almost indescribable. 'The world tips away when we look into our children's faces,' writes Louise Erdrich, coming close to it.[3]

Some women do fall in love with their baby at first sight, but for others, love grows with the child and their confidence in their ability to care for them. But when it does eventually hit, that love is so much more powerful than anything experienced by a woman before that it is capable of propelling her through great whirlwinds of difficulty in early motherhood. Scientists have found that mother-love and romantic love are chemically similar. Surges of dopamine and oxytocin create a bond, switch off critical or negative judgements and switch on pleasure circuits that produce feelings of exhilaration and attachment. Caroline, who has an eight-month-old daughter says, 'I used to think that love songs were about a man and a woman. Now I think they are more appropriate to a mother and baby. I can watch her for hours, I know every detail, the curls at the back of her head, the lines under her eyes.' Wendy also uses music (albeit banal) to attempt to describe the depth of her love for her children. 'I found myself singing Cliff Richard's song about the girl in your arms, but actually the child in your arms is always the child of your dreams and that's quite extraordinary.' 'I had not long attained my nineteenth year, when I became a mother,' writes Melisina Trench in her diary in 1787. 'The delight of that moment would counterbalance the miseries of years. When I looked in my boy's face, when I heard him breathe, when I felt the pressure of his little fingers, I understood the full force of Voltaire's declaration, "Le chef-d'oeuvre d'amour est le coeur d'une mère."'[4]

We don't have to produce children from our own bodies to feel this way. Mothers who adopt earn their child through a tortuous process of assessment which often takes longer than nine months. Juliet adopted a three-month-old baby after three failed IVF attempts. 'I met her on a Monday for two hours and I was so wound up and excited I could hardly speak. She fell asleep in my arms the first time we met and I was glad to leave because it was so overwhelming emotionally. The next time we met I spent all afternoon looking after her, and when I put her to sleep in her cot and realized that I couldn't take her home, I burst into tears. I loved her completely, in two days – that was all it took – and there was I thinking it would take weeks. I suddenly had this flash one day coming home of knowing exactly what people meant when they said they would die rather than let anything happen to their children. When you've only ever been by yourself, you never have that feeling because you are always the most important person, but now I know that if she were in danger I would think of her first and myself second. I couldn't love her more if she had come out of my own body.'

There is perhaps a deep, instinctive need in us to love something more than ourselves, to place someone more vulnerable first and learn how to love unconditionally. But often, it is only as the more negative and difficult emotions subside and we accept and get used to motherhood that love can find enough space to grow. Giving birth provokes a whole range of confusing emotions about identity, relationships with parents and the father of the child, life in general, and women are lucky if undiluted adoring love is all they feel. 'I cried for about half an hour when they gave him to me, I thought, Ugh! He's so ugly!' says Grace. The father of her child was still in Jamaica, unable to get an entry visa to Britain at the time of the birth. 'I wanted the man, I didn't want the baby. I didn't want to hold him, I just looked at him to make sure that he was OK. I felt disappointed by him, he had spit in his mouth and I just felt like dropping him. He had an alien quality and when he moved I thought, Ugh, he's alive. I wanted an angel that looked exactly like my husband. Instead, I got this other thing that looked exactly like me.'

'I was much more spaced-out than emotional, I definitely didn't do the mother-baby bonding thing quickly. I was too dazed and it was definitely a few weeks before it clicked and I felt that really powerful thing that mothers feel.' Natasha is a lawyer living in London. 'When people asked me, "Do you love him more than anything else in the world?" I remember thinking, Should I lie and just say "Yes" because it's easier, or should I say, "No, not really, I feel weird"? I remember saying to somebody that I felt as if I was babysitting somebody else's really cute baby. But I did feel an incredible sense of protectiveness before I knew that I really loved him, the way that I do now.'

The bonding at birth theory advanced by two Australian researchers, Marshall Klaus and John Kennell, in the 1970s has made it harder for women to accept their detachment or indifference towards their newborn babies as normal, natural. Klaus and Kennell studied elk, goats and Guatemalan women and con-cluded that for a short time after birth, mothers were 'in a specially sensitive state which made them more than usually ready to "fall in love" with their child'⁵ provided that they had skin-to-skin contact immediately after childbirth. Babies are particularly alert in the first 45–90 minutes after birth, which is why that first eye contact with one's baby can be particularly powerful. But Klaus and Kennell maintained that if skin-to-skin contact was not experienced at this time, there was a danger that the mother would be emotionally distant and even abusive.

The need for early bonding pervaded childcare manuals and spread rapidly through labour wards. The NCT remained adamant about the need for early bonding until it was dropped from their manual in 1994 when the theory became suspect. Repeated, subsequent research has found no scientific evidence of the bonding theory, but it was too late to slay the myth that a mother's capacity to love depended on early contact, on a single moment. Women who missed out on early contact because they were unconscious from a Caesarean, or in need of further med-ical attention, or because their babies were rushed into intensive care, could easily blame early separation for any difficulties they had in mothering their child. Women now had to bounce back immediately and take a keen interest in their baby to prevent future emotional neglect, when in reality few mothers have the strength or the inclination after childbirth for anything more than a cup of tea. 'The superglue bonding theory is not what I think of as normal, I don't know why women think that it should be,' says Christina McKenzie, who has been a midwife since 1978.

Constant early contact between mother and baby may be pleasurable, but it is not an essential requirement for the devel-opment of a healthy future relationship. Relationships grow with time. It might take weeks, months or years, but the overwhelming majority of women fall deeply and passionately in love with their child as the memory of labour fades, health and physical strength begin to recover and confidence in one's ability to mother grows.

When babies take so much from us physically through pregnancy and labour, when their demands seem so relentlessly tedious or difficult at first and deep sleep the most coveted luxury, it can be hard to find love for a small baby who seems to be depriving us of so much.

Grace only realized how much she loved her son when he was four years old and ill with salmonella. 'I could feel this child slipping away from me. I thought he was going to die. He was dying in my arms. It was then that I knew that I didn't really love his father, but that I loved this child. He's too much a part of me now.' For others love grows as their baby becomes more rewarding and gives love back. 'Initially he was just a bundle of needs and potential.' Kate gave birth by Caesarean. 'But now, at nine months, he's beginning to do much more. A small child is so much more cuddlable and responsive.' Jane Lazarre describes in *The Mother Knot* how she only really felt that deep love for her son on the night before he was due to start at nursery school at two and a half, when she realized he would no longer be completely dependent on her.

> Here it is, I think, sighing with relief. Here is the mother-feeling they talk about. It comes when your child is old enough to love you back, when you have known him for a while, when you are no longer physically suffering, when you have grown used to your life's changes, when you have no choice but to love him.[6]

As we fall deeper and deeper in love with our children, the tiniest details of memory become supremely important. 'When I lift him up out of the bath now, I always do it in the same way as the midwives did to show him to me when he was born, because he still looks the way he did when he came out, all naked and cute,' remarks Natasha. 'I remember fantastic moments of recognition with him during those first few nights in the hospital when it was really quiet, and lovely conversations with the midwives late

into the night,' recalls Sue. It is living with our children and tending to their tiniest, most intimate needs which fosters the deep
love that we feel. I can smell and feel their skin even though they
are not with me now. Their toys and clothes capture something
of their essence and seem less inanimate. I love the way that my
children have taken over my life, and produced such rich emotions in me. I love the way that I am ordered to stand in a line and
be a currant bun by someone less than half my size, the way that
an ordinary, dull little house, car, garden, bed, pair of shoes now
reverberate with memories of their fresh attitude. For those
shoes become giant when a two-year-old clatters around the bedroom impersonating a grown-up, the bed turns into a boat or a
trampoline, and the garden fascinates with woodlice and earth-
worms.

As love grows, so too does anxiety for that beloved child's welfare. A sense of 'skinlessness' and heightened vulnerability to
threats from the outside world begin in pregnancy. Often, we find
ourselves crying at the slightest provocation. We worry about
the health of our baby, and the effects of stress, diet and even
ambivalence about being a mother on the growing foetus within.
Pregnancy opens a Pandora's Box of risk which extends well
beyond the birth through the growing life of a child. But we
don't realize that when we are pregnant with our first child. We
think that if we could just get past the next landmark, beyond the
threat of miscarriage, beyond that amniocentesis, then everything will be all right. But once each threat passes, another arrives
and then another, because so much of the health and welfare of
our children is beyond our control. I spent many Wednesday
afternoons talking to women who had just given birth at St
Thomas's Hospital in London researching this book. Shock and
emotional distress were easily visible on their pallid faces. The
walking wounded mingle with the joyful on a labour ward and the
hot hospital air is pungent with emotion and drama. Every week
there was someone who had experienced unparalleled levels of

anxiety and trauma – a stillbirth, the birth of a baby with cerebral palsy, or, in the words of one of the midwives, 'I'd leave bed number 27 alone, her baby's a bit dodgy.' 'I am now very much more aware of the mortality of things.' Belinda had a previous stillbirth and delivered her first baby at the age of forty. 'It's an awareness that things happen very certainly and cruelly and I didn't have those feelings before birth.'

Then, as we bring these tiny beings home, anxiety levels soar even higher. They seem so fragile and helpless that couples have been known to telephone the hospital in blind panic when their baby first cries. We feel so large with sudden responsibility way beyond our capabilities that we become preoccupied by concerns about feeding, sleeping, nappy rash and teething. The threat of cot death or sudden illness while their bodies seem so small and defenceless is always there. Sometimes it's hard even to believe that babies know how to breathe on their own. Few mothers can get through the first year without checking that their baby is still alive when it is asleep. We worry about getting them to sleep when they are tired and then we worry about when they will wake up or why they haven't woken up. We worry when they cry and then when they don't. Why aren't they crying? Are they just passive or is there something seriously wrong?

Landmarks of child development become obsessions: the first smile, the first hard stool, the first solid food, the first coo, and then if babies don't sit up or stand or grip their spoon when the childcare handbooks say they should, mothers worry. Low-grade panic sets in about the nutritional quality of food, additives and food colourings, hormones in milk, hidden sugars in yoghurts, whether or not he or she is eating enough, ready to wean or old enough for piano lessons. Every simple household object becomes potentially harmful and the dangers of the world outside zoom into focus. Cars, pollution, meningitis, dangerous dogs, BSE-packed beefburgers, drugs, abduction, paedophilia, become terrifying threats, when previously a woman may never have given them much thought. Now that she has a child to protect 'pets are disease-carriers, plants poisonous or potential allergenics, sunshine causes cancer, sandpits are thick with dogs' poo and haunted by would-be rapists'.[7]

Once I thought nothing of jaywalking, or running for a moving bus. Now I walk miles in the wrong direction to find a zebra crossing. When we walk along the street I find it hard to believe that my children will stay on the pavement. ('You know what? They don't,' commented a friend.) We expect to be able to protect our children. We buy socket covers, table corners, fridge and cupboard fasteners, curly kettle flexes, reins, stair gates and car seats to limit the risks, but we cannot watch over them all the time, and the slim chance that something might happen to them becomes unthinkable. And the knowledge that sometimes we have no alternative but to expose them to harm only makes us feel more inadequate and guilty. We have all held a crying, hungry baby too close to boiling water as we struggled to strain, cool and mash potatoes for lunch. We have all had to take our eyes off one small child while we see to another's needs.

'I certainly felt for the first few months that the skinless feeling would be intolerable, for how could you care so much for one person who was subject to infinite possibilities?' says Sue. 'But I actually think it's better to be that way now, as I wonder how people can tolerate looking at the newspapers. There's something wrong in our ability not to be affected. There ought to be a Geldof effect every day. The skin that I am reapplying to myself I am much happier with, so it's a reconstruction in a way because it's not blind sensitivity, but sensitivity with a purpose.'

For families on very low incomes there are the very real anxieties over providing their children with basic food and clothing, keeping them warm in the winter, finding them a safe place to play on run-down inner-city estates or giving them a happy Christmas. 'Nothing hurts you more than when your kids ask you for something and you look around all four corners and you can't see any way of getting it,' comments an unemployed father. 'At that particular time you feel just like picking up a knife and slitting your throat . . . sometimes you wish you didn't have kids . . . and I love them more than anything else in the world.'[8]

Every single woman I interviewed said she found it hard to watch the more horrific aspects of television news once she had given birth. All of those external dangers such as motorway pile-ups, murders and even war become potential threats to the precious being that loving parents are determined to protect. 'Whenever I hear about a child who has gone missing, it feels much closer to home, like it might be my own. Probably for at least a year after she was born, the news would send me into tears nightly.' Sheila found that her anxiety began to ease once her daughter went to nursery school and she got used to the fact that they could enjoy themselves apart as well as together. 'When we were together all of the time, that threat from the outside world was much more present because I couldn't imagine her on her own in the world; but now, even at two, I can.'

The huge, new concentric circle of emotions that envelop a woman once she has a child, mutate and become more complex as that child grows; they never disappear. The sudden swings from depression to exhilaration mellow, but anxiety and fears of accident, death or being separated in some way from that child haunt us more and more. For when a baby is just born, we have only fantasies of possibility to love and lose. But as a child grows, we grow to love them as people and mourning their loss becomes unthinkable. Parents often anticipate grief in the early days, reluctant to invest too much emotionally in someone who may not be born alive or survive prematurity, or handicap. 'A child's not really your own until it's one year old,' my grand-mother used to say.

A recent study of prognoses by doctors to mothers of critically ill newborns concluded that they consistently underestimated the infant's chances of survival to the mother in order to prepare her for the possibility of death. Parents of ill or premature babies were also found to withhold feelings of love for their child in order to protect themselves from greater grief should the child die.[9] A study in 1985 of mothers living in extreme poverty in a Brazilian shantytown found that the weaker, more passive babies were neglected and that the community had developed its own ideology in order to legitimize that neglect by seeing life as a power struggle between strong and weak. Passive infants were, it was believed, lacking drive for life and therefore it was in their own best interests to let them die.[10]

The emotions which drive motherhood inevitably fluctuate according to the pressures and cultural constraints of a woman's environment. In eighteenth-century France and Britain, one in three children died before the age of one year and only half of all children born alive were expected to reach the age of twenty-one, so parents could hope for the health and survival of their children but not expect it. For centuries throughout Western Europe, sex and reproduction were inextricably linked, with women continuing to bear children until the menopause. Few women understood that there were times of high and low likelihood of pregnancy during their menstrual cycle. Children were seen as 'God's will' and as essential providers of additional income from an early age for the poor and as guarantors of the family line for the rich.

At times of high infant mortality, families needed numerous births to achieve surviving children. And when their children died, they were not isolated in their grief, for the loss of at least one child in every family was common until this century. Religious belief was far more prevalent and so God was more readily available to offer consolation, for children were believed to be on loan from God until he recalled them to a 'better place'. But from the 1870s the silent social revolution of family planning began to take hold. Between 1890 and 1920, half of Europe's 600 provinces experienced a 10 per cent decline in fertility. Couples who married in the late 1860s had an average of six children, but by 1924 that number had dropped to the 2.3 that we recognize today.[11] Medical skills began to lower infant mortality and increase life expectancy, children began to cost more than they contributed in earning an extra wage for the family because the government now required them to go to school, and for the first time ever, the element of choice entered reproduction. The notion of 'family planning', of choosing to have children rather than attempting to space them, often ineffectually, through sexual abstinence or withdrawal, only developed in the twentieth century. Inevitably that new element of choice has intensified the emotions of parenthood.

Mothers have always loved their children and mourned their loss deeply. But if they lived at a time when death and serious disease were common and integrated within their communities, then the intensity of that emotional investment was bound to be different. In her book *Forgotten Children*, the historian Linda Pollock, who studied all available resources, successfully refutes the idea that children were less loved in the past, a theory advocated by other historians such as Philippe Aries and Edward Shorter. But she willingly accepts that the death of a small baby was not mourned as deeply as that of a small child. 'The loss of my infant daughter, which seemed heavy at the time, shrinks into nothing when compared with this,' wrote Melisina Trench after the death of her two-year-old son. 'She was merely a little bud; he was a lovely blossom which had safely passed all the earliest dangers, and gave clearest promise of delicious fruit.'[12]

It is hard for the modern Western mother to imagine killing her baby rather than see her become a slave, as Sethe does in Toni Morrison's novel *Beloved*, when we have never known the humiliation and desperation of slavery.

> For a used-to-be-slave woman to love anything that much was dangerous, especially if it was her children she had settled on to love. The best thing she knew was to love just a little bit; everything just little bit, so when they broke its back, or shoved it in a croaker's sack, well maybe you'd have a little love left over for the next one.

We cannot imagine being driven to murder out of love, because 'though she and others lived through and got over it, she could never let it happen to her own. The best thing she was, was her children.' But we can easily identify with the deep distraught anxiety experienced by Stephen in Ian McEwan's *The Child in Time* when he loses his small daughter in a crowded supermarket and never sees her again.

The emotions and the experience of mother- and fatherhood are heavily influenced by the social and cultural conditions in which we live. We choose to have children and we invest more emotionally, materially, physically and psychologically in our children's welfare to justify that choice. Now that the statistics of child survival are far more favourable, with only nine out of every 1,000 babies dying before their first birthday,[13] we are allowed the luxury of expecting them to survive. Fewer children in each family means greater emotional investment in each one and devotion to one child is probably the greatest strain of all, for if that child were to disappear through abduction or death we would have little to live for.

The profound love that we feel heightens every other emotion; we feel greater anxiety over their welfare, we are more reluctant to separate from them and trust them to flourish alone and we feel guilty whenever negative emotions towards our children emerge, because they didn't ask to be born, we chose to have them. Anger or hostility to children was expressed openly and often brutally in the past before twentieth-century notions of psychology and sentimentality about childhood as a separate, magical state took hold. People still treat children badly, but it is no longer acceptable. The same hostile feelings still arise, but we are expected to restrain and repress destructive urges.

Mothers now expect so much more of themselves. We expect to love our children unconditionally every minute of the day and then feel inadequate as mothers when we resent the self-sacrifice. 'I wanted to be with her and I didn't want to be with her,' says

Imogen of her firstborn. 'I remember one night she started crying and as I was walking towards the pram I thought, No! I don't want to have anything to do with you. I don't want to pick you up, I don't want to do this. It was like a feeling of total rejection towards her. It was terrifying.'

As children grow and their demands mushroom, these feelings of hostility, ambiguity and being compromised grow too. They intensify and complicate and can swing from extreme hate to love in a matter of minutes. There are times when I don't want to hunt the house for a pencil sharpener, or draw Pingu for the hundredth time. There are times when I deeply resent scraping yet another plate of half-eaten tea into the dustbin, when I cannot summon up enthusiasm for yet another indifferent painting or laugh at yet another terrible joke. But that doesn't mean that I hate them, just because I hate 'it'. There is no reason why any woman should love every aspect of motherhood and there is nothing new about having such mixed feelings. 'I feel, at times, deeply pressed down, on account of my beloved children,' Elizabeth Fry (1780–1845), who had eleven children, wrote in her diary. 'Their volatile minds try me.' What's new is our assumption that these feelings are not natural or indigenous to motherhood and that the expression of them indicates that we are less than adequate mothers.

As children grow and reward us more for our efforts, we find ourselves soothed, appeased by their charms. When children are clever enough to learn how to make us laugh, how to apologize through physical affection, or when their hurt expressions produce enough guilt or love to kill the rage, we swing suddenly to the opposite end of the spectrum where we would happily move a mountain for the benefit of our child. 'You wonder how you can feel two such conflicting emotions in such a short space of time,' ruminates Maggie. 'They can be doing something really lovely, concentrating on something in an angelic way and your heart pours out to them and then two minutes later they're upending the cot deliberately and you think, I want to strangle them. There's never a doubt that one emotion completely outweighs the other, the pleasure compensates for the annoying bits and also the knowledge that they will change – the thing that's been irritating you for several months suddenly disappears and they're doing something else, equally annoying.'

A child's passionate need for you is either an exquisite privilege or a leech-like drain depending on your mood, how tired you feel and whether or not you have had any time alone. Laura has four boys and gave up teaching to mother full-time. 'I remember when they were little they would get into bed and kick me in the stomach. You'd want them there, but then they'd wake you up early in the morning and start poking you. One of my children used to stroke my cheek, which was wonderful, but sometimes it would drive me insane because he just wouldn't leave me alone. When you want it, it's wonderful; but when you don't, it's just ghastly. It's almost as if they could eat you up when they're little, you feel yourself being devoured. You trawl the house for washing the whole time and feel like your life is being sucked up by the hoover. There are some women who don't take to motherhood and that must be really hard. I love it but I still stand in parks on cold, dreary Saturday afternoons and watch people without children who are going shopping or to the pub and am extremely jealous. But then I think, How could I possibly not have done this?'

Ambivalent feelings of motherhood begin in pregnancy. However much a baby is wanted, there are times when women feel overwhelmed by the irreversibility of the situation. 'Every time my period came I was hugely disappointed, but there was also that relief that we didn't have to go through this great life change yet,' comments Sue. Deciding to become a mother is often as riddled with uncertainty and ambiguity for women now as it is for men. There is so much more to lose career-wise, financially and socially now that women are more independent than ever. Hannah is a management consultant and mother of a six-year-old daughter. 'It's like a greenhouse growing monsters. You didn't know what the monster was, or whether it was going to break the greenhouse. What's it going to do to me?'

Conflict between the interests of mother and child is natural and ongoing. New scientific research suggests that mother and foetus are in competition for nourishment during pregnancy and play an elaborate game of chess to ensure that neither party kills off the other. The placenta invades the mother's arteries in order to tap into her bloodstream to feed the growing foetus. But if it were to invade too deeply it would kill the mother, so she produces 'natural killer' cells which notice if there is over-invasion and kill off over-aggressive cells. Research also suggests that the illnesses of pregnancy such as diabetes and pre-eclampsia occur when the foetus upsets the equilibrium between mother and child in order to ensure its survival, even though such a strategy risks killing them both.[14]

Mother and child have traditionally been seen as a harmonious blissful unit, the Madonna and Child, where mother is utterly self-sacrificing, accepting, understanding, devoted, encouraging and loyal. But we have needs too. However much we love our children or being a mother, that ambivalence, that need to preserve our own sense of self and wellbeing as distinct from theirs is healthy and permanent. Mothers nourish their babies in the womb generously and continue to do so after childbirth. But not to the extent of self-destruction. We co-exist with needs which often seem to contradict each other, for a child's demands are limitless. They would suck us dry if we let them.

Children are so demanding and so easily hurt that we have no choice but to put them first. Then when we feel our own needs surfacing and jostling with theirs we feel guilty about having them at all. When my second child fell head-first down the stairs as a toddler and was clearly suffering from concussion, I took her into casualty and we were kept in for twenty-four hours' observation. As I lay beside her sleeping body on the hospital bed, thankful that we had been spared greater injury and that she was now in professional care, self-blame began to fill the vacuum left by relief. We had both been in the bathroom at the top of the stairs. Getting up from the potty, she pulled up her leggings and headed for the stairs. I turned to empty the potty, warned her to wait, I heard her say 'I just put my foot here and then I put my other foot there' and then she lost her balance and fell. If I had left the potty and held her hand, this would not have happened. I was to blame even though I knew that she had walked up and down those stairs countless times by herself and not fallen before, even though I knew that our children are always just a fraction of an inch away from danger.

Then as she began to recover and sat up, taking an interest in food and her surroundings, a new, selfish and 'less-than-good-motherly feeling' emerged when, after eight hours of nil by mouth, I began to crave a cup of tea. When you are in hospital with a small child, the child has needs you don't. Food was for her, not for me. She slept soundly through the night on a large hospital bed with sheets. I dozed uncomfortably under a blanket in my clothes on a camp bed beside her. The loo on the ward was for children not for parents and I couldn't bring myself to leave her alone, defenceless, in a strange place, to travel further afield for the visitors' loo or the canteen. She was not yet old enough to be able to understand that if I left her there, I would be back soon. I was not allowed to take her with me and she clung to me whenever I tried to leave. The only opportunity to tend to my own needs was when my husband was there to relieve me. As she got better, I became ill – exhausted from lack of sleep, intense anxiety, personal neglect and the complete abandonment of my own life. Ladled on top of the self-blame for not preventing her accident was the guilt about feeling that I had any unmet needs at all, when she was so precious, so cherished, so vulnerable.

Resentment can quickly flare into rage. My children produce unrecognizable, terrifying depths of anger in me, not just the crossness they see. There is the slow-burning residual anger when I think of all the things that I could be doing instead of this.

There is the fiery flash of murderous rage when a child's irrational recalcitrance drives me over the edge. There is anger at myself for not being strong enough to resist the urge to shout or manhandle an obstreperous small child into her coat when the temperature is subzero. There is the anger tinged with disappointment when your child is unable to get the point of fractions in her maths homework or screams, 'I hate you, you're so annoying,' when you try to get her to practise the recorder. And there are the old angers from our own childhood which resurface as we mother our own children. Anger at the mother or father who we never felt gave us enough emotionally or spiritually. Anger at the father who left or never kept his promise to take us to the circus. 'One of the worst aspects of being a parent for me,' writes Anne Lamott, 'is the self-discovery, being face to face with one's secret insanity and brokenness and rage . . . that way down deep, way past being kind and religious and trying to take care of everyone, I was seething. Now it's close to the surface. I feel it race from my centre up into my arms and down into my hands and it scares the shit out of me.'[15]

We do not know how strong we are until we have to push out our babies. Then, as mothers, we have to find unprecedented levels of strength to cope with such extremity of emotion as we discover what we can tolerate and which actions could drive us to murder. A child's anger is undiluted hate. When my two-year-old throws a temper tantrum, I watch with awe and envy her ability to express such rage. 'I had a fantasy very soon after she was born of throwing her against the wall and watching her splattering down.' Imogen is a journalist who had her first daughter in her late thirties. 'I realized at the time that this was a reflection of my anger towards her. I was very, very angry for the first eleven weeks, because of what her existence had done to me.'

Peggy has six children and a husband who earns enough to be able to support them all, so that helps. She says that there have been times when she has been so angry that she has understood how people living in tower blocks with far less money and poorer

living conditions could hurt their children. 'I do smack them for
the big things, for stepping off the kerb or hurting someone
else. But when it all gets too much, I lock the front and the back
door and go upstairs, leaving them alone downstairs for a while
while I cool down.' As children grow older, they find more to
fight over; getting dressed, eating, what they are or aren't allowed
to do, buying toys or sweets on every shopping trip, going to
school or doing their homework. 'Five minutes of every day
there's some fight or other,' Suzanne says of her two daughters,
aged seven and four. 'Even if it's just getting the older one to
wash her hair. "In a minute" never comes with her, but after a
screaming match she'll do what I've asked her to. They just try it
on, kids, push their luck, and if you're just a little bit stressed out,
you can see how mums can bash 'em.'

These negative emotions are not ones that women consider to
be integral to good motherhood for 'good' mothers are bound to
be more understanding. 'I think I'd be a good mother,' says Kate,
who has two sons aged five and seven weeks, 'if I didn't lose my
temper so much.' Charlotte has three sons: 'I do get angry with
them. But I am trying now not to shout because I think that all
they hear is the shouting and not what you're saying.' 'Sometimes
I just want to shake her,' says Hannah, mother of a six-year-old,
'and then afterwards I get angry with myself for being angry
with her because it's usually because I'm knackered and she wants
more attention but I haven't got the energy for it.'

Mothering is stressful daily and expressing anger can be essential when the pressure begins to mount. Mothers who claim that
they never shout or get angry with their children may be expressing their hostility towards their children in more subtle but also
more damaging ways; scrubbing a child violently in the bath when
he won't wash himself, vigorous hair brushing, damning praise,
sarcasm at the child's expense or 'forgetting' promises are all veiled
hostile acts. Failing to react to situations, for example by being
unduly careless of safety in traffic or crowds, is hostile to the
child's interests. So is too rigid a control over a child's clothing or

movements. Children feel the hostility of these actions but find them harder to understand than other more overt expressions of anger which they know they feel themselves daily.

If you get angry when your endurance is being pushed to the limit, you can apologize afterwards and explain your reasons in ways that your child can understand. Compare your feelings with his when a toy is snatched from him by another child or he cannot do or have what he wants. Ambiguous feelings about motherhood are positive feelings. When we lose our temper the subsequent guilt usually makes us better mothers, more concerned for our children's welfare, and our children learn to see us as independent beings who get upset and angry just as they do. A child's demands are limitless for they are inherently selfish and will inevitably find you nurturing as well as denying at times because all of their needs cannot and should not be fulfilled. If the 'perfect' mother were one who fulfilled their every need, children would never learn to take responsibility for themselves, while the clashes that result when you deny them things because you are tired or at the end of your tether will encourage the child's developing identity as separate to yours. They learn that we are all fallible, that we get angry and make mistakes and that if we then apologize for them all is forgiven. They grow to understand that we have different needs and identities which they must respect. But the most important aspect is that both mother and child need to know that they can express their hostility towards each other without losing love. The child psychologist Donald Winnicott believes that there is one consolation when a baby cries through anger: 'that angry crying probably means that he has some belief in you. He hopes he may change you. A baby who has lost belief does not get angry, he just stops wanting.'[16] And so it is with toddler tantrums, when children hit and scream their hate at us, for anger is an essential component of love, and indifference its true opposite.

We are catapulted back to the rich, raw emotions of childhood as mothers. My sensitivities merge with those of my children, their flesh feels like an extension of my own. When they feel sad, I feel sad too. When the eldest is anxious about remembering her lines for the school nativity play or excited by her impending birthday I am anxious or excited too. But there is one big difference between the emotions of childhood and the sudden flood of mixed emotions which can overwhelm women in motherhood. Adults have learnt how to defend themselves through time from the damage caused by such extreme emotions. We know that change is stressful and can anticipate sadness or anxiety when we move or they start nursery school or when we are living through relationship difficulties, but children cannot. They have not yet learnt how to protect themselves from the extremes.

They need to know that the boundaries that surround them are strong enough to take them when they reach these extremes, that when they bang on the walls in violent anger those walls will not give way and that when they feel great grief over a broken toy you are there to console them. Every day, I have to suppress the urge to tell them to stop being so childish. I have to remind myself that the reasons for their anger or distress may seem insignificant to me but mean the world to them. 'Each child of four is also three and also two and also one, and is also an infant being weaned, or an infant born, or even an infant in the womb,' wrote Winnicott in *The Child, the Family and the Outside World.* 'Children go backwards and forwards in their emotional age.' We break down barriers as mothers in that we love unconditionally and have to learn how to empathize with a child and see things from their perspective, but we also have to protect them from our basest emotions. Nothing upsets a child more than seeing their mother crying. An overanxious mother holds back a child's most basic instinctive need to explore and discover the limits of danger for themselves.

But perhaps the hardest task emotionally is living with the daily loss of motherhood as children slowly separate from our influence when they enrich our lives so completely. 'Woman's two great tasks are to shape her unity with the child in a harmonious manner and later to dissolve it harmoniously,' wrote the psycho-analyst Helen Deutsch in *The Psychology of Women*.[17] It is this ultimate contradiction which provides ample reason alone for the ambiguity of motherhood. For we give so much and then have to find the strength to let them walk away.

'Do you have to cut the umbilical cord?' one new mother asked her obstetrician as she stared down at her newborn baby, reluctant to be separated. 'Only literally,' she replied. But the truth is that from birth onwards mother and baby drift slowly, inexorably apart and each stage of child development marks the severing of that link. A baby's vision is poor at birth and depends entirely on close physical contact with the mother, for comfort, for warmth and for food. But as the weeks pass, the baby begins to see further than the mother's face and learns where his or her body begins and the mother ends, sucking his fingers and finding his toes.

As babies learn to sit up and crawl, they become keen to explore the new wider world that has come into vision but will need to come back to their mother or mother figure at regular intervals for reassurance that she has not disappeared. Small chil-dren between the ages of six months and three years are acutely anxious about the possibility of losing their mother figure but they are also programmed to learn through adventure. They need mother-love in order to separate and gain confidence through exploration. American research with baby monkeys has shown that the mother figure is essential for healthy development and separation. Some of the monkeys were reared normally by their mothers and others were separated from their mothers in cages. A third set of monkeys were fed from a wire-shaped mother dummy with teats that would produce milk if they were sucked, and a fourth set had similar wire dummies covered by a furry cloth. The baby monkeys kept with their mothers would explore and then go back to their mothers, but the ones with wire moth-ers or alone were withdrawn and inhibited and crouched in the corner. The monkeys with the cloth-covered wire mummies did better than the ones with the wire dummies because they could explore and then return to the cloth to cling to.

Babies and small children return repeatedly to their mothers for physical contact in order to regain a sense of calm stability after excessive stimulation or too much change when they are alone. If mothers give them as much love as they need when they ask for it then they are building confidence in their children, provided that they release them from their embrace when they want to go. As children grow older, those periods of physical distance between mother and child grow longer.

Mothers too feel deep physical attachment to their child. Many women find it impossible to leave their babies when they are small. It is as if there is an invisible umbilical cord which still connects them. Then, as the umbilical cord dissolves, as babies wean from the physical dependency of the breast and can crawl or walk instead of being carried everywhere we feel a yearning sense of loss for the phase of babyhood that has been left behind. 'Some of the biggest losses in your life are when you have very small children. These are losses of irrecoverable times and not really talked about. I found it terribly upsetting when I had a baby because I'd lost the pregnancy which I'd enjoyed. I was thrilled to have the baby but I'd lost the bump. And then when your child reaches five, it is hard to believe that you will never have a small child again, that I will never breastfeed again,' says Hannah. It is only when we hold another baby, another small child, that the memories come flooding back. 'In the growth of children . . .' writes Louise Erdrich in *The Blue Jay's Dance*, 'in the ageing of beloved parents, time's chart is magnified, shown in its particularity, focused, so that with each celebration of maturity there is also a pang of loss.'

The growing conflict and hostility between mother and child described earlier is integral to this slow process of separation. Conflict triggers separation as the child strives to establish his or her independent self and the mother asserts her own independent needs and regains a sense of control over her life. Dr Robert Trivers, Professor of Anthropology and Biological Sciences at Rutgers University, New Jersey, believes there are parallels between human and animal behaviour. He studied city pigeons in Boston. 'When the chicks were very small and in the nest they were treated with extreme solicitude by both parents, and you saw no evidence of conflict but as the offspring grew larger, you would see the parent avoiding the offspring entirely, flying to a neighborhood ledge to avoid being besieged.' Trivers also saw some striking examples of mother-offspring conflict amongst baboons and langur monkeys especially at the time of weaning. 'The mother is no longer allowing the offspring access to her nipples. The young monkey will often vocalize and try to pressure the mother into nursing and this is very striking, because these monkeys have been selected to be silent to keep predators away.'[18]

Having a second child forces mothers to separate from their firstborn. Fiona Shaw describes this in *Out of Me*. Before going to hospital to have her second child, she 'took Eliza to friends to finish her sleep and as I kissed her, I thought I was kissing away something forever, something she would never have again'.

It hurts to lose the intensity of that one-to-one relationship with our only child. Imogen felt this strongly. 'I went from being so involved with her to not having a moment for her. It was hard to read to her at night, and the baby's needs with colic were so immediate and urgent that I was grieving the first few weeks. I thought, I've lost my baby, I've lost my Beatrice, but of course I hadn't.'

Other women find that they want nothing more than to curl up alone with the new baby and resent the intrusion of a large toddler. Gemma had 'been warned to be prepared to have different feelings to your older child when the next is born. You may not like or love them for a while so when that did happen I thought, That's OK, a lot of people have been here before. I didn't blame myself although I was quite amazed at how different my feelings were towards this child I had loved and adored just six hours earlier.'

With more than one child, our emotional energies are spread more evenly and our children are less suffocated by our attentions because we have less time and energy to give. We give them the space to discover things for themselves while we are tending to another's needs, and anger or resentment at the selflessness of motherhood are spread more evenly among them. When one child provokes a row by beating up his sibling or engraving initials into the wood of your favourite chair, the other child understands that it is bad behaviour which incurs your wrath and not him per se and finds it suddenly possible to play the immaculate angel. With more than one child we are to see them as self-determining individuals who need to propel themselves forward and away from us, rather than genetic clones, affected by our every action and damaged by our mistakes.

Having a second child allows a woman to lay a great many of her anxieties over her firstborn to rest. For instance Wendy found weaning her first baby difficult emotionally. 'I got completely worked up about how I couldn't stop breastfeeding, that you're a bad mother if you stop and that my baby would not love me if we did not stay close. But the second time around I knew that my baby would be fine and that I would be much more logical about it.'

I didn't think that I would be able to find the space in my heart to love another child as much as I loved my firstborn. But a whole new file opens with each child and it feels as if we have an unlimited capacity to love. But if the second child is to be your last child, the sense of loss as that child grows up is even greater. Anne: 'Everything becomes terribly, terribly poignant with the second child. You know what you ought to be doing and when you lose your temper, or don't have time to build a train set, or when you're not very amusing at midnight you think you've blown it and wish that you had a bit more patience or a bit more time, or a bit more ease because you know that you won't get that chance to get it right again.'

The arrival of a second child shows us that it is impossible ever to be truly fair. They are born into different circumstances, one enjoying the luxury of being an only child for a while, the other born into the luxury of an established family home. Inevitably as mothers we behave differently to each child. By the time Anne's second child was born, her literary agency was thriving and she feels guilty about not being able to give her son as much attention in his early years as her daughter. 'He's had far less of me than Polly. He had a very good nanny but he's had a completely different experience and that does worry me. I had a lot of quiet times together with Polly and we're very umbilically bonded as a result whereas I haven't had that with Adam. While he hasn't had as much attention, he hasn't had as much anxiety from me either and he hasn't had to cope with me changing in the way that my daughter has had to, so I suppose he will look back on his childhood in a hugely different way.'

As our children grow older the emotional landscape of family life becomes more complicated for the child's own emotions and interpretations of love and equality come into play. As they grow into distinct individuals, mothers encounter aspects of their personality which they may not like. Feelings of favouritism are common and however much mothers try to hide their feelings, as children grow older, they develop a seventh sense to the family landscape and tell you so. Mothers are expected to be fair and equal in their treatment of their children these days when it isn't always humanly possible.

Some mothers favour their daughters over their sons because they are more like themselves, others favour a stronger child over the weaker. Lydia's four boys are aged between twelve and five and she loved them all equally as babies and toddlers, but as they grew older and their own emotional needs came into play she found one of her sons increasingly difficult to satisfy. 'You're supposed to love them equally but they're different individuals and sometimes your personalities clash in such a way that they bring up these feelings that are not the maternal ones that are written about. It's frightening, but very real and not often talked about so a lot of women suffer in silence.'

Lydia knows that one son has qualities that will stand him in good stead as an adult, immense charm, sparkling eyes and a determination to get what he wants. But as a child he provokes feelings in her that she doesn't like. 'It's like an affront to your love for them, it's as if they're rejecting you. When I'm on top of it I overcompensate by making him the focus of attention, but at other times he just makes me feel as if I want to pinch him, I would like to put my hands around his arm and squeeze it very hard so that I know that it hurts.' Lydia discovered that the boy had overheard her discussing with a friend how difficult he had been. 'I didn't know he had overheard me and then two weeks later we had an argument about something and he threw it back at me. He said, "How would you like it if you heard your mother say that you were the most difficult child of the bunch?" and I thought, He's right. I wouldn't like it, but on the other hand I can't button my lip. He's very astute, he sees it all and it makes me feel terrible. I've gone to bed many a night and thought, That argument was disastrous, they'll remember that when they're in therapy.'

Certain modern pressures must make the emotional aspects of motherhood harder to deal with. Choosing to have children and having fewer children inevitably accentuates feelings of anxiety over their welfare and the sense of loss as they grow older. We are more reluctant to let them go, less able to trust that they will survive without us. In 1990, only 9 per cent of seven- and eight-year-olds went to school on their own compared to 80 per cent in 1971 (Policy Studies Institute). We hold them close, we never let them out of our sight, fearing abduction or assault, even though the statistical likelihood is as rare as ever.

But the ultimate feelings of anxiety and loss come with the conflict and separation of adolescence: when your fourteen-year-old daughter walks down the road twenty metres behind you because she finds your presence so excruciatingly embarrassing, when they don't want to go out with you or on holiday with you any more, when they stop confiding in you or allowing you into the bathroom at bathtime; when they scream 'I hate you,' or 'You hate me,' or, 'You've never understood me,' and introduce you to their friends as their grandmother – that's when you know that they are finally moving out of your sphere of influence for good and that the definition of what it is to be a mother is moving into a different gear. Eventually we look at our children and see that their lives are no longer entwined with ours and that can be very painful. 'Like most of today's mothers I was glad to turn more of my attention to my work,' writes Anne Roiphe in her book *Fruitful*.

Glad not to have to spend so much time planning, watching, thinking about the children. However, the letting go was still hard. The switch from being the person at the centre of their lives to being the last to know, the one that they moved behind, around, was hard, painful, and not a relief at all. If I had listened to the noise in my head at the time I would have heard a constant tearing, a ripping, searing sound as their lives became their own.

6

Exhaustion

People who say they sleep like babies usually don't have one. We get warned by those who are more experienced to expect hell with broken nights, but no amount of warning can adequately prepare us for the sheer torture of night after night without deep prolonged sleep. Then it is hard to believe that it is possible to feel so tired, so consistently. The exhaustion of motherhood can be so profound that it makes us so much more susceptible to the other problems common after childbirth such as ill health, depression, lowered self-esteem, angry outbursts, and poorer social or sexual relationships. That deep tiredness doesn't just come from sleepless nights. There is the tiredness connected to ill health and feeling under par which is so common after childbirth. And there is the emotional exhaustion which comes from the utter devotion, the self-sacrifice of motherhood and the relentless dedication to children's needs, the anxiety, the physical exertions of pregnancy, childbirth, the lifting and the carrying, the daily arguing and nagging to get things done. The day will dawn when you will wake up and think, I'm not *that* tired any more – but don't be surprised if it takes two to three years after giving birth for the blanket to lift rather than the two to three months you've been led to expect.

Sleep disturbances begin in pregnancy. The fatigue felt during the first three months is thought by some medical researchers to be caused by the soporific effects of high progesterone secretion from the placenta. Others believe that tiredness comes from the physiological changes of pregnancy. With huge increases in oxygen consumption, cardiac output, blood volume and ventilation the body is working far harder and we are bound to feel more tired.[1] Rapid foetal development is also taking place inside the mother's uterus.

As pregnancy progresses and our body weight increases, we use up more energy moving around. Many women find it difficult to get comfortable in bed during the last three months. Lying flat on one's back hurts, lying on one's stomach is impossible, and our flanks get sore because two out of four essential night-time positions have been eliminated. Each time we turn in the night, the effort to persuade our great swollen belly to follow in the same direction wakes us up. We need to pee more anyway because in pregnancy the bladder gets squashed by the enlarged uterus, and when we lie down the pressure on our bladder increases, and many women find they are getting up two to three times a night in order to go to the loo. In a survey of 100 women, 68 complained of disturbed sleep due to the physical discomforts of pregnancy such as uterine cramping, indigestion, haemorrhoids and breathing difficulties, while up to 70 per cent of pregnant women experience frightening dreams or nightmares.[2]

There is also strong evidence to suggest that the hormonal changes of pregnancy alter sleep patterns with high levels of oestrogen and progesterone suppressing deep, stage 4 sleep in the final three months. Many women feel so tired that they have to nap more, or go to bed early, but still they feel tired, however much they rest. That tiredness can have an impact on a woman's ability to work or maintain personal and social activities.

It is the physiological and hormonal changes of pregnancy which make women more easily tired. Research so far suggests that external factors such as the number of hours worked, or the number of children to care for have little impact on the overall level of tiredness.[3] So however tempting it is to blame those 'if only's' for your tiredness – 'If only I didn't have to work/could sleep more during the day/had help with my two-year-old/could get a decent night's sleep' – you'd probably still feel tired without them.

Perhaps the sleep disturbances of pregnancy prepare women for what is to come. If the first stage of labour extends beyond twenty-four hours there can be substantial sleep loss before the strenuous exertions of the second stage begin. Once the baby is born, some women feel so euphoric that they cannot sleep. In the early days and weeks of motherhood, hormones continue to affect the mother's ability to enter deep, stage 4 sleep, particularly if she is breastfeeding. Newborn babies have an erratic sleep pattern and may only sleep for two or three hours at a time. They are also unable to enter deep sleep to the same extent as an older child until they are several months old and so are more easily prone to waking. They move around a lot in their sleep, acting out their dreams in their facial expressions and their muscles are not yet sufficiently developed to prevent these movements, which wake them up.

When we sleep we go through 90-minute cycles, beginning with stage 1, light sleep, and moving through to stage 4, deep sleep. Only when we have moved through all four stages do we enter precious REM sleep for dreams which some researchers believe is essential for the brain to process the mental stimuli of the day. We need to go through four or five complete cycles during the night in order to feel healthy and with each cycle, the amount of REM sleep increases.

It is continuous, uninterrupted sleep that matters, and not the number of hours. Most stage 4 sleep occurs early in the night and it is during stage 4 that physical recuperation takes place and growth hormones are pumped out from the anterior pituitary. But the largest chunk of precious REM sleep occurs in the later cycles and if a person is woken at any stage within the sleep cycle they go back to the very beginning again. So a mother who is being woken two or three times a night by her baby is experiencing extreme sleep deprivation through REM loss even though she may be sleeping as many hours through the 24-hour cycle as she did before she had her baby.

Sleep deprivation is a known form of torture. It is also a tactic employed by mediators in difficult and protracted negotiations in order to wear down the participants. Animals deprived of sleep in scientific laboratories die very quickly. Our immune system is more active when we sleep, which is why we need to sleep so much more when we are unwell and when we don't sleep we are more prone to illness. Rats deprived of sleep died of infectious micro-organisms that they are exposed to every day.[4]

When we are regularly woken by babies and deprived especially of REM sleep, we quickly build up a sleep debt. When people have a modest sleep debt of just seven or eight hours a week they can suffer from symptoms such as itching or burning eyes, blurred vision, feeling chilly, hunger, finding it hard to resist high-fat foods or carbohydrates and feeling waves of fatigue. They have less energy, are more lethargic, irritable and suffer a severe loss of humour. As that sleep debt increases, so do the symptoms. It becomes increasingly difficult to undertake simple tasks or absorb new information, which is tough on a new mother suddenly faced with a whole new set of tasks and responsibilities. Anxiety increases and there is a slowing-down of mental processes with people finding it difficult to concentrate. Short-term memory is affected and angry outbursts, paranoia, or even visual hallucinations can occur.

Studies have found that poor sleepers are six times more likely to report having poor health than good sleepers.[5] Sleep loss will not only slow down the physical recovery after childbirth including the healing of scars but will directly impact on every aspect of a new mother's life. It is probably a major trigger of postnatal depression and the problems women can face adjusting to motherhood, although few researchers have concentrated on broken sleep to assess its impact. The researchers of the largest survey in Britain on postnatal health found a strong link between fatigue and depression.[6] 'It's not easy to be able to say which comes first with those types of symptoms, but there must be occasions where absolute exhaustion makes you feel depressed,' says Christine MacArthur, one of the authors of the report.

New mothers and fathers walk around in a fog of tiredness dreaming of nothing more than a good night's sleep. Hannah's daughter is now six, but 'She used to wake to feed three or four times a night and I was so tired that I fell asleep everywhere. You live in this funny half-world and oscillate between it and the real world.'

Kate's seven-week-old baby boy has woken up at least three times a night to feed since he was born. 'Half the time I feel as if everything's running into each other. If someone asks me, "What have you done today, or this week?" I've no idea. That's the one thing that dominates everything else. Even if you are tired, you can't just stop, you have to get on with it. You can't not feed the baby, you can't not jiggle it around and get the wind out. However tired you're feeling you can't just collapse.' Kate found that on the days when the tiredness got too much, just lying down for an hour or two and doing nothing helped to revive her a little.

Sleep during the daytime with more than one child is usually out of the question, unless you know that someone else is looking after the baby. Often mothers of one child find that they cannot sleep during the day because they know that at any moment their baby could wake up. Catherine's thirteen-month-old son still does not sleep through the night. 'I got very annoyed by the books that say "sleep while your baby sleeps" because there are babies that don't sleep at all during the day, or sleep in such short bursts that you could never find the time to unwind enough to drop off to sleep yourself.'

As babies get bigger the gaps between feeds get longer and many women find that getting up only once or twice in the night rather than three or four times makes a great deal of difference. If a small baby is in a crib right beside your bed, or sleeping with you then you may be able to stay semi-asleep as the baby feeds. A bottle warmer by the side of the bed is essential for bottle feeders because you can doze in bed while it's warming and there is the added advantage that you and your partner can take turns in feeding the baby.

However, there are pleasurable aspects to being awake in the depths of the night. I had nights with my youngest child when it was so silent that I felt as if we were the only two people in the world, as her sensual sucking sent me slowly back to sleep. When she woke once during the night at fourteen months, I picked her up as if she were a newborn baby again, rocking her gently from side to side. As I held her, I held those moments of intimacy again. Both of us were soothed by a deep physical memory that goes far beyond words or conscious memory, of how things were between us.

But there were also times nightly, when her piercing cries for food stirred my subconscious and filled it with ugly thoughts. When small babies wake us for their night-time feed mothers lie, as Helen Simpson describes in her short story 'Heavy Weather', for the first moments 'like a flattened boxer in the ring trying to rise while the count was made'. My daughter pulled my strings like a puppeteer and I had to go to her even though repeated sleep disruption made me want to smother her rather than suckle her. When it gets too much, when you find yourself crying through the day from weariness, when you feel unable to go on because of lack of sleep, then insist that the father takes over for a while, pay for someone to look after the baby for an afternoon so that you can sleep and tell enthusiastic grandparents that they are welcome to visit, provided that they take the baby out for a ten-mile walk in the pram.

Caroline works for a charity. Her daughter, Isabel, had bad colic for the first few months and would cry incessantly from 9 p.m. to midnight or from midnight to 3 a.m. She rarely slept

with her partner because he was back at work and needed uninterrupted sleep, but there were times when Caroline had to leave
her daughter with him just to stay sane. 'We did have some nights
when Nigel would be downstairs and he'd hear the baby screaming and crying and then he'd hear me screaming and crying and
he'd have to come up and swap over.' Other men are less accom-
modating. Caitlin is a full-time mother with two children aged
three and sixteen months. The younger child still wakes in the
night. 'I've been tired for so long now. Last night I was up at
twelve thirty until she went back to sleep. When I next looked at
the clock it was five, so I moved her back to her bed and then
slept until seven. When I woke the second time and asked my
husband to take her back to bed, he got cross with me because
I'd woken him up but I thought it was reasonable because I'd
already been up once.'

Like many mothers, Caitlin feels too tired to put up any resistance to unnecessary night-time demands for the long-term goal
of sleep, when the short-term solutions of rocking the child
back to sleep or giving him a bottle will bring immediate relief.
But from about six months, babies do not need to wake for food
or drink, and they are more likely to wake for your company; if
they cannot go back to sleep without your soothing them, then
you are setting a pattern that you will find harder and harder to
break as that baby gets older.

Caitlin is in two minds about what to do. She knows that she
could let her sixteen-month-old daughter scream until she goes
back to sleep. But she screams until she makes herself sick,
waking up her three-year-old brother in the process and her
father who is the sole breadwinner and self-employed. 'If you're
working for someone else you can coast when you're tired, but if
you're working for yourself the day's ruined.' Rather than face the
thought of several badly disturbed nights by letting her daughter
scream until she gets used to the idea of going back to sleep by
herself, Caitlin brings the baby into bed with her, so that everyone can go back to sleep quickly. Penny has six children and

found that letting her children sleep all over the house was the best way of getting any sleep herself. 'Some mornings I just let them sleep on the floor in my bedroom so that I didn't have to take them back to their bedrooms, otherwise I'd be up all night putting this one and that one back.'

Night-time waking amongst babies and small children is extremely common. Studies have found that two-thirds of all babies six to twelve months old and 20–30 per cent of all children aged one to three have trouble sleeping through the night.[7] Researchers from the Institute of Education and Child Health at London University studied the age at which babies could be expected to sleep through the night. They found that 70 per cent of those studied slept through the night (defined initially as from midnight to roughly 5 a.m. without waking) at three months, with another 13 per cent of them by six months.

Parents understandably find it difficult to know what to do with a wakeful child now that the advice from childcare experts seems to be so contradictory. Before the more liberal attitudes of Penelope Leach and Hugh Jolly took hold during the 1960s, babies and small children had set bedtimes and large numbers of parents expected them to sleep through till morning, leaving them to cry themselves back to sleep. Now, with a more child-centred approach to childcare, influenced heavily by psychology, we want to do everything possible to minimize distress in a child and we worry about banishing him to the dark lonely nursery to cry himself into submission in the blackness of night, when the more natural state of mothering means holding your baby close at all times. Leaving a child to cry himself back to sleep apparently teaches him to be resigned to his impotence. 'He has learnt life's cruellest lesson: there isn't any point in trying to improve things. Most of these babies will grow into adults who believe the same – suffering is the human condition, and you can't do anything about it,' writes Deborah Jackson in *Three in a Bed*, advocating that children should sleep with their parents.[8]

But need we always put our child's needs first, to the detriment of our own when unbroken sleep is so crucial to our health and welfare? Babies learn aspects of behaviour from our own and they can be taught to sleep, just as we teach them to eat solids from a spoon, or to walk by holding their hands. All it takes is an insistence on your part that night-time is for sleeping rather than playing, rocking, feeding or watching videos. One study conducted at Leeds University in 1994 found that breastfed babies as young as eight weeks could be trained to sleep for longer periods at night, by gradually lengthening the intervals between nighttime feeds through other activities such as nappy changing and walking up and down, so that the baby learnt to distinguish between nighttime and daytime, when it could feed more often.[9]

From six months onwards, many babies who have been sleeping well resume nighttime waking and then continue to wake if their parents reinforce the habit by getting the baby up, feeding with the bottle or the breast, or rocking. Babies then quickly learn to need their mother or father to feed or rock them in order to go back to sleep and we get more and more tired. Parents then excuse the change in pattern by saying things like 'He just needs his dummy put back in,' or 'She just has a bottle and then goes straight back to sleep.' Of course there's always the excuse that few can resist – that beloved baby is so bright that he just doesn't seem to need that much sleep.

So many of the daytime tasks of motherhood are inherently tiring that we do not need to cope with the additional burden of nighttime waking. Just two or three nights of unbroken sleep can cure the symptoms of sleep deprivation described above and make the numerous jobs of mothering easier to deal with. Children have to grow up in the real world, where people sleep at night, and not in an ideal world where they need only sleep when they are tired. 'If children could be left to their own devices and did not need the attention of adults, then no one would be the least concerned about whether they sleep or not,' writes Dr David Haslam in his book *Sleepless Children*. But the reality of life is that children do depend on adult resources of strength and initiative.

It is too simplistic to compare modern mothering and sleeping habits with those of Third World families or of families historically. Many poor families of the Third World sleep together in the same bed because there is only one, and they do not necessarily sleep better because of it. You cannot simply transfer their experience to ours and maintain that this is a healthier way to bring up our babies, that we will all sleep better if we sleep together, as Deborah Jackson does in *Three in a Bed*. Poor families of the past had no choice but to sleep together because cots were expensive so babies risked being smothered by sleeping in their mother's bed. Infectious diseases spread more rapidly when everybody slept together. Few of us sleep easily when we are crammed together in a small space and kicked regularly in the stomach by a child's feet. Margery Spring Rice concluded in her 1939 survey of 1,200 working-class women that, 'Sleeplessness is not often spoken of in this investigation, because it is not considered an ailment, but it is quite clear that a good night's rest in a well-aired quiet room and in a comfortable, well-covered bed, is practically unknown to the majority of these mothers.'[10]

If you can put your hand on your heart and honestly say that you are happy with your night-time rituals then there is no need to change them. Thankfully now there is no right or wrong way to do it and we can choose either to leave them to cry or bring them into bed with us depending on our own needs and the individual needs of our children. But remember that your own health, stamina and mental welfare are important and that children do in part need to be socialized in order to suit our needs and make it easier for us to be able mothers during the day.

All children have good reasons for waking at times. It can be difficult to go to sleep with a temperature. Colds can disturb sleep with coughs and breathing difficulties. Nightmares and sleepwalking are common in small children and if children are living with undue stress at home, perhaps because the parents have marital or financial difficulties, then peaceful sleep will inevitably be affected. Sheila Kitzinger believes that pre-term and induced babies who have had a difficult birth, and babies of mothers who developed pre-eclampsia, tend to have sleep problems. There are a very small number of children who genuinely don't need much sleep at all, but the vast majority of children should be able to sleep through the night and learn to feel secure about their ability to go back to sleep alone when they surface naturally into light sleep during the night, as we all do.

Everything feels more pronounced at night. Anxieties and fears are more acute for both parents and children. If we feel guilt about working, or about an argument, or not feeling very loving towards our children, or denying them something that they wanted, then that guilt can affect our behaviour towards our children when they wake in the middle of the night. Some women find it hard to untangle their hand from their child's last thing at night and separate from such a loved, precious person at the end of the day. Others, usually the women who have been with them throughout the day, cannot wait for the release. The youngest of Charlotte's three children is eighteen months old and needs carrying to bed. 'There are thirty-three steps between here and Matty's bedroom. I know because I count them at the end of each day.'

We have to recognize that our own mixed feelings about motherhood and separation have a bearing on the way we put our children to bed or respond to them when they wake. It was only when I found myself reading a book to my firstborn in bed at three o'clock in the morning when she was two and a half years old that I realized the absurdity of this and finally resolved to break her habit of night-time waking. We both needed to sleep through the night, every night. It was my guilt about not being a good enough mother to her during the day because I left her to go to work which was keeping us all up at night. We went to the Hackney Sleep Clinic and they told us what we didn't want to hear – that we would have to leave her to go back to sleep on her own and that she would get very angry. We lived through several nights of anguish with pillows over our heads, while she banged on her bedroom door screaming that she just wanted us to be her friend. But within a week she was sleeping through each night and was happier during the day. I then felt even greater guilt that I had deprived her of the greater vitality that she would undoubtedly have enjoyed during the days past had I insisted on her sleeping. Who knows, I may even have limited her capacity to grow psychologically and intellectually from daytime stimuli because she was as tired as I was. I also felt physically sick at the thought that we could have been sleeping better for the past two years if I'd only been a little less wimpish about our nights.

Children need deep and uninterrupted sleep just as we do and can suffer from deceptive symptoms if they are deprived of sleep. Instead of being sleepy, they may become hyperactive and manic. They may show impulsiveness and strong emotional mood-swings and they may be irritable or aggressive. If you have to shake your child awake in the morning then this is a sign that they are not getting enough sleep, as are sluggish mornings, or rubbing eyes and yawning at the breakfast table. If you and your partner are resolved to break the habit of night-time waking then there are people and books on hand to help you. Sleep clinics can help (there is a contact number at the end of the book) and two excellent books will give you confidence – *Teach Your Baby to Sleep Through the Night*, by Charles E. Schaefer and Michael R. Petronko, and *Solve Your Child's Sleep Problems* by Richard Ferber.

The tiredness from broken nights can become even more difficult to cope with after the birth of the second child, because we cannot sleep round the clock with the new baby when our firstborn is so much more needy emotionally. Anne gave up work and was able to sleep through the day with her firstborn as a baby, but found external circumstances interfered with rest after the birth of her second. 'I was burying my father and Polly was settling very badly at school and I had to be there for her. That took its toll and I was very tired for that whole year.' If you have fed your baby at 5 a.m. and know that he or she is likely to sleep for two to three hours, you cannot sleep until eight if your two-year-old wakes at 6.30. But we also learn to be less anxious about sleeping disturbances with second children. Gemma has two small children, one aged four, the other one. 'Instead of springing out of bed when they sob, you let it ride with the second. God knows what you do with the fifth.'

Sleep is an essential part of our 24-hour cycle. We're not happy people without it and children need to understand that as well as reap the benefits in their own renewed health and greater energy. What is certain for parents though is that once sleep has been disturbed consistently through the discomforts of pregnancy and regular broken nights for feeding, then we never entirely recover former peaceful sleep. 'You get used to it,' remarks Kate, 'and then they start sleeping through. But then when they're ill and you have to get up for them that can absolutely knock you for six.'

'Both of my labours were good and I didn't feel at all traumatized by them but the worst thing for me was the lack of sleep. It's unlike anything that I've ever known, that tiredness, and although I'm not tired now –' Anne's children are seven and four – 'I am compared to what I was before.'

The price that you pay for the pleasure of having your children jumping up and down on your bed at 6.30 in the morning and enthusing with their ceaseless vitality, tickling your feet or kissing your eyelids and singing nursery rhymes into your ear is that you rarely get the opportunity to sleep late enough in the morning to recover adequately from broken nights. We spend so much of their infancy listening for their cries that it can be hard to sleep deeply with ease even when they are nearly unconscious from an active day. Being prepared for tiredness and costing in time for rest helps, but in the end perhaps the best solution is to accept the new status quo and give in to it. At least then we do not waste useful energy by resisting the inevitable.

Childbirth is hard work and physically debilitating and you should expect to be tired afterwards. But constant, disabling tiredness may be a sign that you are suffering from a medical condition which could be treated. The physical stress of pregnancy and childbirth can aggravate any existing or latent illnesses, but doctors are notoriously slow at arriving at an accurate diagnosis when new mothers are ill, because they are expected to be tired. After the birth of her first son, Kate found herself getting weaker and weaker, unable to walk past the post box on the corner before she had to sit down on the pavement feeling sick. 'I think I had it a little bit before I got pregnant because I used to get tired really easily. But the doctors couldn't find out what was wrong with me, until my skin started to go very dark (which happens in the final stages) and they diagnosed Addison's disease.'

Anaemia is common in women. Pregnancy as well as blood-loss in labour are known to deplete a woman's low iron stores still further. Symptoms include a pale pasty complexion, excessive tiredness, lowered resistance to infection, impatience, shortness of breath, irritability and a general feeling that everything is too much trouble. These symptoms are easily disguised by the tiredness of broken nights and the chaos of new motherhood, but can be easily cured (see Appendix I). Remember too that when a doctor tests your haemoglobin level he has a wide band of what constitutes a normal iron level to compare it with. It could be that you are in the low quartile of this band but that you are suffering from the symptoms of anaemia which would respond to treatment, even though science says that you are not technically anaemic.

Poor diet, low in fresh fruit and vegetables and high in fat, is common amongst families on low incomes or income support.[11] Because they feed their children first, parents in poor families are often found to be deficient in key nutrients such as iron, Vitamin C, fibre and folate, which leads to health problems and extreme tiredness. 'I don't bother with food,' says Cynthia, mother of three. 'You get pissed off with it, you feel that rotten, really tired and weak.' 'When I was living with his [her son's] father, I just ate better,' comments another mother on income support. 'I had

better-quality food. That's something that's really changed. I find
increasingly that I can't afford to buy fresh fruit and vegetables.'

If you find yourself falling asleep all of the time, if your hair
is lank and has a tendency to fall out, and your skin feels dry then
you may be suffering from thyroid deficiency. Low potassium
levels can also cause extreme tiredness. Prolonged exhaustion is
a recognized medical symptom of postnatal depression, although
surprisingly it is rarely cited as a cause. Dr Katharina Dalton,
who pioneered the theory that progesterone deficiency causes
postnatal depression, believes that when tiredness is coupled
with complete mental apathy and lack of physical energy, that
woman is suffering from 'postnatal exhaustion' and that this can
be treated biochemically, although other medical researchers such
as Dr John Studd dispute this and maintain that oestrogen deficiency may be the cause.

With two small children I found that there was never enough
time in the day to recover completely. As the demands increased
I found myself slipping deeper and deeper into the abyss of
exhaustion where the simplest demand from a child felt like a
major obstacle. I found the physical and conflicting emotional
demands of mothering two children of different ages so tiring
that I was permanently close to tears. Colours began to dim
around me. Focus and breadth of vision blurred. The constant
noise of furniture scraping, shouting, arguing, crying and whining shredded my last remaining intact nerves and the brief respite
given by my husband looking after the children was never
enough. I needed more than a couple of hours. I needed days by
myself with no one touching me, talking to me or making
demands which had to be met. I needed to be by myself in a
room, staring blankly out of the window so that I could begin to
think clearly again. I felt like a sponge squeezed dry because of
successive bouts of flu, February's grey rain, lack of sleep and the
24-hour feeding of my children's psychological and emotional
needs. I felt, as Enid Bagnold wrote, 'like Gulliver sometimes,
weighed down by little men . . . I'm a queen bee, with every

muscle dragging. I'm the heart of a cluster, black, dripping, sucking, hanging. They say they can't do without me. But if I died
tomorrow, they'd cling to someone else.'[12]

I had very mild anaemia, so mild that my haemoglobin level
was technically normal. After several months of iron supple-
ments I felt much better and was more able to cope. Greater
energy meant that I was able to find the time for exercise and a
better diet and while the unavoidable, exhausting elements of
motherhood were still there, I felt more able to ride the storms
and enjoy my children in between. I realized, then, how important it is to try to eliminate all other forms of tiredness in order
to stand a chance of staying afloat through the first few years of
a child's life.

If you think that there may be a medical root to your tiredness
then be persistent with your doctor or get second and third opin-
ions. The blanket definition 'new mother = exhausted woman'
disguises the fact that there are different sorts of tiredness and
numerous different causes.

Children have an unlimited capacity to make demands. From the
moment they wake they want you to do things for them. When
they are newborn they need holding, feeding, changing, and even
though each task seems easy enough, requiring little effort, when
it is repeated hundreds of times it becomes mind-numbingly
tiring. 'It's bloody hard work.' Juliet teaches drama and has
adopted a three-month-old baby and therefore doesn't have to
recover from the physical and psychological effects of pregnancy
and childbirth. 'I don't think I've ever experienced being on the
go so constantly, even at work, where I'm not able to stop for
lunch sometimes. It just isn't the same.'

Carrying babies around, negotiating them successfully in and
out of nappies, vests, babygros, snowsuits or buggies is more
tiring for a new mother because of the revolutionary new state
of being in which she finds herself. If she is even slightly anxious about her baby's welfare, her shoulders tense as she holds

him and ache with exhaustion long before he is ready to be put
down to sleep alone. When a baby cries and you don't know why
or cannot soothe away the tears, the resulting anxiety is utterly
debilitating. 'Racked with pain, dizzy, faint and exhausted with
suffering, starvation and sleeplessness, it is terrible to have to
walk the room with a crying child,' wrote an American teacher,
Elizabeth Prentiss, in the 1840s, after the birth of her first
child.[13]

As children get older, their needs expand to fill the spaces
between feeds and nappy changing that you used to use to rest or
wash up. When babies learn to move their exploration knows no
bounds. You sit down at the bottom of the stairs to put on your
shoes. Before you have tied the first lace, the baby has clambered
up the stairs behind you and is hovering precariously at the top.
Pens go into mouths or all over the furniture, cereal packets get
emptied on to the floor, books get ripped off the shelves, and the
most innocuous chair becomes a hazard, for standing on and
falling off.

The physical demands increase as the baby grows heavier and
develops the most admirable of human attributes – resistance.
The baby still needs to be carried and lifted in and out of buggies,
car seats, or on and off buses. He still needs to be dressed and
fed, only now you need the physical strength of a professional
wrestler, the spiritual know-how of Mother Teresa and negotiating skills far superior to those of the UN in order to get
anywhere near your goal.

Motherhood is more tiring than anything else on earth for
one simple reason: there is never enough dream time, time to
think or do anything else for longer than a minute without interruption. There is never time to follow one thought process
through to another while our children are in our care. Every
sense is alert to impending danger. Mothers are always thinking
about their children's needs, or ways of managing the day so that
they may gain precious time for themselves. There is always more
washing or cooking or clearing up to be done. One can easily

slide into a growing sense of unease, of dissatisfaction at never really doing a good day's work.

'I do feel that I have to be very organized to cope with the exhaustion,' says Helen, an illustrator and mother of a five-month-old daughter. 'The only way I get any time to myself in the evenings is by cooking earlier on, then I can manage one or two nights of my own work.' Keelie is a full-time mother living on a council estate with nine-week-old twins and an older son of eight. 'You've got to give some to your husband, some to your first and to these two and they require so much that at the end of the evening you just sit there and think, Five minutes to myself'd be nice. Sometimes when I've had a bad day I don't want to talk, I just want to sit there and be quiet, just quietness. Then when my husband comes in and I don't talk, it's like "What's the matter with you? You got the hump. You ain't said a word to me since I came in."'

Even as children get older, there is rarely ever enough time to blank out, to drift off for long enough to just be. 'Even though I'm sitting here talking to you now, I'm thinking that at half three I've got to pick up the kids from school, and then we've got to go and look at this play scheme that we may use during the holidays and then we've got a babysitter coming because we're going out. You're thinking ahead of yourself the whole time, you have to. So there's never a chance to switch off.' (Charlotte)

'Sometimes I'm asleep as soon as my head hits the pillow,' says Trudi, who has three children. 'Edward's talking really gets me down 'cos he doesn't shut up and I think, Can't I just read the paper? He asks such stupid questions and provokes Harriet and makes her cry. If I didn't have Edward my life would be much easier.'

It is the constant cycle of persuasion, psychological bolstering and lion-taming that makes motherhood so tiring that it can be hard at times to find the joy. When both children were small there were days when I felt as if I was sinking into the role of the nagging grumpy mother that I swore to myself I would never

ever be, because the only words I ever seemed to utter were orders – pick that up, please, don't kick that chair, leave her alone. It is the constant cycle of cooking, feeding and washing clothes so that they can get through each day. It is the constant clearing up so that you know roughly where everything is, so that nobody breaks their legs falling over toys, or falls ill because of an unhygienic kitchen. It is the irrationality of a small child's demands and the intensity of their passion or frustration which is so emotionally draining.

Our love and dedication are so great that we absorb our children's anxieties and disappointments and feel them to be our own. When we are tired, a child's demands seem more unreasonable and tempers are short. Expressing anger uses up precious energy and makes us feel even more exhausted and a vicious circle develops quickly. It is the very repetitive constancy of motherhood that women find so draining and which often makes them feel depressed or angry, for exhaustion distorts reality. There is no escape but even if we were offered a permanent way out, very few of us would take it.

We can now insist on our need for unbroken sleep and optimum health after childbirth in order to be able to cope. We can now avoid the exhaustion from repeated childbirth suffered by women in the past. One mother writing to the Women's Co-operative Guild in 1915 shows just how successive births coupled with the daily care of motherhood undermined her love for her children. After her first baby: 'I had every care and motherhood stirred the depths of my nature. The rapture of a babe in arms drawing nourishment from me crowned me with glory and sanctity and honour.' She developed eczema, had a second baby fifteen months after the first and then a third baby sixteen months after the second, after which, 'Motherhood ceased to be a crown of glory and became a fearsome thing to be shunned and feared . . . Many a time I have sat in daddy's big chair, a baby two and a half years old at my back, one sixteen months and one one month on my knees, and cried for very weariness and hopelessness.'[14]

Dora Wright was born in 1908 in Stockport. Her mother had eight children and Dora decided to limit her own family to one. 'My mother was just worn out, her general health was terrible. I think it attacked her nerves because I remember when I was in my teens, she would always be ill, crying a lot and she looked so tired. I wanted to enjoy my children, to give them lots of time and be with them and my new husband. I didn't always want to be scrimping and saving for every penny.'[15]

Many poor mothers still live with handicaps to health and have good reasons to feel extremely tired. The Joseph Rowntree Foundation report *Life on a Low Income*, published in 1996, found that many mothers miss meals or live on toast, go to bed early in winter or sit in blankets, and live in the dark in order to reduce heating and lighting costs when they have no money to feed the meter. Parents invariably want to give their children the best, and mothers in poor families will stint on their own needs if it means that they can provide for their children. They also want to avoid burdening their children with the stigma of being poor – thus mothers will wear clothes from jumble sales so that they can buy their children new clothes. They often barely eat so that they can pay for school dinners, and so avoid labelling their children as disadvantaged through having free school meals.

Bad housing also contributes to poor health and greater levels of exhaustion. Overcrowding means that there is never a quiet corner to seek refuge, few tower blocks have adequate, safe areas for outdoor play and inner-city estates, with drug dealing, gang fights and syringes lying in the gutters, are not necessarily the best places for small children to roam free. Sonya is Egyptian. She and her husband live in a one-room bedsit in London with their two-year-old son and nine-month-old daughter. There are mice and cockroaches and her son has constant diarrhoea. Consequently she finds it very hard to sleep. 'My son is very active and I can't sleep because we're all in the same bed and sometimes he cries all night. What can I do?'

Ann, now a single mother living on benefit, lived through her

pregnancy and early motherhood in a rat-infested rented basement. The father began an affair when their son was six months
old and soon moved out. Ann feels that such adverse circumstances 'took a toll on my health. I went grey suddenly and it
affected my ovaries or hormones because I had erratic moods
and either bled all the time or not at all. I also suffered from
chronic migraine which I'd never had before. I got very frightened of losing control and hurting the baby because the pain
got so bad and I couldn't cope with the crying. I thought that it
could be helped if practical things improved, if we had somewhere decent to live. This basement was piled high with
rubbish outside and rats and they could get under the front
door. I could see them in the daytime. Everything was a battle,
battle, battle and after three years of fighting I got quite sick
and tired.' Ann did eventually get moved into a flat – on the
thirtieth floor of a vast imposing tower block in Notting Hill,
London.

Working mothers are more likely to feel exhausted than working fathers or mothers who stay at home, although research on
postnatal depression has found they are less likely to be
depressed than housewives, and have a higher sense of self-
esteem. Work is a release from the chores and demands of
motherhood. But a working mother often feels her identity as a
mother threatened unless she can cram all the hands-on 'quality
time' delights associated with 'good' motherhood into every
waking hour when she is not working. But then someone has to
do the washing, cooking, shopping, cleaning, ironing and hanging
up of children's clothes . . .

'Why *are* you so tired?' was my husband's daily question for
years, followed by the rational refrain of the male brain: 'There
must be something wrong with you.' I was always too tired to
explain and it would take more time than I had to run through
the list of diverse but unnoteworthy accomplishments of the
past days and the growing number of tasks that had to be done
in the next twenty-four hours. The two hours between waking

and getting the children to nursery and school are filled on the average day with the following: loading the washing machine and hanging up the last wet load; coaxing breakfast into the children; slurping tea; maintaining some semblance of communication with the ones I love most but hardly saw yesterday; telling the older one to turn off the TV; clearing up the cornflakes and milk spilt all over the floor and the kitchen table; cooking a cauliflower and a cheese sauce for their tea because they will be ravenous as soon as they come in; telling the older one to turn off the TV; searching for clean clothes for the two-year-old and persuading her into them; shouting 'Turn off the TV!' down the stairs; replacing in the cupboard all of the clothes scattered by the seven-year-old around the bedroom as she strives for her image for the day; reassuring her that she looks fabulous; arguing with the two-year-old that a patterned T-shirt doesn't go well with patterned shorts and then letting her wear them anyway; coaxing her back into the patterned shorts once she has taken them off; chucking any old clothing I can find on to my own body; marshalling the children into the bathroom to clean their teeth and brush their hair; full-scale row about both of these issues (external social pressure means that it really matters to me that my children do not go to school with unbrushed hair); clean my own teeth; scrape the congealed cheese sauce off the bottom of the pan and on to the draining cauliflower; search the house for their shoes and that particular pencil she has suddenly developed a passion for; open the post; glance at the headlines; avoid thinking about anything that I have to do after the children have gone to school because it is too frightening; put some spare clothes for the younger into a bag in case she wets herself; shovel a swimming costume and towel for the older into another bag; open the front door; strap tiny into the buggy and then I'm told that the older one needs to have the costume for a woodland animal by Friday. I won't bore you with a further list of things accomplished after work, or indeed the number of things I squeeze in between working, or when I ought to be working, like shopping for food, essential items of clothing and green felt for that wood-land costume.

I am worried that this sounds like whingeing. I chose to have children, I love them more than life itself but we're not allowed to say that it's tiring. 'I must say,' wrote a working woman in 1915, 'that although it is a time when women suffer terribly, yet it is a time when they get very little pity as it is looked upon as quite a natural state of things.'[16] Things haven't changed much. Improvements in the social and medical conditions have unquestionably made aspects of motherhood easier, but we still get tired and we still get very little sympathy for it. If motherhood can now be avoided, then we have no right to complain about the drawbacks. 'It's not something that we can moan about because we wanted her so much,' says Jane of her adopted three-month-old daughter.

Camilla had her first child on the understanding with her part-ner that she would take full responsibility for that child, for he already had two grown-up children from a former marriage. He adores his new daughter and helps care for her, but Camilla feels that she can never complain. 'I had to have a fine pregnancy. I had to have a fine birth. I had to go back to work without a moan. I have to get up in the night and I can't be tired. I do feel that it's up to me to make everything work, but it's worth it. Definitely.'

I know that I am not alone. Countless other working mothers say that they are more tired now than they have ever been and many are far less fortunate than I am. Grace, who works as an administration officer for a local authority, has to 'wake up at six, wash, bath, tidy up, get Malcolm ready for school and then go to work. I finish at five, rush back to get Malcolm something to eat, get him to bed by eight-thirty to nine and then go to bed. On Saturdays I do my shopping and cleaning. I do get exhausted, I burn myself out, but what can I do? How would he do without me? Who would he hug?'

Many full-time working mothers move from crowded, noisy offices, on to crowded noisy public transport, home to noisy children competing with each other for her valuable attention. Even though she is tired, the average middle-class mother wants to see her children and feels duty-bound by modern theories of 'quality time' to pay attention to her children, even though she has yet to take off her coat. Self-employed women cram full-time work into school hours and when the children are in bed, at other times pacifying them with biscuits and television during important phone calls.

Working mothers can just about manage to juggle work, motherhood and their relationship provided that nothing else happens. As soon as somebody gets ill or there's a crisis at work, or an important meeting suddenly gets rescheduled for five o'clock the following day, a working mother has to run fast between all three spinning plates in order to stop them from crashing to the floor. Michelle has a one-year-old daughter: 'Nobody tells you how to do this bit. There's one page in the Health Authority manual which says "If you're ill, see if a friend can help out" but if it's infectious and you don't want the friend to get it, what do you do?' Unless they have a temperature so high that they cannot get out of bed, mothers have little choice but to struggle on, however bad they are feeling.

We have to work, we want to be reasonable mothers and we need 'him' to want to stick around. We do not want to remove an element from the triangle (unless 'he' is more trouble than he's worth), so we have no choice other than to resign ourselves to feeling tired. Resignation due to lack of choice in motherhood is not new. In Margery Spring Rice's survey of working-class wives during the 1930s she found that 'tiredness and strain are considered to be the inevitable consequences of marriage and of a growing family, and must be accepted with the same resignation as getting old'. She found that half of the women in her survey got up at 6.30, went to bed at 10.30 to 11.00, having spent more than twelve hours of the day on their feet. Poor housing meant great physical exertion for many of them. They couldn't just bung the washing into a machine.

Many poor families in cities like London and Liverpool lived in tenement buildings, one or two rooms in a larger house, sharing the same sanitation facilities with other families. These houses were built for one middle-class family, with servants to fetch water and empty buckets. Each working-class housewife now had to carry her clean water up from the basement and carry her water down again to be emptied. She had to heat that water on an open fire or possibly a gas ring.

Average rooms in tenements had no outside larder in which to keep food, coal had to be stored in the sitting room and there was no garden or courtyard in which to dry clothes. 'One is tempted to ask why, if water has to be fetched from a yard or heated in a kettle, is washing-up done after every meal?' asks Margery Spring Rice.

> Or, why, when cooking facilities are poor, fuel expensive, and other work abundant, is cooking performed every day instead of two or three times a week? The answers to such questions are implicit in the accounts these women give of their household difficulties. There is very seldom crockery or cutlery enough for more than one meal and therefore it must be washed up before the next meal. Besides, as the kitchen is also the living room, the sight and smell of greasy dishes would obtrude themselves during the woman's next two or three hours of work.[17]

Perhaps, now that most middle-class and many working-class mothers have better health and living conditions as well as fewer children, we are burdening ourselves with greater emotional exhaustion. Perhaps we have filled the space left by washing machines and flushing lavatories with additional tasks like mixing Play-Doh, making advent calendars out of egg boxes, or pandering to new theories of 'good' motherhood such as those advocated by Jean Liedloff in *The Continuum Concept* who says that we ought to carry our babies tirelessly around until they are three years old. Mothers in the past who were too ill from repeated child-birth and the ceaseless cycle of keeping their numerous children clean, clothed and fed, would have envied our privilege and in all likelihood laughed at our obsession with eye contact and interactive play.

It is as if middle-class mothers have replaced the unavoidable exhaustion from too many children and adverse economic cir-cumstances with a modern exhaustion in the form of a ceaseless emotional strain from worrying about our children's safety and welfare, the effect that our daily habits, actions and attitudes have on their growing psychology and our reluctance to discipline for an easy life. Perhaps we have embraced child-centred theories of 'good' motherhood to our own detriment. Perhaps, now that children are presumed to be chosen and therefore wanted, we are exhausting ourselves needlessly in our misguided belief that if we endeavour to give our children everything within our power and deny them nothing, they will grow up confident and successful rather than constantly disappointed. Perhaps I am my own worst enemy.

Small children can be completely irrational and I have been pathetic in my inability to refuse unreasonable demands and say no. When both my children were small variations of the follow-ing scene were common at meal times:

Child: 'I want juice.'

Me: '*Please* may I have some juice?'

'Not dat cup . . . dis cup.' She's pointing wildly in the direction of the sink from her throne-like high chair without the slightest clue as to which cup she means, but like the demented imbecile she knows me to be I search for it. She is beginning to get cross and I am beginning to lose patience. Why am I doing this? This is utterly insane, I wonder as I pour the juice into yet another beaker, hoping that it might be the one that she thinks she means.

'Not dis cup!' She's screaming now and the words dissolve into plaintive wailing and I'm beginning to get worried: what can she possibly mean? I assemble all of the available plastic cups on to the table in front of her and attempt to control my rising anger.

'Which one do you want?' I say firmly through gritted teeth. 'What's wrong with this one, it's a lovely red colour, it's got Mickey Mouse on it. There's a little handle here for you to hold.'

I know well that to try and apply rational adult common sense to an irrational eighteen-month-old baby is more pointless than swapping seats on the *Titanic*, but still I do it. Baby has meanwhile forgotten what she originally wanted and has dissolved into tears from the sheer frustration of not being able to make me understand. I feel guilty about not being able to understand her needs, for shouting and for getting angry, and feel inadequate about my inability to just rise serenely above the situation and say, 'Forget it, kid, stick with the beaker.' Instead, I try to give her what she wants even though she doesn't really know what it is, and I am now the one who is exhausted, emotionally drained and feeling inadequate.

If it isn't the right cup, it is plates, spoons, books, toys . . . so that we sit surrounded by a sea of mess, unable to curb irrationality with order. It is as if a child's chaotic and unformed mind spreads like a virus to the parent. I have learnt one lesson from all this – irrational toddlers have no short-term memory. If you wait just two minutes before fulfilling a request they have usually forgotten what they wanted and have moved on to something else. When mothers didn't have time to serve their children like little emperors because they were too busy scrubbing clothes against washboards they learnt this profound piece of wisdom naturally.

But there are also historical reasons beyond our individual control which have made the experience of motherhood change so radically and become that much more demanding. As we saw in Chapter 4, motherhood was not considered to be a full-time occupation until the end of the nineteenth century. Children were encouraged to fend for themselves at an early age and they were often looked after by other household or extended family members as well as by their mothers, soon after they were weaned.

Mothers were responsible for basic aspects of the care and welfare of their children. It was only with the Renaissance and then with the growth of psychology in the late nineteenth and early twentieth centuries that the roles of educator of morals and resident shrink were added to a mother's growing list of responsibilities. As science realized the importance of 'good' mothering, women paradoxically became increasingly to blame for their children's actions and defects. It was becoming harder for mothers to feel as if they were doing a good job unless they joined the exploding ranks of women adopting the additional practices of child-centred mothering.

'At home in Nigeria, all a mother had to do for her baby was wash and feed him, and if he was fidgety, strap him on to her back and carry on with her work while the baby slept,' writes Buchi Emecheta in her novel *Second-Class Citizen*. 'But in England she had to wash piles and piles of nappies, wheel the child round for sunshine during the day, attend to his feeds as regularly as if one were serving a master, talk to the child, even if he were only a day old!'

We now know from the work of child psychologists that we have to do more for an under-five than just keep her safe and fed. Previous generations of mothers avoided eye contact with their children so that they didn't have to strike up a conversation and could get on with their chores. Now mothers are encouraged to spend every spare minute of their day in stimulating, structured play so that their children reap the benefits of early education. Many mothers adore these aspects of modern mothering. The highlight of one weekend for me was spent sitting on the floor of the China Room at the Victoria and Albert Museum teaching my youngest how to use a pair of scissors while the eldest coloured in a replica of a mask from an ancient Chinese tomb. But the point is that mothers are expected to do everything possible now for their children whether or not they want to, and whether or not they personally would be better off with a rest.

The modern ethos is that babies breastfeed on demand, which often means all of the time, and breastfeeding can be inherently tiring. We carry them in baby holders so that they can be close to us, and because we know that babies feel more secure if they can feel and smell their mother all of the time; many women feel reluctant to put their babies down even when they have to. Truby King mothers were encouraged to leave their babies alone in the pram so that they could get on with their own chores. For centuries babies were left to cry in the belief that it was an essential way of exercising their lungs. Now mothers have to soothe their babies' tears wherever possible because crying is understood to be a baby's sole method of communicating that something may be wrong. Modern child-centred theories no longer allow mothers to leave their babies to cry themselves to sleep even if they are exhausted to the point of dropping themselves.

'I just feel that I ought to be perfect. I'm hard on myself and I think I ought to be giving her more attention. I feel bad about doing what I want to do when she's asleep, rather than what I ought to be doing as a good mother. I feel guilty for trying to read the paper while she's sitting in the high chair and I think, I'm ignoring my child, what must people think? I know that everybody is just doing their best, but it always comes back to the fact that I feel that I ought to be doing more,' says Juliet.

The modern attitude to children is so child-centred that it is easy for some mothers to forget that they are in charge. We are told by modern manuals such as Deborah Jackson's *Three in a Bed* that 'the more we interfere with and attempt to train our young, the more we are tampering with things we do not fully understand. We should be fulfilling our babies' expectations of us, not creating our own expectations of them.' Old-fashioned methods of discipline may have been hard on the child, but they made mothering easier when a child was bludgeoned into submission and meant to be seen rather than heard. Encouraging a child to be confident and to stand up for his or her own beliefs and needs means that it is hard to know what to say or do when your six-year-old turns around and says, 'You go to bed when you like, you do what you like, so why can't I?'

The modern abhorrence of smacking and the knowledge that shouting at your kids is both unseemly and ineffectual forces many women into more subtle forms of child control which demand astonishing efforts of patience and energy that most simply do not have. Explaining to a three-year-old why cars are dangerous, or why it is unacceptable to hit other children in terms that he or she will understand, are skills we expect now of mothers, whereas in previous generations they rebuked their children with a firm no or a quick slap of the wrist so that they knew it was wrong before they understood why it was wrong.

So strong are the modern theories on discipline that many middle-class mothers invest energy they haven't got in resisting their natural inclination to scold or shout at their children in public. You can hear the strain in mothers' voices as they repeatedly try to persuade their aberrant toddlers to conform socially, in parks, playgrounds and supermarkets, rather than shout or yank at them as do the mothers they despise. There is collective horror at my local 2 o'clock club whenever a mother yells at her child. It is awful when you see children being the victims of perpetual verbal abuse, always shouted at and ordered about rather than talked to as human beings, but many modern mothers are so frightened of crossing the divide, of sliding into an abyss of anger and hatred from which they fear they may never return, that they are reluctant to scold at all and make the daily work of motherhood much more tiring.

An anecdote from my local 2 o'clock club illustrates this perfectly. There was a small slide for babies and toddlers in the garden. I was helping my child up the four steps at the back of the slide behind an even smaller baby. On the plastic roof of this slide sat a four-year-old girl, kicking her feet backwards and forwards so that the heels of her shoes hit the babies smack in the face as they struggled up the steps. Instead of scolding the child and removing her from a slide that was far too small for her anyway, her mother held her feet straight out in front of her so that she wouldn't hurt the smaller children as they passed beneath her. The girl had a twinkle of glee in her eyes. She knew that she had won a small but important victory and merely had to steel her wit and confidence for the next confrontation.

We also exhaust ourselves worrying about their welfare. Our increased awareness about the sources of infection means that we work even harder to keep our homes clean, and blame ourselves when our children get ill. 'He had a weepy eye when I brought them home and at first I was blaming myself, thinking that it was because I was breathing on them, and they were constipated and I thought I'm doing the milk wrong, that I'm not sterilizing them properly, but you gotta stop yourself thinking that, otherwise you go round the bend – I can't put this dummy in their mouth 'cos it's been in the air for a little while!' (Keelie) Our children are so precious to us that we are reluctant to let them out alone to play or to walk to school by themselves when just over a hundred years ago the majority of our children would have long been contributing to the family income through their own labours.

The modern stresses of motherhood mean that mothering is still inherently tiring, despite the radical improvement in health and standards of living. But we do have advantages over countless generations of mothers, since we can deny or limit our children's demands so that we can feel less tired and have greater strength. Constant fatigue is a warning sign that your mind and body are being overstretched and that you are potentially endangering your health if you continue to pander to modern pressures to do everything well, to 'have it all'. Something has to give. You either have to work less hard at your job or at being a mother. You have to put selfish pleasure and self-indulgent pursuits back into your lifestyle, rather than denying your own needs because of your children.

Children repay us for our efforts in the pleasures we get from them. A beach isn't the same without a child to dig in the sand with. Parks come to life when we examine acorns or feed the ducks. As children get older, 'in' family jokes develop and they learn how to tease us and bring us back down to earth just as we do to them. The pleasure we gain from their physical affection heals wounds in seconds and can replenish much of the energy that our children have succeeded in draining from us earlier that day. Then there is the pleasure gained from their achievements which seem so much more marked and admirable than anything we have ever accomplished; the pleasure in drinking the first cup of weak, sweet tea made and stirred carefully, the astonishment that they can swim at all, let alone the pride in the grace and style of their front crawl. But the fundamental truth is that, however much our children give to us in bucketloads, we always have to give them more and that is why we get so tired, for that giving never really stops, but ebbs and flows with their changing needs.

When your youngest child reaches the age of four or five he will be more rational, want more time alone and be able to play happily with friends unsupervised. From four onwards children are more easily able to do things for themselves such as going to the lavatory or operating the video-recorder. Consequently you will feel considerably less tired.

But the tiredness resulting from our emotional input seems to increase as the years go by and our children become less and less easy to influence. Reminding a child hourly that he or she has yet to do his piano practice or his homework, encouraging them to eat good food, and having to beg your offspring to turn off their computers because you are worried about eye damage are particularly tiring pursuits when they are not for your own benefit and rarely reap results. Arguments become more vicious and more hurtful and harder to win as children get older, bigger, more articulate and able to fight back. Our children get to know us so well that they can find our Achilles heel and wound us painfully, yet if we were to resort to the same tactics they'd be threatening us with calls to Childline. Sleepless nights for infant feeding and nightmares soon get replaced by late nights as we lie rigid with worry, waiting for the crash of the front door as they come home.

There are ways of limiting facets of that tiredness if we are resolved enough. If you hear yourself regularly defending your child's broken nights with weak excuses such as 'He just wants a drink, so I refill his bottle and he goes straight back to sleep', and crave uninterrupted sleep more than anything else, then take greater control of your nights and be persistent, with consistent indifference to your children when they wake at night until they stop. Adopt star charts, talk constantly about the rewards for a week of uninterrupted nights and refuse to pander to even remotely reasonable requests at night until the pattern of waking is broken.

If your child is sleeping, you are no longer breastfeeding and you still feel chronically tired every day then go to see your GP so that the possibility of a medical complaint can be eliminated through tests. Cost in time for selfish pursuits two or three times a week even if you are working full-time and if you find yourself giving more to your child than you feel physically or emotionally able, hold back for just a while until your reserves build up again. Resist the temptation at all times to be a supermother. So much is required of the modern mother that it is impossible for the average woman to be good at everything. Play to your strengths and avoid your weaknesses. If you enjoy reading and drawing with your child, but loathe playgrounds and fairgrounds, then avoid the latter or let some other family member take them.

But, above all, avoid persecuting yourself about the possible negative and detrimental effects of your everyday actions on your child's future development. We all make mistakes but unless those actions are deliberately malevolent and born from complete lack of love, our children will not be damaged by them. They grow up shaped and influenced by the culture they live within, by school, by friendships with other children and other adults, and provided they know that they are loved they will eventually forgive you. We must never be so presumptuous as to think ourselves omnipotent in their upbringing. They have their own characters and their own unique way of being which lies beyond our influence from the moment they are born. If we were able to avoid just some of the many absurd licences that we give to our children in the misguided belief that we are preventing future psychological distress, then perhaps we would have enough energy for the inevitable, unavoidable efforts of motherhood, and be able to enjoy it more.

7

Relations with the Father

For the vast majority of parents, the arrival of a baby is the fulfilment of a dream, the most exquisite result of romantic love imaginable. Holding a new baby moments after birth, we see our physical characteristics married permanently to those of the father and face the prospect of a shared life together, linked genetically through that child. But it may take time for that dream of a deeper, closer relationship to come true. In the first few months of life, a baby often seems to produce the opposite, driving parents apart and revealing differences between them that were hitherto unseen.

As a couple in love we are equal partners. But from conception onwards the balance changes as each partner enters a transitional period of adjustment to parenthood; and we do not necessarily change in the same way or move closer together. Each parent looks towards the baby rather than each other. There is less time for each other as lovers and much more to argue about as we attempt to share new responsibilities. The birth of a child revives memories of childhood for each parent and those recollections are bound to differ. One parent may have had a happy childhood and want to repeat it. The other may have had an unhappy time and want to do things differently. Inevitably those experiences clash and both partners will have very different ideas about how they want to be as a family.

It takes time for a couple to arrive at a new way of being. There is 'his' adjustment, 'her' adjustment and there is 'their' adjustment, all going on simultaneously and unlikely to be synchronized. But the vast majority of couples do eventually emerge from the chrysalis of change provoked by the births of first, second and even third children far stronger, emotionally enriched and happier. The pleasure gained from having children more than compensates for the sacrifices. Children cement partnerships, they make family what it is and give parents added reason to work through marital difficulties. While the media focus on the rising divorce rate, statistics show that parents usually do stay together through the storms of any relationship for the sake of their children.

However, when relationships are already weak, they can deteriorate faster after the birth of a child than at any other time. One of the largest surveys conducted in America over seven years found that relationships can change in four basic ways after the birth of a baby: 12–13 per cent of the couples interviewed found that relations deteriorated to such an extent that they were in danger of separating; 38 per cent of couples experienced less dramatic decline but were unquestionably more distanced from each other than they had been pre-pregnancy; 30 per cent of couples managed to stabilize the situation so that there was no deterioration in their relationship but no new sense of closeness either, and 19 per cent of couples managed to overcome their difficulties and found that their relationship improved.[1] What most of us do is to put our relationship on hold for a while until we have the time and the energy to build on it further.

Pregnancy can be an intensely romantic, intimate time for couples. When men welcome the news of impending fatherhood, women often find that the father of their child becomes their main source of emotional support during pregnancy, for they are reluctant to confide in doctors and midwives and are unlikely to have close friends who are also pregnant.

But differences in outlook and attitude between the sexes are already beginning to emerge. In an ideal world, both partners want a child with equal enthusiasm and plan for it together. But in the real world few men feel ready for fatherhood in their twenties and thirties. It is usually the woman who, spurred by her biological clock, takes the first step by abandoning contraception, and this can alter the balance in a relationship until long after the baby has been born. Some women feel that they have to protect their partner from the more tiring aspects of babycare because they were the one who made the choice. Karen wanted to have a child far more than her partner and now that her baby is six months old she finds that she is trying to shield him from aspects of babycare. 'I don't want him to be unhappy with his child or with me. I get upset when he doesn't appreciate that because I think that I am really doing my best to keep him happy, which is pathetic. It's the worst way to try and maintain a relationship. You only need to read *Jackie* magazine to know that when you do that, that's exactly when men walk all over you.'

It is the woman who lives through the physical experience, attends hospital appointments, antenatal classes, buys books on babycare and baby gear and gives birth. A woman begins to adapt psychologically to the prospect of having a baby as she feels it kick and turn inside her, but a man has no physical change to root him with the reality and has to make a conscious commitment to the mother of that child. Some men (approximately 50 per cent) become deeply interested in their partners' pregnancies and report a growing attachment to the foetus by feeling it kick, talking to it through the stomach wall and looking forward to the prospect of fatherhood with excitement. The rest are either more distant and consider their role to be sturdy reliable oaks for their woman to depend on, or they are so distant that they refuse to believe this is happening. Some research shows that women tend to be more concerned by the way that the new baby will affect their relationship, while men are generally more concerned about how their life will be restricted by a baby.[2] It is not uncommon for men to react to the news of pregnancy with swelled pride at their virility and a brief spell of passionate sexual activity, followed swiftly by a sudden need to be absorbed day and night by their work or their hobbies.

The emotional balance in a relationship can also be destabilized during pregnancy. A woman can feel far more needy, irritable, tearful and vulnerable during pregnancy, but men seem to stay the same. Some men love the added dependency and feel more confident in their relationship because of the greater attachment that pregnancy brings. Their partner is now wedded to them and less likely to go off with another man. They may feel them to be more beautiful pregnant or feel guilty about intermittent negative feelings such as finding pregnancy to be ugly or sexually unappealing and having fantasies about other women. They may get irritated by their partner's mood swings and dependency and they may interpret angry outbursts as personal criticisms. If things get really rough, men may even doubt their paternity, have an affair with another woman in order to mitigate feelings of being trapped or even leave altogether if they feel that commitment to the mother or fathering that child is too much.

Women on the other hand find themselves suddenly defenceless and dependent upon a man they may not altogether trust. Old-fashioned gender roles of the male protecting the more fragile female begin to emerge and this sudden emotional imbalance in a previously egalitarian relationship can come as a shock. He goes out to work exactly as he has always done; she does the same but longs for afternoons in bed. He wants to be able to go out to the pub, to socialize or indulge in numerous leisure pursuits; she wants to go to bed at nine o'clock, eat jumbo bars of Fruit & Nut in front of the telly, decorate the nursery and refold the babygros.

While the father may become increasingly concerned about earning money to provide for his progeny, the woman who has always earned her own living may find herself financially as well as emotionally dependent on a man who may not be entirely committed and that prompts worries about how she will support herself and her child. A woman may feel vulnerable sexually because she doesn't feel attractive or sexy and may worry as a result that she will lose him to another woman. I remember that 'just don't have an affair' was a daily refrain in our house during both pregnancies because the mere thought, when I was so physically, emotionally and sexually vulnerable, seemed like the ultimate betrayal.

As pregnancy progresses, some women find that they are in such discomfort and so unwieldy that they reach remarkable heights of solipsism. It is hard to even conceive of the fact that a man may be going through any kind of emotional or psychological turmoil when he so patently avoids all of the physical discomfort of pregnancy, let alone labour. The first time it occurred to me that my husband might be having a hard time too, was when I was eight months pregnant and he began to fill every spare minute constructing an elaborate cardboard three-dimensional model of a Roman amphitheatre. While my hormones dictated that I had to wash the kitchen floor sixteen times, he prepared for labour by taking his mind off the whole thing with a hobby that demanded such powers of concentration and precision he has never repeated the experience.

Some fathers find pregnancy and the prospect of childbirth so psychologically taxing that they channel their anxieties into physical symptoms mimicking pregnancy. It is known as the couvade syndrome, where men experience symptoms such as weight gain, toothache, gastrointestinal symptoms and loss of interest in sex while their wives are pregnant. Studies indicate that approximately 20–25 per cent of men experience symptoms which are often not recognized as pregnancy related. Researchers have found a 20% rise in the nurturing hormone prolactin in expectant fathers and the stress hormone cortisol doubles, increasing their sensitivity and alertness beady for bonding.[3] Anthropologists have also described ritual couvade, where men act out childbirth or follow a strict diet and avoid the use of weapons during their wives' pregnancies in order to protect both mother and child from evil spirits. A Swedish study of couvade found that older men were more likely to experience couvade and concluded that a possible explanation for this may be that older men anticipate and experience greater change in fatherhood.[4] Whether it is empathy, anxiety or a public acknowledgement of paternity, the existence of pregnancy symptoms in men indicates that many men live with considerable psychological upheaval and fears about labour and fatherhood.

When it comes to labour, the differences between men's and women's physical and emotional needs polarize still further. A woman has to do all the work, but she can thrive on the emotional support of her partner during childbirth. A man stands helpless beside her, only able to offer a limited range of services. Some men pour every ounce of available energy into intense massage and vigorous bullying to 'breathe' and 'push'. Others read books between contractions and show more interest in the scientific wizardry of the monitor than the mother. It's hard to know which way your man will fall until you actually get there.

The presence of the father during childbirth was unusual historically but not unheard of. During the nineteenth century, French kings and many upper-class fathers were present at their wives' labours. In some rural, isolated areas the father would have been essential, and sometimes the only helper. However, throughout history all cultures that have excluded men from the scene of childbirth have done so because there is little for them to actually do. In cultures where fathers are expected to participate they are given very specific jobs to do such as following prescribed hunting rituals or simulating labour pains but they are rarely allowed at the scene of the delivery.[5]

In recent years, however, there has been a cultural revolution in the nature of childbirth in many Western industrialized countries. In 1970, only 15 per cent of fathers were present during labour in Britain, but by 1990, that figure had jumped to 92 per cent.[6] Most men and women want to be together during labour, they want to share the experience, as they intend to share the experience of being parents and this is a change that would have been welcomed by many women in the past. The assumption now is that the father ought to be there, yet all of the research into the positive and negative effects has produced inconclusive and contradictory results.[7] Some research has shown women to have a more positive conception of their experience of childbirth, with less pain, fewer complications in labour and enhanced feelings of being well supported and sharing a family experience. But other research has shown the opposite – that there are no measurable differences in the level of pain, duration of labour, or obstetrical intervention and that the father can transmit additional anxieties, expectations and even feelings of failure when it is not possible to stick to the birth plan – demands which a woman in labour clearly does not need.

If the father is relied upon too heavily by the medical staff as an unpaid comforter alleviating staff shortages, then that can also have a detrimental effect on the labouring woman, for she may as a result receive less advice and support from a trained professional. Research in America and South Africa has shown that women do better in labour if they have, rather than the father beside them, an experienced *doula* (someone who, although not a trained midwife, is there with the sole purpose of supporting the woman in labour and ensuring that she gets all she needs or wants).[8] *Doulas* have experience of labour and labour pain, their only commitment is to support the labouring woman, therefore their own emotions or anxieties do not come into play and they understand the hospital environment. In the research conducted in Ohio, USA, *doulas* were found to be far more interactive verbally and physically with the mother and stayed closer to her throughout, particularly during the second stage.

It is hard sometimes for men and women to accept that they have a right to decide for themselves whether or not the father should be there, when pressure from family, friends and even the medical staff assumes that he will be. There are many gains for men and for family life. The vast majority of men find it intensely emotionally rewarding and feel immediately closer to the baby and the mother as well as immense respect, even awe, at her achievement. But a minority of men can feel shocked by what they have seen and some researchers believe that these men can develop psychosexual problems as a result.

Some fathers feel isolated within a medical environment normally associated with illness and death and powerless to help their wives. Witnessing a loved one in great pain is deeply distressing. If complications arise and the health or life of either baby or mother is threatened then men can be deeply traumatized. Seeing the sweat and exertion on the doctor's face as he heaves away at your baby's head with forceps is shocking. Just like women, many men are surprised by the fact that they are as likely to feel overwhelming relief once the baby has been born rather than an emotional high. The delivery room is not necessarily the right place for every man. Each couple must decide for themselves what is right for them individually and as a couple.

Ideally, the presence of both partners during childbirth is a uniquely binding experience, fostering intense intimacy between two people who are already close, and creating the potential for closer emotional ties between father and mother and father and baby. Many women say that their partners are far more support-ive in the subsequent weeks and months of early motherhood after they have witnessed the supreme efforts and joy of labour. Some research indicates that new fathers are able to compensate for the mother if she has had a difficult birth or a Caesarean by becoming more closely involved with the baby, physically and emotionally.[9] But if the father of your child is not present at the birth he can form just as close an attachment to your newborn baby simply by picking him or her up and sharing those precious early days.

If we want our men to be active fathers, then it can be argued that they should be present at the birth, however difficult or upsetting it may be. I needed my husband to be there even though we both knew that there wasn't much that he could do to help. I needed him to share the experience of our children's births, however difficult they might be. My trauma was to be his trauma and I saw no point in protecting him from it since the result was to be our child. He was upset by the birth of our second child seeing me in pain and holding the baby for half an hour after her birth while they tried to stabilize me after heavy blood loss and another Caesarean. But perhaps the most upsetting moment for us both was at the end of the day, when he had to carry our older child away from my bedside after she had held her baby sister for the first time, for she screamed 'I need my mummy too!' along the hospital corridor, when she realized that I wasn't coming home with them. When he returned to the hospital later that night, he drew the curtain silently around my bed. He put his arms around me and we sobbed uncontrollably together, sobbed for our firstborn, sobbed for ourselves and we sobbed with relief. It was a moment of shared intimacy that I will never forget, for it was the first time after years of marriage that I had seen him cry.

Biological differences between men and women are starkly highlighted during pregnancy and childbirth and it can feel at times that what was once a close and mutually supportive relationship is drifting inexorably apart. But if this is your first child you are united by the fact that pregnancy, labour and parenthood are uncharted waters for both. Neither of you knows what to expect, or what will happen in labour. You're both likely to be anxious, fearful or even terrified about what sort of a parent you might become or how your relationship will change. This is a uniting experience as well as a potentially divisive one and the proof of that union comes with the arrival of that child, a unique genetic marriage, produced through a unique labour from a unique pregnancy that only the two of you can share.

As working men and women with mutual and independent interests we stand side by side, more equal than we have ever been throughout history. But with the birth of a first child, egalitarian notions between the sexes dissolve into pronounced and old-fashioned gender roles, with the mother quickly assuming the lion's share of domesticity and babycare as she nurses the physical and emotional wounds of labour, and the father quickly returning to work, ever intent on providing for his new family. All studies show that relationships tend to become more patriarchal after the birth of a child. Many women wouldn't want it any other way. They want to be with their babies and many plan to stay at home as the primary carer during their children's early years.

But for the mother who plans to return to full-time work after her maternity leave, and hopes to share aspects of childcare equally with her partner, life becomes more complicated. She finds herself suddenly at home alone, feeling emotionally unprotected and dependent, while he maintains his links with the outside world as he has always done. She has sudden, complete responsibility for her new baby, finding herself acting the housewife, grappling with the new world of mother-care while he returns to the sanctuary of a world he knows well. There can be conflict over money and how it is spent, who does what in the home and how they intend to bring up their child. And sometimes we find ourselves staring incredulously at the man we thought we knew so well when parenthood brings out attitudes or behaviour that we have never seen before – wonder at the closet love and tenderness that only a baby can extract or disappointment with the man who is reluctant to share in the baby's care or perceive the baby's needs in the same way as we do.

Inevitably we feel suddenly more dependent on our partner

when he is the only other person who can give us any time off at this early stage. I have interviewed capable, confident women who have been astonished by the way that they long for their partners to come home when they are at home all day with a small baby. Then as their home becomes their castle because they have lost their other territory of work, aspects of housework which they never previously considered that important, zoom to the fore.

'The first few months I couldn't wait for him to come home and then when he got home I found him intensely irritating,' says Hannah. 'He was on my patch and I didn't have another patch like he did. I remember going for him one day with, "You've just put your briefcase there and I've just tidied this house, you know." I can't believe that I actually said that.'

Keelie has always felt herself to be independent, capable and able to withstand her partner's teasing or sarcasm. But now that she has just given birth to twins she feels acutely vulnerable. 'When my old man's sarcastic I get really upset, with tears in my eyes, and I don't want to be like that. I try to reason it out but it's horrible to feel that emotional and dependent. He takes the car to work and I feel stuck in the house.' By the time Keelie has fed the twins and got them ready to go out, she only has an hour or two before she has to be back to give them another bottle and she sometimes finds that she forgets to buy the items she set out for. 'If I have to phone him up and ask him to fetch something, I feel really terrible, like I ought to be able to do it myself. But I can't always do it and we have fought about it because he says I ought to be able to find the time for it. He can't understand how I can forget to buy nappies when I go to the chemist, but I do. He is getting better about it. It's new to him as well, but I've sat him down and said, "How are you coping?" He hasn't said that to me. He expects me to cope.'

The roles of mother and housewife seem to fit so neatly together from birth onwards. There is just enough time to squeeze in the odd household chore in between tending to a small child's needs. The tiniest baby can tell the difference between essential chores and self-indulgence, gurgling happily while you scrub the kitchen floor but screaming his head off whenever you pick up a book or telephone a friend.

Men on the other hand tend to feel the full impact of father-hood when their baby is six to twelve months old and weaned from the mother.[10] Men who were helpful during pregnancy often regress after childbirth into stereotypical views about motherhood in order to appease their own feelings of ineptitude in childcare. Several studies have shown that many fathers do less housework after the birth of their baby than they did when their partners were pregnant because they assume that if she is at home all day long then she can easily fit in the cleaning and the cooking while he is out earning the family wage.[11] If a new mother is breastfeeding, then she has no choice but to get up in the night. The pattern is quickly fixed whereby the mother always gets up even long after she has weaned her child from the breast.

A father can put down the baby with the excuse that he is frightened of dropping it, but a mother cannot express such fear in case it should reflect badly on her mothering capabilities. A man will 'forget' to change a nappy, dress the baby in the first thing that comes out of the drawer or give up trying to spoon-feed a weaning infant by concluding that he is no good at it. In the weeks after giving birth to their first child, Natasha found it impossible to rest when her husband volunteered to give her a break, because he would bring their baby son into their bedroom whenever he cried, insisting that he was hungry. 'That would just drive me totally crazy because I couldn't get away from him. I'd hear him crying in the distance and know that sooner or later he would bring him in and of course when he did and I put him to the breast he would feed.' Natasha and William are lawyers living in London who have shared an equal partnership for years. Now, with the arrival of their son, they are having to work out a new way of relating in order to be able to care for him. They intended to be 'modern about it and share the responsibility' but found that harder than they imagined. Two weeks after giving birth, Natasha began to express breast milk so that William could give it to the baby during the night and then he would go to work the following day. 'I knew that wasn't what most men do but I let him think that that was normal. He was outraged when he discovered it wasn't. We were both really tired and both secretly felt that we were doing the harder job. He felt like he was up all night and doing everything and then going to work all day long and I just felt that even if you are tired, you go to work all day long and get away from the crying baby while I am with him twenty-four hours a day, and that there was no competition. I knew he was doing a lot but I felt that I was doing more. I do think that it's one of those terrible injustices of life because being with a newborn baby the whole time is incredibly draining and fathers will never know what that's like.'

Within days of giving birth the mother is established as the primary carer, supposed to know instinctively what is right for her baby. The father then finds it hard to look after their baby without asking for advice from its mother, or without that help being seen as some sort of favour. Studies show that men almost always assume that they are helping their partners in baby and child care rather than sharing in the day-to-day job of being a parent.

Men find it uncannily easy to watch television or read a newspaper while they are minding the baby. Mothers of older children stand astonished by the way that their partners can ignore the repeated question of a small child at least ten times before answering. Most mothers find it impossible to ignore their children to that degree, however much they might want to. A mother's time belongs to her child unless she has made alternative arrangements, whereas a father's time is his own unless he has the baby thrust into his arms or has a specific request to collect a child from nursery school written down in his diary.

Arguments can erupt quickly because there is so much more to fight about and both partners are likely to be very tired and overstretched It seems churlish to argue over who does which menial chore. After all, loading a washing machine, mixing up baby milk powder, changing nappies or pureeing carrots are not difficult jobs – but when you have to do them dozens of times a week, you start counting.

Then of course there are the disagreements about how you do things, not just whether or not you do them at all. Mary is an Alexander teacher who had her first child at the age of thirty-six. She cannot remember doing much housework, or it being an issue in her relationship before her baby was born a year ago. They were both working and shared the housework equally. Now that she is at home most of the time, 'I find myself feeling resentful although that's not right. I seem to do things as necessary whereas John will do a great blast of cleaning partly because he's not here most of the time. But I do get irritated. He accuses me of interfering, saying that I undermine him when I suggest that she ought to be eating something else . . . if only I could just let him get on with it.'

Arguments over babycare can be particularly acute when both parents care passionately about their child and both have their own ideas about how children should be brought up, based on their own experiences of childhood. Many of the family influences which shaped you as an individual resurface when you become a parent and become crucial to your new way of life as a family. The father who resents his strict, orderly upbringing may want to be more relaxed with his own child, while his partner may want to reject her more liberal upbringing and create a more formal environment for hers. Alternatively, the parent who is happy with his or her own upbringing, may want to repeat it. Either way the template is unlikely to correspond exactly to that of their partner which can lead to an unprecedented level of arguing.

'We've never fought so much as we have done after having a

baby,' says Natasha. 'Essentially we have different attitudes as to how it should be done because it's the most important thing in the world to both of us and we've never had to do something like this together before. I guess we were very compatible, only fighting about houseworking things, but that's what a baby is times a thousand, except that now it really matters. I feel that, because our son grew out of me and I breastfeed him, he really needs me and that he won't be OK unless I make him OK, whereas William feels that he's a sturdy, healthy little soul and absolutely fine. I'm constantly concerned that he's dressed properly and not in direct sunshine and William just feels like I'm nagging him the whole time. He never thinks ahead about what food is in the house, or what we'll have for supper, so why would he do that for a baby? But I'm always pureeing sweet potatoes or reminding myself to get some bananas. I've resigned myself to that now and I do enjoy the nurturing, but I guess it's part of that whole man–woman thing where men feel as if you're attacking their manhood if you tell them what to do, whereas women just see it as constructive criticism.'

If women quickly assume the lion's share of childcare and domestic responsibility, they set standards by which they expect things to be done and find it hard to allow men to be fathers in their own way. A woman measures what a man does at home and with the baby against what she does, whereas a man measures his investment against the often minimal efforts employed by his own father and expects praise. When she criticizes him for not doing things in the way that she would like them done, he takes umbrage, feels inadequate and is even more likely to abandon tasks.

'Tie it under her chin,' Caroline ordered her partner as he put on their baby's hat so that he could take her out for a walk while we talked about new motherhood for this book.

'Where else would you tie it?' he replied bitterly as they both fussed and fumbled over the buggy, which groaned under the weight of sunshades and brightly coloured jangling toys. When he returned an hour later, he looked worn out and frazzled. He had lost one of her many toys. When he went to the park café, he found that he couldn't carry the cake and the cappuccino and push the buggy to the table outside, so he took the food out first and then went back for the baby. But by the time he got back to his table twenty-five birds were eating his cake. Caroline smiled knowingly with just a hint of smugness. The same thing had happened dozens of times to her while he escaped the sole responsibility of parenthood at work.

When a woman who has always earned her own living suddenly finds that she has to ask the father of her child for money, it can be deeply humiliating, depressing her sense of self-confidence still further as her dependency is highlighted in ever more poignant ways. Keelie's husband refuses to open a joint account or to give her a cashcard to his account. His attitude is well meaning in that if she needs something, she only has to ask for it, but Keelie feels that merely exacerbates old-style patriarchal notions of 'her indoors'. 'He's not tight or anything, but it does get me down because I have to ask for it. He thinks I'll spend it all on myself, which is what he might do, but I haven't bought myself anything since I've had the twins. My first thoughts are always on their needs, not mine.'

Having a baby is an expensive business at the best of times. If a woman has given up work or has only a short period of paid maternity cover, this adds imbalance to the relationship and can be extra stressful, highlighting what many people now feel to be outdated notions of marital relations. She feels less and less able to provide for herself and her child and therefore less and less able to determine how their money should be spent. On the other hand, he feels under even greater pressure to earn more to provide for his family, and that perhaps he has a right to control their joint expenditure.

When couples have viewed their financial affairs as separate, semi-private entities pre-parenthood, it can come as a shock to discover that you have little choice but to pool resources. One woman I interviewed, who has a four-month-old baby daughter, had already spent her maternity pay and found that she was having to persuade her partner to part with some of his savings so that she could cover her standing orders until she went back to work. He was resisting this bitterly – a symptom perhaps of his own problem coming to terms with responsibility and becoming a parent.

Another couple who adopted a baby after several failed IVF attempts were finding the financial imbalance a severe handicap to good marital relations. 'We had a lot of difficulties when I stopped earning money and I felt very very angry about that because it added to the fact that because I wasn't bringing in any money, I didn't have any value, and while I know that society doesn't value motherhood, I expected my partner to. For me part of being a good mother meant that she had to have everything – I would compare the toys she had with the toys my friends' children had. As I didn't have any money, I wanted John to spend money on her, but from his point of view – his parents split up when he was thirteen and he feels his father worked hard all of his life for his family and never felt appreciated for it – there's a withholding, a reluctance to make an investment in his new family. When there were just the two of us we could pretend that we were individuals and keep our money separately but now we've got to provide for her and I want us to put things on a much more equal footing. I want us to have a joint bank account and organize our finances differently but he's not keen to do that. I think he's worried that if he does share, he'll get rejected, just like his father was.'

Couples who have always pooled their money and lived through times of high and low income, because one of them was unemployed or studying, tend to cope with the transition more easily because they have already made the shift from separate individuals to interdependency. But as more and more of us live financially independent lives before having children that transition is less easy to accomplish. Prospective parents need to discuss their financial affairs openly and how they plan to share resources before the baby arrives. They also need to be prepared to discuss money regularly as their needs, and the needs of their family, change.

When new mothers discover that they love being at home with their babies, the prospect of having to go back to work because they need the money can be a source of sadness. It can also create tension in a relationship if the woman resents the fact that her partner doesn't earn enough money to enable her to stay at home. Penny has a six-month-old daughter and definitely doesn't want to return to her job as a teacher, but her husband wants to be relieved of the responsibility of being sole bread-winner since his earnings are not enough for the three of them. 'It feels so unnatural to me, but I would earn more than we would have to pay out for childcare and we are really beginning to need that income now because I haven't been earning for a while and that is a source of tension between us. We're trying to be grown up about it, but it does mean that an awful lot of subjects have become taboo because they're about money and what we would do if we had a bit more. I feel I'm being pressurized to spend money so that I have to go back to work and he thinks I'm trying to prove that we can live on his income alone so that I can stay at home.'

Paula is a health visitor who earns more than her partner, who runs his own health food shop, and she pays the mortgage on their home. She has been surprised by how much she has enjoyed being at home alone with her daughter and doesn't want to go back to work but knows that she has no choice. 'Six days out of ten I'm totally supportive of him because I want him to have time to develop his work, but then I find myself thinking, Why can't you go out like lots of other men and earn the money so that I can stay at home and look after the baby?'

Kate's husband is unemployed and looks after their ten-month-old son while she works as a hospital administrator. She feels that she has no choice other than to work to provide for her family but would much rather be at home with her son. She feels that if he were earning the money she would get far more done at home. 'A man has a single-track mind. He can look after the baby, but he can't seem to clean or tidy up. It's meant that I have unwittingly become a bit of a nag and I come home and take over, which just isn't going to work in the long run. He tries to justify his position by saying that it's hard work. I know it's hard work being with a baby all day long but it's hard for me to accept when it's what I'd like to be doing. It substantially changed our relationship and we're still thrashing about trying to resolve it.'

When parents are on such a low income that they fall within the definition of poverty, the absence of cash inevitably adversely affects their relationship. The less money there is the more likely a couple are to argue unless their relationship is particularly strong. Parents who care for their children do not want to see them deprived. They will buy goods on credit and delay bill paying if their children need clothes and shoes. Many parents don't want to burden their children with the social stigma of poverty and pay for their school meals. Consequently there is next to no money for their own needs or pleasures. They can't afford a social life, and this increases a sense of isolation and mutual dependency, so undermining self-esteem.

The idea of the father figure as sole breadwinner is becoming increasingly outdated in Britain, with only 34 per cent of families with a child under four conforming to this traditional pattern in 2004. When it comes to families of children of all ages, less than a quarter depend solely on the fathers income.[12] Families now depend upon women's earnings but the old-style gender roles of mother and father are still well pronounced and harder to change. When mothers go back to work, differences in earnings and economic power highlight assumed gender roles still further. Men still earn consistently more money than women in every skill and profession, in spite of more than twenty years of equality legislation.

Men therefore have to be left unhampered to earn that living for the family, while the mother assumes the bulk of the childcare around her own work.

Many women in low-paid professions find that the costs of childcare eat up so much of their income that it is hardly worth working and resign themselves to ad hoc part-time or flexible working until their children reach school age. It is usually mothers who decide on the type of childcare to go for and who track it down, not fathers, and mothers almost always pay for it. The implicit reasoning is that a childminder or nanny is a mother, rather than a father or parent substitute.

Becoming a parent affects a woman's daily life so much more than a man's. Full-time working mothers spend approximately 1.6 hours more each day than their partner with their children.[13] Mothers usually take their children to and from the nursery or the childminder, are more likely to take time off when the child or childminder is ill, and take children to the doctor. Mothers shape their children's way of life by shopping for clothes and food, devising ingenious new ways of mixing mince with pasta, deciding which TV programmes they can or cannot watch, ensuring that they have the right educational toy for the right age, organizing their social lives and transport, talking to their teachers, taking an interest in their homework and feigning interest in their repeated jokes. Fathers only usually involve themselves in one of all of the above if they are asked to do so by their child or its mother. Volunteering for such pursuits rarely comes naturally, leaving mothers all too often with an overwhelming feeling of acute responsibility.

When a mother feels on top of things, senses that her children are thriving on her efforts and isn't too tired, there is great pleasure to be gained from such power, and from the knowledge that one is being a loving, good mother. But at other times when we lack self-confidence and energy, working mothers become easily angered by the fact that they have to cajole their partners daily with a sledgehammer in order to feel even temporary relief from that responsibility. 'I was the boss,' writes Jane Lazarre in *The Mother Knot*. 'But it was half the responsibility I needed to be rid of. Frightened that I couldn't trust you, I had to let you take it on yourself. It took almost two years, but that finally is what engaged your interest. Once I had to ask *you* if he needed a polio booster, and I was happy for days.'

The compensation for all this new and difficult inequity in our adult love relationship is the extraordinarily powerful emotional enrichment that comes from loving our child. 'The leaping heart that I used to feel for Dan, I now feel for Joe when he walks into the room,' says Sue of her eighteen-month-old son. It is so much easier to love a small defenceless baby that grew inside your body, when their tiny faces change and grow more interesting daily and when they respond so positively and reward you so generously for your efforts. Full-grown men are far more complicated.

Many women find that they are so enraptured by the physical presence of their baby, and feel so drained by the intensity of their emotions and the work involved in caring for them, that they have little emotional energy left for their partner. 'You give so much physical nurturing to your child, you don't need to give it to your husband,' says Camilla. 'I don't mean to exclude him, but it's just so easy to give it to a child. They're so responsive and your love for them is so overpowering.'

New parents touch the baby far more than they touch each other and either can feel jealous or feel the loss of adult emotional enrichment. Sometimes it is the mother – 'We had been together for twelve years before our daughter was born and our relationship was so important to me,' says Imogen. 'It was the first really good thing that had happened in my life and I felt as if she had come and smashed it into smithereens. Then when she was three months old, we started to put her to bed earlier and suddenly we had evenings together again – oh the pleasure! It was like I was clawing back a little of my life.'

But more often it is the father who feels emotionally abandoned. If you find him asking you to cut his toenails or make the coffee more often than usual when previously he has always managed to master these difficult tasks all by himself, then he is probably either feeling jealous or in need of emotional input. The intensity of love that many women feel for their child is far greater than anything that they have ever felt for their partner. You think you love someone and then you discover how much more love you can feel for your child. But eventually, once both parents have adjusted fully to parenthood and retrieved more of their life together as a couple, they discover that they have even more love for each other because of the common bond of their love of the child. If he is jealous then ask him to compare the amount of attention and love that you give to the baby with the amount of time and attention that you give to yourself rather than to him.

If both partners can accept that their relationship needs to be put on hold until they have enough energy, time and enthusiasm for each other then they are more likely to be able to give each other enough space to adjust to the lifestyle revolution of parenthood. You cannot go back to those exclusive times when you only had each other to consider, but you can make small windows of coupledom to reinforce your relationship in the new triangular family shape that you have created. Just a few hours out alone together will remind you both that love for each other came before the love for your child. Just a few hours alone together can give parents images of togetherness to cling to. Caroline left her eight-month-old child with a babysitter for the first time when they went to Center Parcs. 'We went to the pool and swam in and out of each other's legs and really played with each other like we did when we were courting. It was lovely, and now whenever we feel we are never going to have those happy heartfilled times again, we think back to that afternoon and know that we will. It's just a question of making the time to do it.'

Often the old gender definitions work to help us in the months after childbirth. We wallow in the nest of new motherhood and find it hard to leave our babies unless the more detached and worldly man drags us from there. Women are often too tired and too wrapped up in their babies to find any extra resource for the initiative of organizing time out together as a couple. We need the man to do it. 'Gender roles suddenly made sense to me,' says Wendy, a keen feminist, university lecturer and mother of two. 'The father has a role to play in pulling you back into the real world and at times he has to be quite insistent. I hadn't thought that would happen and that fits in with a whole load of ideas about women and men that I wouldn't have subscribed to previously. I used to think of that bit of a man which is so emotionally detached and connected to the outside world as a sort of disability, but it now seems purposeful, in dragging the mother out of the nest. But then you have to allow them to be like that at other times.'

Men can change radically when they become fathers. All of the emotions, the psychological upheaval and the exhaustion described in previous chapters can affect men too, and many women discover hidden reserves of love and tenderness in their partner. 'His pre-baby personality was marked by distance and reserve and a serious inability to get close to people.' Sue's husband writes novels. 'Watching him accept Joe completely and open new channels of feeling in him that I haven't seen in him before is really nice. What I want now is for those feelings to come back to me. I don't think that we've got to the point yet where we are looking at each other as people again. He sees me as a mother and I see him as a father, but there are lovely things about that.'

If a second child arrives before the parents have found time to be alone together then that can increase the distance between them. Suddenly there is even less 'down' time because the father looks after the eldest and is forced to form a closer bond while the mother looks after the baby. It is harder to rest or take time off to be alone together when the baby sleeps, because the needs of the older child fill that space. If that child is still finding it hard to sleep through the night, or without one or other parent, then whole days and nights can pass without a couple touching or talking to one another.

'We are really bad at getting the kids to bed.' Wendy's children are three years and eighteen months. 'When I was pregnant with Joe, Maya still needed walking up and down to get to sleep but I was so exhausted that I just couldn't do it so she slept with me throughout my pregnancy. And now that Joe is here, Pete and I haven't shared a bed for a long time because he looks after Joe at night and Maya comes into bed with me. I remember reading an article about a woman who had fertility treatment and had three children. One had died in the womb, one had died as a child, and the tensions had been so great that she'd split up with her husband. Pete asked me which of the things I found the saddest but I couldn't see that there were three things. I just saw that two of her three children had died, but for Pete the saddest part was the relationship splitting. That hadn't even occurred to me. The scales are now rebalancing a bit, but they are still way out there with the kids.'

In many ways the transition to parenthood for couples is harder now that there are no set roles within a relationship. The 1662 Book of Common Prayer stated that the primary purpose of marriage was the procreation of children. Now that we subscribe to more romantic notions of companionship in marriage, where relationships have to continue to feed each other and grow in spite of the children, it is perhaps harder for men and women to marry their own relationship needs with those as parents. For centuries, material considerations such as marriages between estates and allies and the continuance of the family line or business through the procreation of children mattered far more than romantic love. Families needed children to contribute to the household economy through their own labours and to provide some vestige of pension for the parents in old age or if they became incapacitated. Now, we search for complete personal, sexual, emotional and even intellectual fulfilment from our relationships and expect to be able to maintain that equilibrium through the impact of children.

Historically, mothers have always been able to depend on other sources of support such as an extended family living within the home or close by, or a multitude of household servants. Now, mothers depend almost entirely on the father of their children for any time off. Never before have women depended so much on the fathers of their children for physical and emotional support; inevitably such dependency places strain on a relationship.

When servants provided much of the childcare in middle-class families, both parents were seen as amusers, educators, companions and figures of authority. Mother and father were allied and the domestic divisions between them may have been less sharp, but their roles within marriage were more specifically defined, with the man as breadwinner and the woman running the home. Now, we have to work at our own domestic arrangements until we arrive through trial and error at some sort of compromise, unless we subscribe to the traditional male breadwinner/female housewife template.

Men and women in modern relationships are unlikely to sit on exactly the same spot on the continuum between complete traditionalism and complete egalitarianism and often find that they have to renegotiate the terms of their relationship as parents when they are probably exhausted, overemotional and easily anxious – not the ideal circumstances. When presented with the new responsibilities of parenthood as well as a sudden lack of free time, each partner is likely to feel as if he or she is giving up more than the other and inevitably the renegotiation of those terms leads to arguments.

Studies indicate that romanticists are more likely to idealize parenthood and become disillusioned after the birth of a baby than those who value the friendship and partnership aspects of their relationship most.'[14] Disagreeing at such a time of profound change is healthy and not necessarily an indicator that you are on the road to divorce. By arguing constructively parents are able to air their grievances and create opportunities for compromise in ways which will eventually enhance reconciliation and foster greater happiness within the relationship. Children will not be adversely affected by such discord because they see you resolve the conflict positively.

But if the fighting is constant, and a manifestation of loathing rather than adapting to changed circumstances, then children can be very badly affected indeed. Studies indlcate that couples give out distinct warning signs when they feel under severe attack in an argument. Men will become defensive, then evasive, while women exhibit sadness and fear. When couples fight seeking resolution they will argue until they see these warning signs and then retreat offering concessions and compromises, because mutual happiness is more important to a loving couple than winning the argument *per se*.

But when couples feel so deeply unsupported within their relationship that they lack confidence in its surviving, they are more likely to ignore these warning signs and push their partner beyond those boundaries in an attempt to score points and feel better about themselves by making the other suffer. Children raised by parents whose marriages are characterized by criticism, defensiveness and contempt are more likely to do badly at school and show aggressive and anti-social behaviour towards their classmates. They may find it harder to concentrate or to soothe themselves when they become upset and they may have more health problems such as colds and coughs as well as high general levels of stress hormones in their urine. When relationships have passed the point of no return in that they are dominated by hate rather than love, then children may well be better off living with one or other parent.

When relationships cannot survive the difficulties of early parenthood, it is important to remember that the children are not to blame. Their arrival has merely highlighted the fissures in an already weak situation. And even though there may be less conflict once the relationship has dissolved, single parents live with greater loss as a result. There is loss of money, friends, family, possessions and sometimes their home. There can be loss of identity, confidence and security, and hardest of all is the loss of shared parenting. Single parents can find themselves in emotional turmoil after separation or divorce – rejected, angry and jealous if they have been abandoned, and guilty or worried about the children if they feel that they should have done more to keep the relationship together. With no one close enough when you are ill, tired or grumpy, to take up the slack, and no one there to share the highs and the lows of parenting at the end of the day, single parents feel more isolated. 'I sometimes feel our relationship is too clingy,' Grace says of her six-year-old. 'He clings to me because he doesn't know who his father is and I worry about what would happen to him if something happened to me.'

We live in stirring, exciting times, when the rules within relationships are more fluid and unconventional than ever and are being defined by the individuals involved rather than by social constraint. Fathers have in recent years become far more involved in the intimate details of their children's lives and are often no longer the remote providers and disciplinarians of the nineteenth and early twentieth centuries. We expect so much more of them because we want our children to have strong relationships with them and because egalitarian notions dictate that if both parents work, both should take care of their children.

Women have determined much of this change but we must continue pressing men to take on more responsibility for their children. Ideally, children should have as strong a relationship with their father as they do with their mother, for research indicates that the 'healthiest' families are the ones in which the power is shared.[15] If parents work together and make conscious decisions as to who is going to do what, children grow up learning valuable lessons about compromise and co-operation. They learn to appreciate diversity and the inconsistency of life by seeing that each parent has different things to offer and different reactions to events.

Fathers are crucial to a child's upbringing. Research shows that paternal involvement with a child, particularly from the ages of eleven to sixteen, raises that child's educational and career aspirations and that good paternal involvement from the ages of seven to eleven reduces delinquency levels.[16] Type A – driven, successful businessmen who are absent from the home most of the time – are as potentially damaging to their children as the father who leaves, even though they may be providing well materially for their children. If you encourage your partner to take an active role from early on, by giving him the baby and reassuring him that you are as new to babycare and therefore as inept at it as he is, or by insisting that he gets home at bathtime, you will be nurturing their bond that much earlier. You will also be gaining time to rest and recuperate, time to feel your own life coming back, which is not as selfish as it may sound.

The number one cited cause of marital distress in new mothers is feeling unsupported and misunderstood by their spouse. If the father is more involved with the daily care of his children he more easily understands your tiredness, you are less tired and the balance between you is more equal. By sharing care and fostering a healthy relationship you are being better parents because you are less likely to have unmet emotional needs which you unwittingly expect your children to fulfil. Some research shows that mothers are nicer to their children when the father is present, smiling more often and paying more attention to them.[17] And when children grow up in a stable family environment, they are given greater freedom to explore and set their own pace for interactions with the grown-ups. Research in Ohio has found that single parenting can lead to an overprotective atmosphere. The mother or father is more likely to consider that their children need to stay close to them because they have sole responsibility for their welfare. That single parent is also more likely to impose their own ambitions and goals on the children.[18]

Men become more than just lovers when we mother their child. We depend upon them far more than we ever did when we were childless. Their earning potential, their ability to steady volatile emotional situations with a little more rational detachment, their contrasting slant on life and how to live it, allow us to be better mothers. They are as crucial to the healthy upbringing of our children as we are. But we have to be prepared to relinquish more of the motherhood preserve if we are to bring out the best of fatherhood, and, more important, we have to allow them to father in their own way, by learning from their own mistakes rather than expecting them to do everything as we would.

I could have avoided an awful lot of marital discord when our children were tiny if I had found the strength to resist the urge to interfere when he was trying to give me some time off. But I found it hard to lie in bed on Sunday mornings when I could hear the baby crying implacably downstairs. I could hear him trying to feed her breakfast, squeaking toys to distract her and even trying to drown out her cries with Radio 4. I've lost track of the number of times that I've got out of bed and interfered. Usually if I picked her up out of the high chair she would quieten down a little, surprised perhaps by my sudden appearance. But immediately marital relations are tense. I've intruded on his space and I can't resist undermining his confidence in his childcare abilities, angered by the way I'm forced to abandon my lie-in because he's just not doing it right.

We cannot expect to maintain the monopoly on motherhood simply because we create and give birth to our children. 'The power of the womb, marvellous as it is, does not have enough wattage to light up a whole lifetime,' writes Anne Roiphe in *Fruitful*. If we give the fathers of our children up to 50 per cent of their care, we also give them 50 per cent of the guilt and 50 per cent of the self-blame. But then we also have to give up the good bits too and be able to stand back and watch our beloved children turn to their father for comfort, affection and advice rather than to us.

When the youngest one calls for 'Daddy' in the middle of the night, or looks at me as if I was a complete moron as she sits on the loo waiting for her bottom to be wiped and says 'I said *Daddy*', it is not easy not to feel rejected. I take great comfort from the knowledge that my daughters are as safe and happy with their father as they are with me. As I watch him being a father, images of my own childhood and losing daily contact with my father through divorce resurface. I realize that giving my children a loving father who will not leave them is perhaps my greatest achievement.

Acceptance, compromise and understanding are the key words. Most marriages and relationships with enough common ground between the two partners and the flexibility to change survive in spite of the conflicts over money, responsibility and who does what. Research shows that the total decline in a relationship after the birth of a child is unlikely in the vast majority of cases. Most couples manage to absorb the change and cope with it and feel that the rewards that come from having a child far outweigh the costs. The arrival of a child does not initiate severe marital distress nor will it bring already distressed couples closer together. But couples who are able to focus on what unites them and learn to accept that their pre-baby lifestyle will never return usually have a happier time.[19]

All relationships ebb and flow with time and general levels of satisfaction tend to decline during the first fifteen years whether or not there are children. The giddy honeymoon heights of fresh love cannot be sustained over a lifetime. People get bored or irritated by each other and crave new sexual stimulation. But once we have got used to the new equilibrium, we discover that children do not take from our relationship, they give abundantly to it. Children give edge, commitment and stability to a relationship that inevitably has to change. When couples have few areas of common interest through their work or hobbies, children provide a focus and give them plenty to do together. Suzanne's daughters are seven and four. 'If you didn't have kids to talk about I think as the years go on you'd end up not saying a word to each other because basically that's all you talk about apart from "Bloody hell! Look at this phone bill!" You'd have to find an interest together if you didn't have children, otherwise what would you talk about? You'd probably be divorced within five years.'

Children give our relationship space to breathe and grow by shifting our focus away from each other. And as each partner changes through becoming a parent, the relationship can develop in unforeseen and very positive ways. 'Having children has made us much more appreciative of each other and of what we can do in our spare time. Because there is so much less free time together, we feel more wicked and teenage about it.' Gemma works full-time in television and has two children under five. Her husband has made peace with his own unhappy childhood by becoming a father. 'I used to be the strong one, but now that he has confronted the person that he was, he is much stronger. He's made friends with himself and the balance is much more equal between us. Even though there is much more local tension to our day, the children have brought us closer together.'

As children grow older with their own friendships and a keen desire to follow their own pursuits, more space opens up in the lives of parents for each other. We discover that we need to foster a united front in order to cope with questions over discipline or morality as our children get older and we need an ally with whom to escape when we feel unable to cope with a recalcitrant toddler or teenager. But above all we need to be able to share our worries and our sense of joy at their achievements with the only other person in the world who has an equally vested interest in their welfare. We see the world afresh through the eyes of our children and can feel closer to our own wider families and the community in which we live. Through our children we share a biological link to the future and to each other. Wendy feels that the connections are even wider. 'Children teach us to see the joy of what is ordinary and what is universal. The fact that everybody goes through this parenting thing and gets off on the same thing about their kids makes you feel as if you are linked into the wider world, not just amongst human beings but even with animals. It's like the final step out of adolescence, welcoming the relief of being ordinary.'

8

Sex and Sensuality

The effect of pregnancy and giving birth on our sex lives is so profound that it is often long-term rather than temporary. All of the parts of a woman's body which we normally associate with sexual pleasure change or get hijacked for other purposes. The sense of abandonment and embarrassment about one's body and bodily functions in labour are unlike anything we have ever experienced before. We cannot see our genitals, but everybody else can as they prod and poke at the foetus to ascertain its position and measure your cervix for dilation, always somehow managing to rest their thumb on your clitoris. Ultimately, many women say that their sexuality and sexual self-esteem flourishes. Many men and women say that they only discover respect for a woman's body, however flabby or un-Barbie-like, after the wonders of pregnancy and childbirth. Sexual intimacy after such an intense shared experience deepens and becomes richer in the years ahead. But before that sexual utopia can possibly be reached new mothers and their partners have to go through a long and sometimes painful process of healing – physically, psychologically and emotionally.

Research consistently shows that the majority of women

experience an overall decline in the frequency and enjoyment of sex during pregnancy. When a couple are expecting their first child it is tempting to think that they will 'get back to normal' soon after the birth of their baby. But for the vast majority of couples, there is a gradual rather than sudden resumption of sexual activity, as both partners come to terms with being parents and attempt to find the time. More than 50 per cent of couples have not returned to pre-pregnancy levels of sexual activity one year after the birth of their child.[1]

We attempt to sever the connection between sex and pregnancy when our enjoyment of sex is purely recreational. But as soon as a couple decide to abandon contraception and try for a baby, the sexual act assumes a whole new mantle of significance. The pleasure and passion can be far more intense without the hassle of contraception as an almost primeval urge to procreate takes precedence over years of efforts of avoiding conception. If pregnancy is then elusive, the need to conceive can diminish the pleasure of lovemaking, as spontaneous passion gives way to temperature charts and making love at the right time.

Dicing with the danger of conception can be very sexy. We have to choose to abandon contraception in order to have a child and are far more knowledgeable about the ways that motherhood can limit our lives. Consequently the decision can be harder, impossible sometimes to make and it may be that by taking risks and leaving more room for chance, we are allowing fate to make the decision for us. 'When you're regularly having sex with someone, it's just so murky,' says Ann. 'Some days you're very clear about it. You think, I must use contraception, and you do. But other days you get swayed by a different mood. You become soft and lose that power to think clearly and you don't take care in the same way.'

When a woman is pregnant, she can find it a hugely sexy time. There is no need for the hassle of contraception, and as a couple they have achieved a romantic goal and suddenly have the prospect of an even closer future. The blood flow to the genitals increases during pregnancy which may make the woman feel sexier, achieving a more intense orgasm with greater ease, and the vagina becomes more lubricated due to the increase in oestrogen and progesterone. The woman may feel fulfilled and magnificent and the man may feel particularly virile, proud and loving as a result of his success at impregnation.

But for many, if not most, couples that romantic ideal is short-lived, for as pregnancy progresses, a woman's discomfort is such that the mere thought of sex just makes her feel worse. One survey found that couples had sex half as frequently during pregnancy as they did before.[2] Nausea, tiredness, bloating, tender breasts, the frequent need to pee, indigestion and heartburn every time you lie down are not normally considered to be lust-inducing symptoms. The hormonal changes of pregnancy can also greatly reduce a woman's libido and there seems to be more point to sleep than to sex. The increased weight of the baby presses down on the cervix and can make penetrative sex uncomfortable as the penis bumps directly against the cervix (which points straight downwards during pregnancy) rather than behind it. Sweating, breathlessness, tiredness and aches and pains increase considerably during the last three months. Feelings of pressure and swelling in the genital area increase, she may have piles and feelings of sexual arousal may accentuate that feeling of heaviness and make orgasm more difficult.

Even if the physical symptoms of pregnancy are not a hindrance to sex in themselves, the additional psychological upheaval and uncertainty can dampen any hint of lust in a woman, and sometimes in men too. The ability to abandon oneself happily to sexual activity doesn't happen in a vacuum, but depends upon equilibrium and a certain amount of calm in the rest of our lives. When a woman's body is so busy reproducing, her mind is bound to be preoccupied with her changing identity as she plans for and perhaps fears for the future, and inevitably feels a certain amount of anxiety about the baby's welfare and about giving birth. The deep ambivalence of pregnancy (see

Chapter 5) experienced by many women even when their pregnancies were planned can inhibit sexual feeling.

The hormones of pregnancy may make a woman bloom with health, but the shape of pregnancy is not one that we normally associate with sex. Chloasma, weight gain, stretch marks and waddling do not help to raise a woman's morale when it comes to showing her body to her lover and it can be particularly hard to feel sexually appealing in a large vice-like bra or a flowery tent-shaped dress. A woman with a large pregnant belly gives out a clear warning sign that she is unavailable sexually, already 'banged up'. Men often do feel turned off by their partner when she is pregnant and may express worries about harming the baby through intercourse or find the prospect of being 'watched' by the baby inhibiting.

Much has been made in recent years of the sexual pleasure of childbirth. Dr Grantly Dick-Read, the father of natural childbirth, first coined the phrase 'ecstatic childbirth' during the 1940s and Sheila Kitzinger has been a forceful and persuasive advocate of the potential sexual pleasure in childbirth. 'It can bring positive enjoyment,' she writes in *The Experience of Childbirth*, 'and precedes the sensations of delivery rather as intense sexual pleasure builds up to release in orgasm, and this even when it involves some pain.'[3]

She uses sexual innuendo throughout her bestselling handbook in order to give the experience of childbirth a romantic glow. She compares 'the gradual opening of the vagina' with 'the uncurling petals of a rose' and the pleasure of the second stage of labour with a child's delight at the body's ability to defecate. She quotes extensively from women who say that they have found childbirth exhilarating and pleasurable, and merely skates over the horrors of labour complications as if they are unlikely to happen.

While I share in her dream that, one day, all women may be in complete control over their bodies and enjoy the experience of childbirth, the fact of the matter is that only a tiny minority of women find childbirth sexually exhilarating. There is a small number of women who have found childbirth so sexual that they have reached orgasm, or begged the midwife to masturbate them. But for most of us having a baby is not the same as having sex and while there are similarities they may not be erotic or particularly pleasant.

Giving birth is physiologically similar to sexual arousal in many ways. As the first stage of labour progresses, the woman's blood pressure and pulse rate may rise. The hormones of childbirth are sex hormones. Oxytocin, which we know is produced in response to nipple stimulation, causes the uterus to contract in orgasm as well as in labour, and later in afterpains. The rhythmic crescendo of contractions; the groans, sighs and panting; and the warmth of bodily fluids as the membranes seep or break are deeply reminiscent of sex. There is mounting anticipation as the woman has no choice other than to let the physical sensation of labour take over. Labour is genitally focused and is a time of intense emotion. During the second stage delivery positions can feel remarkably similar to sexual positions, particularly if the woman is lying on her back, with her feet in stirrups. The expression on a woman's face as she pushes her baby out is remarkably similar to those during orgasm and after she has given birth she may utter repeated exclamations such as 'Oh my baby, my baby', feel overwhelming joy, tears of relief and exhaustion, as women do after lovemaking. Giving birth inevitably throws up deep and often troublesome associations with sex and it can be deeply traumatic for women who have been raped or were sexually abused as children.

There are also psychological similarities in that a woman in labour has to balance seemingly contradictory qualities of abandonment to the physical process of labour with an element of control. Anne had two good experiences of labour and thinks there are strong similarities between sex and riding and sex and childbirth. 'It's about power, mastering this strong beast in a psychological rather than in a physical way. You're controlling this horse but really it could go its own way. When you gallop, you can't actually stop, which is why it is so much fun.'

But the danger of linking sex with childbirth is that women who have yet to give birth only have their largely pleasurable experiences of sex to compare it with. Childbirth may be exhilarating, intense and extraordinary but for most women it isn't nearly as much fun as having sex. Meg Southern, a midwife who has herself had children, sums up the difference when she writes:

> It is a sexual event, not because the sensations were similar to those I feel when making love – labour was too fierce and savage for any comparison. But there were similarities in that my priorities were altered to concentrate entirely on the task in hand, I was overwhelmed by rhythmic waves of sensation to which the only response was to open up to them and let go.[4]

There is also a worrying association between the stoic resilience of suffering labour without pain relief and the myth of female masochism during sex. 'The cry of a woman in travail has become a commonplace of literature,' wrote Margaret Llewelyn Davies in 1915, 'and the notion that pain and motherhood are inevitably connected has become so fixed that the world is shocked if a woman does not consider the pain as much a privilege as the motherhood.'[5] Psychoanalytic theory and Freud helped to inculcate the link between female masochism, motherhood and sex. Freud saw female sexuality and motherhood in phallocentric terms. Women had babies because they didn't have a penis and the self-denial and passivity of motherhood and female sexuality was considered inherent. A woman's journey to mature female sexuality went hand in hand with motherhood. She had to renounce the pleasure of the clitoris for the vagina and accept subjugation by the penis and the passivity of intercourse, just as she had to accept the passivity and masochism of motherhood. 'The only logical way to reconcile woman's commitment to suffering with the overall cultural commitment to pleasure was to assert that, for women, suffering was pleasurable,' write Barbara Ehrenreich and Deirdre English in their study of experts' advice to women, *For Her Own Good*. 'The psychoanalytic construction of the female personality found mounting cultural acceptance from the thirties on, and by the forties and fifties – the height of the permissive era – the Freudian faith in female masochism stood almost undisputed.'

Medical progress has given women greater choice in child-birth and they no longer have to accept that extreme pain and suffering are unavoidable. Women in the past had longer labours and often suffered pain from medical complications which have been eliminated in the modern world, such as urine retention and distortion of the pelvis due to poor nutrition and rickets. Chloroform was a powerful new form of pain relief during the late nineteenth century but it was difficult to regulate the dose and could kill. But doctors had little choice but to give in to pressure from women for chloroform because they would simply lose their custom to another doctor if they denied them. 'I feel proud to be the pioneer to less suffering for poor, weak womankind,' wrote Fanny Longfellow to her sister-in-law after the birth of her third child in 1847. She was the first woman in America to give birth under the influence of ether. 'This is certainly the greatest blessing of this age, and I am glad to have lived at the time of its coming and in the country which gives it to the world.'[6]

It is only now that we can be near certain of surviving child-birth with the luxury of a living baby and an epidural if need be that we can even entertain the thought that childbirth could be sexually fulfilling. The drop in the maternal death rate and therefore in the fear of death, and the prevalence of relatively safe methods of pain relief has allowed us the luxury of considering how we labour, rather than merely praying for survival. But that doesn't mean that we have to enjoy childbirth or feel hard done by if we haven't experienced sexual pleasure during delivery.

*

Thirty-six hours after I had delivered my first child by Caesarean section after an arduous but failed attempt at a natural breech birth, a junior house doctor settled down for an intimate chat on the chair next to my bed.

'And what are we going to do about contraception now?' he asked cheerfully, hugging his clipboard for moral support.

I could barely move, still used a catheter and everything hurt, even breathing. My breasts throbbed and my nipples stung. I was already hallucinating from sleep deprivation and I never wanted to go near a penis again. I wanted to tell him to piss off and leave me alone. Instead I stared incredulously at him and said politely, 'I beg your pardon?'

When it became clear that he was not going to leave until he had a satisfactory answer to write down next to my name, I mumbled condoms to get rid of him and watched him cross the ward to talk to a woman who winced with pain as she shuffled slowly around her bed to pick up her baby.

'Piss off and leave me alone,' she said when he asked her the same question. 'If you think I'm ever going near a penis again you need your head examined.'

Women who have just given birth have numerous good reasons for loss of sexual desire. All of the changes of early parenthood that have been discussed in previous chapters affect a woman's libido: the physical, hormonal and minor health problems resulting from pregnancy and childbirth, mild depression and problems coping with a small baby, conflict about working motherhood or not working at all, the emotional intensity, anxiety and exhaustion of suddenly being a mother, change in the equilibrium of your relationship and low sense of esteem or identity. Just one of these problems is enough to send a woman's sex drive plummeting to zero. Since most new mothers experience several of the above it is perhaps surprising that anybody has sex at all in the first year of motherhood.

Pregnancy handbooks and doctors indicate that sexual relations get back to 'normal' in about six weeks but this is largely fiction. There are no set rules. Many couples do not resume sex for months after childbirth and most couples find that the frequency of sexual relations is severely reduced for years, if not permanently. Research shows that 30–60 per cent of couples have 'resumed' sex within six weeks, but they've probably only done it once and it was more than likely a bungled and unsatisfactory experience. A survey of 1,200 women in Birmingham found that only a third of women did not experience problems on their first attempt at intercourse after childbirth.[7] NCT research has found that 50 per cent of women felt their sex lives were less good after birth usually because of persistent pain.[8] Do what feels right for you as a couple, be honest and open with each other about your feelings in order to avoid misunderstandings and remember that resuming sex after giving birth is always a gradual process.

The physical stress and pain of childbirth lingers on. Approximately 70 per cent of women who give birth experience tears or episiotomies and up to 15 per cent of these women still have a painful perineum three years after giving birth. Fifteen to twenty per cent of women have the surgery of a Caesarean to recover from. As a result, most women find penetrative sex painful in the weeks and months after giving birth and fear the prospect of experiencing even more pain when the experience of childbirth is still so fresh in their mind. After an episiotomy or tear, the surrounding tissue swells up and can pull on the stitches and cause considerable pain if the wound has been sewn too tightly. A doctor's proclamation that a new mother has 'healed up nicely' at her six-week check-up sounds absurd when she knows that she is still experiencing discomfort.

If you experience pain during intercourse for longer than six months and the pain does not seem to have been gradually decreasing during that time then you should consult a doctor, for there may be a good medical reason. If your scar is very red, or there is pus and a smelly discharge then you may have an infection which will need treatment. Bad stitching can leave you with a lump or ridge of scar tissue, a thin loop of skin usually at the back of the vagina where the labia meet, which feels as if it could tear easily, or with a narrowed entrance to the vagina.

Specialist physiotherapy such as ultrasound can be used to help stretch hard or unyielding scars but the problem needs early identification as this treatment is far more likely to be successful in the first six months. Alternatively you may need to consider being recut and resewn, an understandably unpleasant thought. But it is worth remembering that this is a minor operation and it has solved the problem for many women.

If you can locate an exact spot of pain then you may have a specific problem. If the pain disappears when you move your finger to either side of the sore spot then you may have a trapped nerve-ending which may need to be removed. Granulomata are little areas of scar which have not healed properly and are sore and red; they might heal up on their own but may also need cauterization with silver nitrate. Very occasionally bits of the lining of the womb get caught up in the scar and become tender during menstruation.[9] If your GP is unhelpful then ask to be referred to a specialist or go to your local family planning clinic. You are not making a fuss about nothing. Your GP may not have found the root cause of your problem, but you do need to be insistent and determined if you are going to get your symptoms treated seriously.

There are other physiological changes after childbirth which can make sexual intercourse painful or hold a woman back sexually. The vagina is often dry due to hormonal changes (high levels of prolactin and low levels of oestrogen) which will inevitably be more acute and prolonged in breastfeeding mothers. Some research indicates that breastfeeding mothers have lower libido and lower rates of sexual congress than bottlefeeding mothers because their hormonal make-up is so different.[10] Breastfeeding mothers may be more tired because of more frequent night feeding and the physical drain of feeding another growing creature from their own body.

Nearly a third of women suffer from haemorrhoids after childbirth which may itch, burn or bleed. Thrush is a common infection after childbirth because it thrives when there is a change in the pH of the vagina or when antibiotics are used. Large numbers of women are now routinely prescribed antibiotics after childbirth in order to limit the possibility of serious infection, but antibiotics also destroy beneficial bacteria which help suppress such fungal infections. The itching and discomfort of thrush will make a woman feel under par and unsexy and make intercourse less than pleasurable. Even when women do not tear badly during childbirth, they will have experienced considerable internal bruising and abrasion, particularly if the membranes broke early in labour and did not lubricate the vaginal walls during the second stage. The use of forceps or the ventouse cap can lead to considerable bruising which may be tender for weeks, even months.

On top of the physical manifestations of childbirth, there are numerous psychological reasons why a woman should be apprehensive or uninterested in sex. First, her entire sexual anatomy has changed shape and it takes time to come to terms with the loss of a tighter, neater vagina. 'I don't feel as if my vagina's really mine any more,' says Emily who gave birth to her son seven months earlier. 'It hasn't gone back to being the way it was and I don't know whether it ever will. It's never such a private part of your body again – I mean, how many people exactly have been up there?'

Karen's doctor stitched her episiotomy too tightly after her first delivery. 'I felt so alienated from my body. I felt like it had been one way for thirty-nine years and now it was different. I felt so angry at first but now that I'm used to it I don't care that much any more.' Vaginal slackness can result in a ballooning of the vagina during sex which means that air is drawn up into the vagina and expelled noisily, which can be embarrassing.

Some women find the medical intervention experienced during childbirth deeply inhibiting. For others, the pain of labour can affect their sexuality and subsequently make intercourse painful. A subconscious connection has been made between sex and pain, therefore penetrative sex produces pain. If the pain you feel is clearly located in a particular part of your anatomy then the root cause is probably physical. If your pain is more generalized it is more likely to have a psychological cause. Your mind may well have decided that you are not yet ready for sex – in which case it will eventually ease its hold over your body as you heal, mentally as well as physically.

Many men are hesitant about resuming sex after they have seen their partner giving birth and in pain. They may fear hurting her, and both may fear pregnancy, for childbirth focuses the mind on the consequences of even the most casual, pleasurable sexual encounter. Most men don't find the whole process of pregnancy and childbirth particularly sexy and will withdraw sexually until they feel that their partner looks and feels less like a mother and more like a lover. But as the memories of childbirth gradually fade, and a woman's body slowly regains some semblance of its former self, those fears and inhibitions do eventually subside.

Many couples feel the need for even greater honesty and commitment as a result of what they have been through together, which can in turn lead to greater sexual intimacy. 'I think Kevin held the picture of the birth in his mind very strongly,' says Hannah. 'I wonder how much women's sex lives change after birth because men's experience of birth influences the way they see women. They can't help but relax more about women's bodies after they've seen them give birth. They've seen something that's so intense that it's bound to change the way they relate to their partner.'

Many couples feel that a woman's breasts are no longer erotic when they are enormous, tender and leak milk at the slightest touch. Sometimes women who were sexually abused in a way which included regular breast contact find that breastfeeding triggers traumatic memories which inevitably dampen their sex drive until those feelings are laid to rest or breastfeeding ceases. The breast assumes its natural function of feeding after childbirth, isolating men from touching an area of a woman's body which they now feel belongs to the baby. Some men feel their own sexual desire dampened by their partner breastfeeding, although it may take months to discover that it is the man's psychology which is holding back sexual progress. Michelle, an American journalist living in London, breastfed her child for over a year. When she and her partner eventually talked about their lack of a sex life he complained, 'Your body belongs to the baby.'

'Now we're making up for lost time, but it will make me think seriously about breastfeeding this long again if we have a second child. I will have to ask myself – do I want not to have sex for a year?'

Numerous other aspects of new motherhood can affect a woman's libido. Even the mildest depression reduces interest in sex in both men and women. Anti-depressants may help to lift the spirit a little but are known to kill completely any hint of desire. Loss of libido is often the last symptom to disappear as depression lifts. Acute tiredness is another known lust killer. Tired lovers take longer to get aroused and find it harder to reach orgasm.

'Sex was impossible because I was always asleep. Sex is so important when you're seventeen or eighteen but after having children you wonder whether it really matters. John was completely stressed out about his job and I was so tired that the idea of us both wanting sex at the same time was ridiculous, like having simultaneous orgasm, so we'd laugh about it rather than do it. What does it matter?' says Charlotte, mother of three. It only makes you feel good and there are other ways of feeling good.'

If a woman's sense of respect in her body is at an all-time low because of the distortions of pregnancy and childbirth, she may find it harder to feel relaxed about her partner seeing or touching her. Josie has a five-month-old son. 'My body isn't what it was and I do feel quite conscious about showing it to my husband. I don't want sex that might come from looking at each other, more just the cuddles really. I do feel quite conscious about revealing the whole of me. Pete's sex drive is lower than mine so now it's more equal between us. I don't get frustrated about it or feel this is a terrible situation because we're so much closer than we were before we had Joe.'

Sue was always acutely aware of her sexuality before she had her first child, who is now eighteen months old. 'Sex was one of the most important things to me. That's what I felt I was about, and now I've had to completely reappraise myself and so it's still very much in a state of flux. I definitely feel less sexy now. I was always aware of the way men lusted over me and now I'm not sure where I stand any more. I feel like a mother and I feel very different about my body – it's two stone heavier.'

Karen and her partner Ben have a six-month-old son and have had no sex since their son was born. Karen says that she never had much confidence in her body but now that she has had a baby, 'It's rock bottom. When I first came back from the hospital and looked in the mirror I got very upset by what I saw, and I still find it very difficult to think about what I'm going to put on in the morning. I feel so uncomfortable about the way that I look.' The arrival of the baby has also upset their lovemaking rituals, for they used to make love early in the morning before they went to work and now that is impossible because their baby is awake.

Men and women have so much to get used to as new parents that understandably making love is not at the forefront of their minds. Anxiety and preoccupation with their baby's needs can envelop a couple and distract them from each other. Both partners are also coming to terms with their new identity as parents and may find themselves feeling older suddenly, less carefree and more responsible. The memories and atmosphere of one's own childhood can resurface vividly and for most of us those memories do not equate sexuality with parenthood. While we may have giggled over or been disgusted by our parents' bodies, it is hard to imagine them ever actually doing it together, for pleasure.

The long sensual snog turns into a peck on the cheek and slow casual lovemaking before and after breakfast on a Sunday morning seems unimaginably indulgent when there is cereal to be spoonfed lovingly into growing babies' mouths or ducks to be fed in the park. When there is no choice but to do these things, couples need only take a few small steps to persuade themselves that this is what they want to do as responsible parents and give up all hope of being sensual, sexual beings again. If couples insist on calling each other 'Mummy' and 'Daddy' when they are not with their children then there is even less hope of ever disassociating themselves from the strictures of parenthood.

If a couple's relationship changes radically, as described in the previous chapter, then their sex life is bound to be affected. If a couple are tense and in conflict over who does what or who is more tired then the atmosphere is hardly conducive to intimate lovemaking. 'To begin with my scar was sore, John's arm was sore, I felt squeamish about my breasts and the main problem was that I was so cross and tired most of the time that I just didn't feel like it.' Kate's first child was born by Caesarean and is now ten months old. 'We had a lovely, sexually active time during my pregnancy but it's been hard to re-establish that and I have found it harder to have an orgasm because the baby seems to have a sixth sense and wake up.' Kate is the breadwinner of the family, although she would rather be at home, and finds herself resenting much of what her husband does or doesn't do. 'We'd have to have a totally harmonious day for sex to be possible, for us both to feel we could get in the mood. I don't have the energy any more for apologizing or cajoling or persuading.'

Sometimes couples find that sex itself is the main source of conflict between them. Men haven't changed physically or undergone the tremendous hormonal upheavals of pregnancy and labour and go on wanting sex for sex's sake or in order to feel loved in their relationship. But women sometimes find that their sex drive plummets. Irene and her partner had a very active sex life before they had their two daughters and even though the youngest is now four, Irene hasn't found her sex drive returning. 'I don't know whether it's hormonal because I'm definitely not tired like I was in the first year, when I felt like my boobs were for my baby. But I definitely can't have sex if I see anything that is to do with the baby. My sex drive has really dropped and I don't know why. There's only one time in the day when we can have sex which is when they've gone to bed in the evening. I've lost that sense of naughtiness, that frivolity. If there's a toy in the room I can't do it at all. Now when I want sex it's for that sexual good feeling, it's not because I need to feel loved. He's been so patient with me and sometimes I feel really sad about it because I know that it could threaten our relationship. If he had an affair for sex I'd crack up but I'd understand.'

Women have always found slow seduction sexually appealing. We like to have time together as lovers, before the possibility of sex even arises, and the biggest turn-off is feeling pressurized to make love when a woman hasn't had sufficient time to get in the mood. When women are juggling childcare, their children's emotional needs, household chores and their own working lives and thus inevitably find themselves feeling far more tired, they need seducing more than ever. When you have dragged two children to two separate places for their education before enduring all of the habitual pressure of a day's work, collected children at the end of that day's work, cooked their tea, coerced them into doing their homework, sorted out fights, arranged for someone to pick them up the following day because you have to stay late at the office, bunged a heap of washing into the machine and tried hard not to argue with your mother on the telephone because she has called just at the moment when both children are demanding your full attention, the last thing on your mind is sex.

Mothers are in the greatest need of seduction – flowers and kind words, evenings away from their children, and their men to turn them on in bed. Men take note – mothers simply haven't the energy to do all of the ego-boosting that they indulged in pre-children. The only way they can possibly consider getting sexually aroused is if they just lie there and you do all the work. After thirty minutes of highly skilled cunnilingus they're bound to be more responsive.

Clara, a historian, has one daughter, aged four. 'What I'd find really sexy, what would really turn me on is him picking up Lily from nursery, him cooking supper and cleaning up everything, him putting her to bed and *then* we have sex. To me that would be wonderful but he says, "If I did all the housework then you wouldn't find me attractive." He sees no connection between sex and the rest of life, but to me they're integrally connected.'

Women tend to need to feel loved and understood in order to enjoy sex, and often women feel that their partner does not empathize with their problems as new mothers. The sexiest thing that a man can do is to offer genuine understanding and tempo-rary relief from her responsibilities without a grumble or a murmur of self-congratulation. The sexiest thing that a man can do is to refrain from pressurizing his partner into having sex and offer numerous opportunities for non-sexual cuddles and close emotional support. Loss of interest in sex is not the same as loss of love and it will be temporary provided that men allow women time to heal mentally as well as physically.

Modern Western societies have lost the cultural taboos which allowed men and women to separate sexually from each other after childbirth and protected women from unwanted sexual advances. Numerous Third World cultures protect the new mother from sexual practices by seclusion for periods of roughly forty days. The Abelam society in Papua refrain from coitus until the baby can walk and the Alorese in Oceania wait until the child can sit up. The Masai are forbidden to have inter-course until the child has cut its teeth and Bengali Hindu women who are breastfeeding abstain from intercourse for at least three months postpartum.[11]

Historically couples refrained from intercourse while the mother was breastfeeding because sexual activity was believed to curdle the milk and many historians believe that mothers handed their new babies over to wet-nurses under pressure from their husbands who were anxious to resume sexual relations. In upper-class houses in seventeenth-century France, the maid might be encouraged to keep the new mother company in her bedchamber, or separate bedchambers were established and a mistress engaged in order to prevent the master's sexual advances towards the new mother.[12] Until well into the twentieth century children lower down the social scale slept in their parents' beds and as they got older the boys slept with their father and the girls with their mother.

The consequences of sex – pregnancy and, with that, possible death – were greatly feared and contraception was rare before the 1920s and expensive. Withdrawal and abstinence were the most popular forms and the rhythm method was simply not an option because there was little understanding of a woman's menstrual cycle and times of high or low risk. While women may have been ignorant of their reproductive system, they knew well what made them pregnant and would sit up late night after night sewing or otherwise usefully occupied until their husbands had fallen asleep or abstained permanently, risking their husbands' unfaithfulness Mary Norton Hardie had her first baby in 1923.

My husband was really very nice about it all and I slept in a different bed with the baby . . . I wasn't frightened, I was terrified. I wouldn't have gone through that again for a man. I refused to sleep with him in the bed – not that he demanded it. He realized that I was terrified of having more children and he was very good, though we did have one or two sessions. But we were so careful and he always stopped before he

completed. I managed seven and a half years when I didn't
sleep with him to avoid being tempted.[13]

She did eventually succumb and went on to have six more children.

Modern culture is now so obsessed with sex that we consider
ourselves to be less than whole if we go through periods of
abstinence. Couples can feel under added strain to resume sex
and often feel inadequate if they are still not copulating happily
nine months after the birth of their first child. But they are completely normal. Perhaps a more sane way of looking at it would
be that it would be odd if most couples were copulating happily
and regularly when they have lived through so much change after
the birth of a child. Couples need to take time to rediscover one
another again. As parents, you start a brand-new relationship
because both of you will have been changed radically by the
birth of that child and you can never go back to being the way
that you were, sexually as well as emotionally. You have to start
afresh within a changed and changing relationship and develop
new rituals and sexual routines which will enhance that relationship.

There will be times when you can be alone together but you
may have to make time or snatch it when the child is asleep. If
penetrative sex hurts, explore each other in other ways and
develop new depths of intimacy through touch and words. If
you want to avoid any form of sexual contact at all, then talk
openly about your feelings to reassure your partner that it is sex
that you are rejecting and not him. As each parent begins to
settle and accept their new way of life as normal, sex works its
way back into their lives (although less frequently) and many discover that it is a more intense and enjoyable experience because
they have had children. One quarter of the women interviewed
in one survey a year after giving birth said that they enjoyed sex
more now than they had done before they conceived.[14]

Sometimes sex is actually just what you need to make you feel young, irresponsible, attractive and relaxed again, even though the thought seems completely unappealing. 'Sometimes I get very gloomy.' Mary's daughter is one year old. 'And I attribute it to resentments over the washing-up. Then we have sex and I feel better and I see that I needed sex but didn't realize it.'

'Having a baby was brilliant for our sex life in the end.' Imogen suffered quite severe postnatal depression after the birth of her first child. 'Partly because you had to seize the moment, which can be deeply erotic. It did something wonderful for me because she centred me in a way that I had never been before and you have a better sex life because you feel more in tune with your body.'

Knowing that your partner has seen you in the most compromising of positions and that there are no physical secrets between you, can help women to be more relaxed with their partners and less self-conscious about their bodies. Many women find orgasm easier to achieve and more intense after they have given in to the ultimate submission of labour. And then there is the added emotional intensity of making love to the father of the child you hold so dear to your heart, the man with whom your future is now so inextricably linked.

Charlotte, full-time mother of three, has found another advantage. 'I'm more confident now and happy to be sexual because there's a sort of shield that protects you as a mother. You can walk behind a pushchair in shorts and not feel available.' Many childless men find mothers deeply attractive and many single mothers find their sex lives are greatly enhanced, even though the logistics of organizing time out from one's child can be great indeed. 'I feel better about myself now, more confident and more sensual. Now that I've got a child I get more men, ones who want to be serious,' Grace finds. 'But I am so much more assertive now that I've had a child. I know what I want and I can handle men now that I have no fantasy expectations. I know the reality of being abandoned and bringing up a child alone.'

*

When childless, women need sex to feel loved and nourished emotionally, and sexual contact is often the only time that we are touched as adults. But the work of motherhood is so physical and sensual that women can find that their needs from sex diminish. They want sex for that good feeling, but the need to love and be loved is fulfilled so perfectly by their child. 'No one had told her what it would be like, the way she loved her children. What a thing of the body it was, as physically rooted as sexual desire, but without its edge of danger,' writes Mary Gordon in her novel *Men and Angels*. 'The urge to touch one's child, she often thought, was like, and wasn't like, the hunger that one felt to touch a lover: it lacked suspense and greed and the component parts of insecurity and vanity that made so trying the beloved's near approach.'

The physical and emotional sensations that come from caring for the flesh of one's flesh are a hair's breadth away from so many aspects of adult sex, yet they are worlds apart. Kissing, hugging, playing, tickling and chasing are instinctive aspects of loving motherhood, just as they are in loving sex. We wipe their genitals clean and caress their bodies with oils and lotions, not to excite them or ourselves sexually, but to extend and nurture the extraordinary physical bond between us. We nuzzle their mouths with our breasts, take their fingers between our lips as we stare lovingly into their trusting eyes and gobble their bottoms in play. We hold their small bodies close to our own as much as possible, enveloping them with our warmth as we did when they were in the womb.

The sensual pleasure that babies bring inevitably affects the way that a mother relates sexually to her partner, when so many of her emotional needs are being deeply satisfied. 'In all relationships that she had hitherto known, in childhood, in friendship, in love, in mating, the partner fought, the partner struggled to live, to command, to break away, or to break in,' writes Enid Bagnold in her novel about early motherhood, *The Squire*, first published in 1938. 'But here for a short while she held in her arms the perfect companion, fished out of her body and her nature, coming to her for sustenance, falling asleep five times a day in her arms, exposing its greed, its inattention, its pleasure and its peace.'

'I feel such passion, it's like a passionate love affair.' Imogen has two daughters but says of her first daughter, who is now six years old, 'I'm still obsessed with her body, I just think that she's got the most beautiful body and I can't take my hands off it. When I was first falling in love with her it amazed me how incredibly physical an experience motherhood is – I had no idea it would be like this. It's exquisite, absolutely exquisite. It must have something to do with the fact that you allow yourself to totally love someone and put everything else in second place.'

'I could just cuddle them all day long.' Sophie has two daughters aged six and two. 'It's wonderful when they put their arms around your neck, or when they're tired and just want to snuggle into you. Who else gives you hugs whenever you want them!'

The sharp contrast between the beauty of a child's youthful, fresh flesh and adult decay can easily destroy romantic notions of our partner's attractiveness. 'The smoothness and sweet smell of their children, the baby's densely packed pearly limbs, the freshness of the little girl's breath when she yawned,' writes Helen Simpson in her short story 'Heavy Weather', 'these combined to accentuate the grossness of their own bodies. They eyed each other's mooching adult bulk with mutual lack of enthusiasm and fell asleep.'[15]

There is a very definite line between pernicious sexual abuse and the innocent physical affection of mothering which is essential for a child's healthy emotional and sexual development. Now that there is such media attention on the hidden prevalence of incest and paedophilia many parents and even grandparents worry about where that line may be and become self-conscious about being physical with their children. There has to be intent from the adult, and while most of us gain immense sensual satisfaction from nurturing our children we do not want to have sex with them. But there are other more subtle and invidious forms of abuse which parents may not be aware of. New theories of sexual abuse have sought to widen the net beyond the obvious immoral horrors of child fondling and rape. A father who introduces his daughter jokingly as his 'girlfriend' or comments regularly on her appearance in sexual terms makes a daughter feel as if she is the object, albeit untouched, of her father's sexual attention. The mother who grasps for cuddles when a child has not come to her for physical support seeks emotional enrichment that she may lack elsewhere.

'Subtle abuse is behaviours that may not be intentionally sexual in nature but serve to meet the parent's emotional needs and/or sexual needs at the expense of the child's emotional and/or developmental needs,' writes Christine Lawson in her paper on sexual abuse by mothers.[16] Examples of subtle sexual abuse occur when a woman frequently shares a bed with a child, baths or massages a child at an age when it is inappropriate for her to do so, asks the child to massage or bath her, obsessively washes a child's genitals, or repeatedly gives a child an enema. This behaviour is an entire world away from the day-to-day physical nurturing of mothering, yet associations are regularly made between the physicality of motherhood and adult sexuality.

Breastfeeding can be an intensely intimate and sensual time for mother and baby. Links between adult sexuality and breastfeeding have always been romanticized by men who find it hard to see a child suckling in non-sexual terms.

Bind me in your arms, hit me with your thighs,
Choke my heart with your milkswollen breasts . . .

wrote the fifteenth-century Bengali poet Vidyapati. Balzac dwelt upon sexual masochism in breastfeeding in *Memoirs of Two Young Married Women* when Renee says, 'When they [babies] fasten there they cause both pain and pleasure – pleasure which stretches into pain, pain which ends in pleasure. I cannot explain to you the sensation that radiates from my bosom to the source of life: it seems that a thousand rays start from that centre to fill my heart and soul with joy.' Balzac's description is perhaps better suited to orgasm than breastfeeding.

More recently, the Natural Birth Movement has emphasized the erotic connotations of breastfeeding. 'When the child stops crying, receives caresses, is sucking satisfactorily, relaxes and then sleeps in her arms it gives confirmation to the mother that she can handle the child. It is like a coitus where the feelings are flowing, both parties have orgasm and sleep in the certainty of love,' writes Sheila Kitzinger in her book *Women as Mothers*.[17]

The myth that some women experience orgasm during breast-feeding is pernicious and frightening for women because of the connotations of incest. There are physiological similarities – the stimulation of the nipple causes the release of the hormone oxy-tocin which has mood-enhancing and relaxing qualities and causes the uterus to contract. But that is all it is, a contraction, not an orgasm enjoyed in the full abandonment of sexual congress between two consenting adults – or any other kind of orgasm in the normal course of events.

Touch, too, is essential for a small child's healthy develop-ment. The experiments with infant monkeys at the Wisconsin Primate Center in America I mentioned in Chapter 5, have high-lighted the importance of touch between parent and offspring for healthy sexual development of the young. They were put into separate cages where some were fed purely by wire teats and others fed by cloth-covered wire models of their mothers. There were also soft dummy mothers who produced no food and the baby monkeys far preferred to nuzzle up to these than to the wire dummies with the lactating nipples. They would cling most of the time to the cloth substitute and only leave it when they were hungry to feed from the wire. The research followed these monkeys through to adulthood and observed distinct sexual repercussions from their upbringing. None of the mon-keys raised without mothers could perform sexually. The males were completely unable to perform intercourse even though they were provided with ample opportunity to learn by observation, and the females would collapse helplessly on the floor unable to co-operate. When these motherless females became mothers (through artificial insemination) they were unable to nurture their young emotionally and some were abusive towards their infants.[18]

Touch locates us in time and place. Babies first learn about their own body boundaries and develop their own neurological capacities through being touched. Being touched gives the baby pleasure and induces feelings of security when they are held confidently. As the horizon of a baby extends, they learn to find pleasure from their own bodies, sucking their fingers and toes, enjoying the sensations of urinating and defecating and they quickly learn how to rub their genitals to make them feel better when they are anxious. In the first twenty-four months of a child's life, when their understanding of language and reason is limited, the emotional reassurance that comes from touching our children is crucial to their healthy emotional development. They need to be picked up and carried or cuddled most of the day. They need to be kissed and tickled and made to laugh in order to feel loved.

Healthy relationships with children are sensual, not sexual. We may admire their physique and their youth and feel nourished emotionally when we hug them but that is an entire galaxy away from wanting to have sex with them. The most erogenous zone of the body is, after all, the mind.

Sexual activity produces babies and having babies alters a woman's attitude to sexual activity. The physiological toll of pregnancy and childbirth alters the contours of a woman's body and can reduce sexual confidence for a while. The exhaustion and anxiety of new motherhood can dampen libido considerably and the emotional shift from woman-to-man to mother-to-child is so profound that many feel little need for sex at all. Giving birth affects our sex lives long-term rather than temporarily but few of us realize that until motherhood is upon us. Gradually as the demands of small children change and we get less tired many women discover a new level of sexual intimacy with their partners. It is possible to feel closer sexually after living through the shared experience of childbirth and shared love for the growing child once both parents have recovered. But that is more likely to take years rather than weeks. Forget the sexual abandonment of childlessness. That will never return. But you can begin again.

9

Friends and the Outside World

There is a vast chasm between the expectations and lifestyles of the childless and those with children. Few of us understand just how much motherhood changes our relationships with old friends until it is upon us, drawing us away from the childless ones and closer to those with children. Our priorities change radically as mothers, spontaneity and freedom of movement are severely compromised and suddenly we are thrust into another world of playgrounds, theme parks and children's party entertainers, which we barely knew existed before pregnancy. We delude ourselves that we will be able to socialize as we have always done by organizing babysitters or taking the children with us. Then when our children arrive we understand that there are two separate worlds, one with children and one without, which rotate in opposite directions and occasionally collide, as they did one day over Sunday lunch at the house of my childless aunt.

My first child was two years old. We arrived hungry at one o'clock to find that the joint was just being put in the oven. As my aunt poured us each a glass of wine, I spotted my uncle scrubbing mussels in the sink for our first course and a large bowl of guacamole standing on the side together with a tantalizing display of spicy corn chips. I asked hesitantly if there was anything that the baby could eat, for it was way past her usual lunchtime, and there was a frantic, embarrassing search through cupboards for something that wasn't either dried, herbal, spicy, far too sweet or alcoholic.

We had come prepared with all of the essential paraphernalia of new parents – baby wipes, spare clothes, favourite toys, plastic spoons and a Winnie the Pooh drinking beaker, but food was the one thing I was counting on my aunt to provide. I had become so used to a diet of macaroni and cauliflower cheese, lasagne and baked potatoes that it hadn't occurred to me that lunch might not be child friendly. I had forgotten that much of the rest of the adult, childless world or those with older children, indulge in spices and shellfish, chilli and curried parsnip soup. The idea of regular eating is also anathema. Grown-ups can survive on Sunday lunch at four o'clock, but small children need fuel every three hours, forcing you to think about the next meal as you wash up the last. As the hours passed and there was still no sign of lunch, we sat getting steadily drunker while my child's whinge factor rose and rose.

When we eventually sat down at the starched white linen tablecloth, elegantly laid with giant silver cutlery, the child was too distraught from hunger to eat and needed the potty. I carried her rather resentfully to the bathroom while my husband guzzled mussels. The bathroom carpet had a shag pile so thick that it looked as if it had been transferred straight from the back of a yak to the floor and would have begun to stink within a week of the average child's bathroom habits. I failed to notice through the blur of alcohol until I had sat my child down on her potty, that she had already done the first of a series of poos on the carpet before butt met the pot. As I desperately tried to scoop it up from the floor with a wodge of loo paper, I saw out of the corner of my eye another brown smudge and then another as Eleanor walked across the bathroom carpet. She had stepped in the first poo and was now spreading it everywhere.

Slowly shit came into vision at every turn and as I tried through a drunken haze to clean it up, I only seemed to be spreading it further. I had to get her out of the bathroom before I could assess the extent of the damage and attempt to clean it up. I cleaned her shoes, dressed her and deposited her firmly on her father's lap. Then I went into the kitchen and took all of the cleaning materials and buckets I could muster and began to scrub the walls and floors vigorously with undiluted bleach, wondering how long it would be before my absence was noticed.

When it was clear that nothing was going to remove the stain from the carpet, I decided that the best thing to do was confess. While aunt and uncle tried to reassure me that it didn't matter and told me to sit down and eat my lunch, I felt a lasting sense of shame and subsequently learnt that they had to replace the carpet. It was five years before we dared accept another invitation to lunch. My second child was now the same age as my first had been but there were no similar accidents to disgrace us and my aunt bent over backwards to get a child-friendly lunch on the table by two o'clock.

As soon as you begin to tell friends that you are pregnant, their attitude or behaviour towards you shifts. Friends without children can feel as if you are moving on without them and those with children smile knowingly and feel free to ask intrusive questions – what type of birth are you having? Was it planned? How is your mother taking it?

When a woman discovers that she is pregnant she has to decide who to tell and when, whether to wait until the first twelve weeks are over or risk telling all now. As soon as she tells anyone she feels suddenly exposed. Her life is now being closely charted by friends and relatives, she is already being defined as a mother-in-waiting and may find herself overlooked by colleagues or bosses at work as a result. Should anything go wrong with the pregnancy, or abnormalities be revealed through antenatal testing, she has to face the prospect of telling everyone and responding to their sympathy as well as dealing with her own disappointment and grief.

Unless a pregnant woman has a close friend who is pregnant at the same time, she slips into a limbo between the worlds of the childless and mothers. The size of her abdomen for some reason makes a pregnant woman public property. Total strangers feel at liberty to pat her on the stomach. Yet she may have fewer people to confide in about her pregnancy. Friends who have never been pregnant cannot know what she is living through and she has yet to make it into that great club of old and new friends with small children, because she hasn't yet succeeded in producing her first child. The emotional dynamic with childless friends inevitably changes as they feel you slipping inexorably over to the other side, and it can be particularly difficult with girlfriends who want to have a baby, but may not have a mate or have fertility problems.

When the baby arrives, lucky women are showered with cards, congratulations, presents and champagne. For ten minutes friends make you feel like a complete star, but this is either swiftly followed by complete silence and social isolation, as considerate people leave you in peace to enjoy those blissful early days, or you have to entertain and exercise great skills of social management in order to cope with a stream of telephone calls and visitors. I remember worrying, as I lay stitched to my hospital bed, still dopey on morphine two days after giving birth, about the fact that two separate sets of visitors did not know each other. I found myself introducing them to each other and searching for common points of reference so that they could have a good time together while I lay there like a zombie.

You long for your closest oldest friend to really understand, to be able to help you come to terms with what has happened in the way that they always have done. But the cultural emphasis on the joys of early motherhood is so great that it is hard for childless friends to really understand what you are going through if you're finding aspects of new motherhood tough. A woman's identity and image transforms overnight from a young carefree individual to a responsible grown-up as friends apply their own precon-ceived notions of motherhood to her new status.

Martha is sixteen and a single mother to a one-month-old baby boy whom she adores. She finds other people's reactions to her situation the greatest change to her way of life so far. 'Adults used to have conversations with other adults and not with me and if they did talk to me, they talked to me like I was a child. Now it's totally different. They talk to me as an adult and people my age won't talk to me as a child any more.' Her close friends no longer confide in her and feel uncomfortable about including her in their social plans because of her baby. 'They seem to think I'm grown up and unapproachable, rather than sixteen with a baby. It must be hard for them to know how to talk to me. I don't think they really know how to take it.'

Childless friends find it impossible to understand how little spare time you have and how tired you are. They still live in a world where they can nip out to the pub or the local cinema whenever they just feel like going out. You on the other hand now need days of forward planning in order to organize a babysitter and get in several early nights just to be able to cope with a night out. Now even shopping seems unimaginably complicated and pointless unless it's for baby clothes or somewhere with 'soft play'. These differences between priorities and the ability to be spontaneous can create conflict between childless friends and mothers. New mothers can feel jealous of a childless woman's freedom when she is feeling overwhelmed by her new responsibilities while friends without children complain that new mothers are obsessed with their babies and boring.

Even girlie chats over a cup of tea become difficult because only the most saintly childless girlfriend doesn't get insulted when you have to break mid-sentence in order to tend to the needs of your child. Then as you return to talk to her, the topic has moved on, and rarely do you get to discuss one subject in depth without interruption until it is resolved. I've never felt less understood and more alone than I did one afternoon when one of my oldest friends sat in my kitchen describing her recent flu over a cup of tea. 'If you get this cough then the only way to get rid of it is to go to bed for three days,' she said without a hint of irony. I wanted to say 'How?' but knew that she couldn't begin to understand what my life was like now, with a job, a four-year-old just starting school and a six-month-old baby who did not sleep through the night permanently attached to my hip.

Childless friends complain that all you talk about is the baby, when that is all you can or want to talk about. 'Unless they're particularly baby-centred they just don't know how to handle it or what to do with me,' says Emily, who has given up a full-time job in the City to look after her seven-month-old son. 'I don't want to go out drinking any more, I'd rather stay at home shelling peas.' Janet echoes her change in social priorities: 'I'm happier to be at home now. I used to be very disappointed on a Sunday night if I hadn't had a particularly active, high-achieving weekend, but now I'm much happier hanging out, because doing nothing with a child is always doing something.'

When women feel isolated at home with small babies and haven't been out yet for an evening alone, they often wonder how long it will be before they can enjoy the social life that they once had again. 'I feel like it's never ever going to be the same again.' Rachel has a seven-month-old son and has been out twice with her partner since giving birth. 'You wonder how long will it be like this. There's this constant projecting into the future and then you feel guilty because you think, I'm wishing this child's life away – why am I looking forward to life without Joe so much?'

But the reality for most women is that our social lives rarely return exactly to what they were. Life has moved on and parents find new ways to maintain social links, which inevitably means moving closer to other people with children. 'I've got closer to friends with children and further apart from those I used to see a lot.' Mary's daughter is one year old. 'I've withdrawn into my world with this baby. In the evening I don't feel like phoning people, I haven't got the energy. So if it's someone I can't phone in the day, they sort of disappear. I lost contact with my closest girlfriend because having a baby was a huge emotional thing for me, that was all that I wanted to talk about, but my friend found this hard to understand.'

Maggie has a son and a daughter aged two and three, a part-time job and a childless brother who is always trying to coax her out for a drink. 'I long for him to have triplets. I want all of the people I know now to have kids so that they will understand why it is that I'm always forgetting to ring, that I don't always remember birthdays, if at all, why I sound so dizzy and why I'm always apologizing I always seem to be saying to people, "I'm sorry I didn't ring you but . . ."'

The impact of children on the social lives of people on low incomes can be even more devastating. They may not be able to afford the money for a babysitter or for the alcohol and the ingredients for a meal if they were to invite friends over. Surveys of families living on low incomes show that many lose contact with their friends because of their financial difficulties and that some deliberately cut themselves off because they cannot face socializing when inevitably the conversation always turns to money worries. 'I have lost all my friends,' commented one mother to a researcher from the Joseph Rowntree Foundation. 'I don't go out much now, but a few years ago when I used to go and see my friends, as soon as they saw me the first thing that struck them was maybe I was coming to borrow something. Even if I had come to say "Hello".'[1]

Couples faced with fewer opportunities to escape their children, or each other, often face greater strain in their relationship. Their children also experience a more restricted social life, unable to invite their own friends over for meals or participate in extra-curricular school activities. They too spend far more time watching television if their parents are reluctant to allow them out to play with the children who have been turfed out by their parents unsupervised. The impact of television on community life has been immense. Hilda Caldwell lived on a new housing estate in Leeds from 1949 where the kids formed a gang and were forever in and out of each other's houses. Then 'as each of the families got their own television, the other kids never came . . . and we were just left with our two kids and us. I felt lost, I missed having the kids around. It was like a party.'[2]

While old friends seem to drift further away, new mothers are thrown together with women who they would probably never have chosen as confidantes if they weren't pregnant or mothers of small children at the same time. Hannah has 'had some of the best laughs of my life in my NCT group. We did some mad things together and there was a deep sense of shared experience, of being able to see each other in a dreadful state, being able to say, "I can't cope. I need to sleep." And someone else would say "OK. You go upstairs and sleep while I look after the baby."'

When you find a good friend at an NCT or postnatal exercise class it can make a positive difference. You need to be able to compare your experiences with other new mothers, share tips and confide in someone you trust when things get too much. 'I've made my closest women friends since I had a baby.' Irene has two daughters, aged seven and four, and runs a shop selling secondhand children's clothes. 'The solidarity I had during those first two years was amazing. Only women know what women have to do as mothers. I can say, "I've said all of the wrong things to Rosie," or "Shit, I've had a really hard day." Even if they haven't got an answer, it helps just to be able to say I'm not coping. The downside is that you make friends with mothers who you wouldn't otherwise be friends with and it takes you about two years to summon up the confidence to think, God, you're a wanker, I really don't like you, and then leave them well alone, by which time you usually have found other mothers that you do want to be friends with.'

Having a child roots people within their local community more than anything else. Shopkeepers and passers-by stop to talk to you and gradually faces become familiar at health centres, playgrounds and the school gates. When parents have a second child they are less likely to feel the same sense of social isolation as they felt after the first because they now have a wider social network into which the new baby fits. When children form their own friendships, their parents have no choice but to talk to new people and share confidences about their children's welfare. It comes naturally and forces many women to be less shy.

'I feel more outgoing with children. You have to do all sorts of things with them, talk to people in the street and take the children to the clinic,' says Kate. 'I was fairly shy before – I found it easy to be quiet and let other people do the talking. But then I got involved in a mother-and-toddler music group in another mother's house so I met loads of people there and that got me actively interested in music, which I love.'

Some new mothers find the atmosphere in mother-and-baby groups intimidating. Mary did. 'I felt quite isolated. People like Sheila Kitzinger say, "Go down to the park and meet other mums." But that didn't work for me, partly because I felt a bit old for all that and also frightened. I'd go down to the one o'clock club and I'd be shaking as I went through that horrible gate and then nobody talked to me. I've never found women to be particularly friendly in those places.'

Sometimes women feel as if they are being judged by other mothers. Kelly is twenty and a single mother with a three-year-old son, who struggles on income support and help from her mother. 'I don't go to those mother-and-toddler groups. It makes me so cross because all you need is one bad example of a single mother to give all the other good single mothers a bad name. The ones who've got partners look at me as if I'm a slag.' Kelly lives on a run-down council estate in Essex and finds herself even more socially isolated by her surroundings. She doesn't want to associate with other mothers on the estate because, 'A lot of them are so odd. There's one woman here who was in a refuge who seems to do nothing but sleep all day long while her kids run riot. They've all got a strange way about them and I don't really want to be their friend.'

When women lack confidence as mothers or feel depressed

they often find it hard to find somebody to confide in. It is now so difficult for new mothers to admit to problems to family, partners and friends, that I was aware as I conducted interviews for this book that I was often acting as an unpaid therapist. I have had hundreds of intimate and draining conversations with new mothers about the trauma of childbirth, the shock of the aftermath, their feelings of being unable to cope and the immense impact of the baby on their entire emotional, psychological and marital state of being because they were unable to talk about these experiences honestly anywhere else.

Imogen went to a mother-and-baby group soon after the birth of her second daughter because she was anxious to get out of the house and avoid the postnatal depression she had experienced after the birth of her first child. 'I was amazed, because there were all these quite wealthy women who clearly didn't need to work, talking about baby clothes and schools as if they didn't have another care in the world. It was as if they weren't living through the same experience as I was – worrying about work and money and abandoning my first daughter by having a second and feeling completely exhausted – their apparent calm, even though I *knew* that it couldn't all be bliss for them, only made me feel worse.'

When you are feeling inadequate as a mother, innocent questions such as 'Is she teething/walking/talking or sleeping through the night yet?' reduce your self-esteem still further. Immediately you are concerned as to why she isn't teething/walking/talking/sleeping through the night yet, and comments such as 'Gosh, she's big (or small) for two' send you into a paroxysm of self-doubt. It takes confidence as a mother to dismiss the probing of other mothers, or ignore their often contradictory advice – confidence which few new mothers have.

The mother who is still feeling her way and pretending to manage as she grapples with the logistics of going back to work, the demands of mothering and sleepless nights, can find the apparent self-confidence of women who appear to know how to do it deeply distressing. I know I certainly did. Motherhood apparently gives some women licence to turn into judgemental know-alls. One woman I interviewed with a seven-month-old baby reduced me to astonished, terrified silence when she stated categorically that she could never be friends with women who bottlefeed. 'I feel sorry for the baby, or if I feel that it isn't being held very much then it is very hard to be that mother's friend.' She had turned mothering into a profession whereby she was going to do everything right – the right foods, stimuli and she would of course not go back to work until her child was at least of school age. But by setting herself up as a paradigm of virtue she was heading for a big fall and I found myself being equally vindictive as I anticipated the prospect of her coping with a recalcitrant, irrational toddler who would not conform to her controlling nature.

Everything about having a baby divides women as much as it potentially unites them. If we are not already divided over the ethics of bottle versus breastfeeding, we soon divide over whether or not we go back to work, whether we let our babies cry themselves to sleep, whether we feed our children crisps, sweets and meat instead of rice cakes, raisins and veggieburgers, and over how we discipline our children. People easily assume that the experience of motherhood is essentially the same for everyone, when in fact there are huge differences in attitude and lifestyle.

Michelle: 'When you have a baby, the circle of people that you know widens enormously. I don't like the assumption that because you have a baby, you have a lot in common with another woman who has a baby. If their child is older, what they're really saying underneath the pleasantries is you've got all this to look forward to and it's no fun. "Wait till she starts teething!" They just want to kill the joy.'

'When I had Zachia I knew nothing.' Isis, a solicitor with a sixteen-month-old daughter, is pregnant with her second child. 'I realized, too late perhaps, that we had to find our own way of doing things. Now with this baby I am going to do it the way it suits me. I really hate dummies, but people kept telling me to get one so I got one and ended up throwing it away. People kept telling me to put her down, but she was a baby that wanted to be held all of the time. People tell you so many things, there's so much confusion and it can be hard to resist what they say and do it your own way.'

It takes courage and certainty to know that you are doing what is best for you and your child when other women so easily and unintentionally cast aspersions, but it is usually over the issue of working motherhood that the heat really rises.

When the pressure is on or a woman finds herself hating her job but unable to give it up for financial reasons, a working mother cannot help but resent the luxury stay-at-home mothers enjoy of being kept women, the time they get to spend with their children and their undoubted greater reserves of energy because they are able to attend a morning aerobics class. Stay-at-home mothers cloud their jealousy of a working mother's freedom and independent income by perpetuating the myth that working motherhood damages children.

'I do have slightly aggressive feelings towards women who rush back to work. I don't know why. I just don't feel they are real mothers.' Sue gave up a high-powered job in journalism to look after her young son. 'There are women I know who have no financial need and go back to work when their babies are three months old. I just know that I'm not going to want to talk to those women much, I don't hate them or anything but they're not going to be my best friends.'

Full-time working mothers have less time for friends, particularly childless ones. They have their friends and colleagues at work but when they are at home at the end of each day and at the weekend, they more often than not want to be with their children, fostering the emotional and physical links that so many have missed or feel guilty about missing during the week. Full-time working mothers don't go to mother-and-toddler groups.

They stand lonely and bored in windswept playgrounds during the weekends unless they bump into other working parents they know locally. Conversations about their children with acquaintances take place on telephones or as introductory small talk with other working mothers before they get down to business.

Confidence in mothering evolves with time and gradually each woman finds a style that she feels comfortable with, often after the birth of the second child. When another mother asks you questions about your child's development or more personal questions about your own wellbeing which may sound judgemental or intrusive, she is more than likely just seeking reassurance and needing to boost her own confidence.

Whole areas of conversation between mothers can become out of bounds in case they should offend. 'Anything that anybody suggested made me feel that I must be doing it wrong and I wanted to do it my way.' Clare has two children aged six and three. Now that she is over the difficulties of new motherhood, she finds that she has joined the conspiracy of silence that surrounds motherhood whenever she comes across a newly pregnant woman. 'I imagined that it would be wonderful from day one so when I hear them say that it's all going to be wonderful because they'll work from home, just put it in a basket and carry on, I never say a thing because one of the things which drove me most mad was people giving me advice.'

When someone with a new baby comes for supper and fusses over the faint bleating of a newborn, you know that their cries sound like a foghorn to them. It would be so easy to point out that he is just tired and needs to sleep. Instead, you watch them jiggle the baby around or check the nappy anxiously. They put the baby to each breast which just makes him cry even more and then pat his back with such force that he pukes down the back of their shirt. Then they mutter about catching something and think about ringing the doctor. You know from experience that these are cries of tiredness rather than cries of hunger or pain. You know from years of mothering that babies cry and then eventually they stop. And you also know that at that moment your guests are so anxious about their baby that they are unable to eat their food, while you long to be able to serve up the pudding. But you cannot say a thing in case it should be mis-interpreted as interference.

The easiest way to become persona non grata at your local mother-and-toddler group is to leave your two-year-old strapped into his buggy with the hood down in the corner of the garden until he cries himself to sleep when he is overtired. It won't be long before some interfering mother lifts him out to comfort him or tells you off for damaging him psychologically. I felt the bile rise in my throat when I took my first baby to the health centre for an injection when she was eighteen months old. As we sat in the waiting room she spotted a ball in the bottom tray of another buggy and tried to take it out. I gently told her to leave it alone because it wasn't ours. The other mother tutted under her breath and said, 'She's much too young to be teaching her that sort of thing.' She could have said other, much nicer things. She could have urged my baby to play with her ball or she could have said nothing at all.

I hated her smug certainty and yet all mothers are in some measure guilty of the same defect. When the investment of motherhood is so great, when we cannot escape from hourly concerns about our children's welfare, mothers inevitably turn professional. I have to squeeze my lips tightly together when I see a baby without a hat on in winter; when I see six-year-olds being pushed around in buggies instead of being allowed to walk, babies with Coca-Cola in their bottles and children eating crisps and sweets on their way to school. I make value judge-ments too. When I see women holding their babies unbelted on the front seat of a car, I cannot understand why they haven't been bereaved or sectioned; when I see mothers punishing their children harshly, or hurling abuse at them, I instantly dislike them, even though I have no idea who they are or what their lives are like.

As children get older, parents become embroiled in ever more complex questions of social etiquette. You get invited to lunch by new friends because you have children of roughly the same age but the children take an instant dislike to one another, and sit sullenly in opposite corners, exclaiming their boredom with deep sighs and refusing to eat even crisps. When my children whinge and whine or throw temper tantrums as guests at other people's houses I could brain them. Children can bully each other into 'lending' things that they do not want to be parted from, fights erupt quickly and it is almost impossible to know who started it. Prompting a silent child to say 'Thank you for having me' when you pick him or her up from another child's house is deeply shaming. I want the floor to swallow me up when my child asks for her party bag in full earshot of her host. And while there are opportunities for forging new friendships with the parents of your children's friends, there is also plenty of uncharted subject matter to disagree over: politics, racism, the ethics of private versus state education.

Children can enhance old friendships with people who are already parents because there is now an extra thread to conversation and activity. But there are also acres of extra room for potential embarrassment. Feeding children the wrong foods, allowing toddlers to wander around with bottles, letting children get down from the table before everyone has finished become potential minefields of disagreement. We were once invited to lunch by close friends. Pudding was barely finished when one of their daughters said confidently, 'I think it's time for the guests to go, I want to be with my imaginary friends.' Her parents didn't tell her to play elsewhere or laugh off her comment as a joke, so we sat there feeling uncomfortable and unsure of our welcome even though it would be too preposterous to pander to the whim of their child and excuse ourselves before lunch was really over.

Differences of opinion over discipline and whether or not to scold another's child often cause the greatest difficulties or offence. When you are in *loco parentis* you have, in my view, a duty to treat those children with the same care, concern and need for reprimand as if they were your own. But when other people's children misbehave, insult or hurt your own children in front of their parents and they do not intervene, it can be hard to know what to do. Caught between risking offending friends and failing to treat the interests of their child as paramount, caring parents inevitably opt for the latter and some old friendships never recover their former intimacy.

The outside world seems at times so hostile and difficult to navigate with a small baby that many women retreat into isolation. New mothers need to focus their energy on the baby and on their own recovery, and often lack the strength and self-confidence to maintain external links as well. Rachel has a seven-month-old son. 'At the moment it's a bit disconcerting because I can't really think about anyone but him and I've got limited resources or tolerance for anybody else. It makes me feel a bit useless, as if I'm no good to anybody else but him. I definitely feel that I don't know who I am and where that leaves me with my social life.'

While Hannah 'felt complete detachment from the world. Motherhood makes you emotionally vulnerable because you are always caring for this small person who is so precious. I remember the first night I went out to see a friend when Jill was five months old. When asked how I was, I said, "Jill's got a tooth." He said, "Great, but how are you?" I replied, "Well, it's her second tooth actually." It was only when he finally got through to me that I realized that I had no idea how I was.'

Such extreme feelings of social isolation among new mothers are peculiar to modern Western industrialized countries. Up until the end of the seventeenth century, few people enjoyed the luxury of ever being left alone. Houses were designed in such a way that sleeping, eating and living often took place in the same room with large numbers of extended family. Eighteenth-century house design began to give families a little more room for privacy with beds in separate bedrooms, but life was largely lived in public on the streets.

In Victorian England, poor families felt great loyalty to their street, and neighbours were in and out of each other's houses helping each other out. Working-class women may have been cut off from the world outside but they were heavily dependent on neighbours and family who were bound to live close by. There was a strong belief that the poor should help each other out and the close nature of the community meant that there were few secrets and most knew what other people needed. If a woman was sick, a neighbour would take in her washing or mind her child. Strenuous efforts were made to keep orphans out of the workhouse and it was even known for a street to rustle up a deputation to dissuade a philandering man or woman from upsetting the family equilibrium.

Nowadays, members of the same family rarely live within walking distance of each other. We move house far more frequently, particularly when we are pregnant or have just had a baby, and move away from local friends and neighbours into new territory. Travelling anywhere with a small baby can feel like a full-time job and so mothers often tend to stay put in their houses, alone, when their babies are small.

A large part of the shock of new motherhood is how difficult normal tasks such as travelling short distances outside home seem to be with a small baby or child. If you want to go by bus you have to be able to hold the baby and nappy bag with the collapsed buggy as you wait for the bus in order to get on before it moves off. Moving buses can be dangerous for small children. Stern conductors will only allow one buggy in the baggage carriers of London buses and so you stagger with baby on the hip, buggy and bags to the back, unable to hold the hand of your other, small, light child, who cannot help but career about the moving bus. You can almost hear the other passengers thinking, If she can't manage with two children she shouldn't be out with them.

It takes courage to master an escalator on London Underground in the rush hour when children can so easily not be seen and get crushed. Driving anywhere means stress from within the car as well as from other cars on the road. If the baby screams and cannot be soothed, if there is nowhere to stop to feed or change a nappy, if a small child is sick or simply miserable, car journeys seem interminable. When I first met Kate, she was waking up three or four times in the night to feed her seven-week-old baby, and having to cope with a very jealous firstborn, aged five, who was having trouble settling at his new school. 'You forget how difficult it is to do things out there with a small baby. We try to go out and do things at the weekend together as a family but last Saturday we got stuck in a traffic jam on the way to Richmond and the baby starts to cry. It was supposed to be fun. He stopped crying when the car moved but when it stopped at the lights or in the queue he starts crying again. You can't reach round and you're not supposed to get them out of their car seats and all you can do is think *shut up*. We had to stop on the way to feed the baby and then Ira fell off his bike, so we had all that as well and then by the time we got home I thought, What a lousy weekend – I wish we'd never gone.'

Blithely, we assume that common activities such as shopping and eating in cafés or restaurants will be pursued just as vigorously with children as they were without. We stand resolute, determined to reveal to our children that there is more to life than Disney by showing them the world that we like to inhabit as adults, refusing to buckle under the pressure to dabble solely with childish things. Then we discover that it is more relaxing to eat cheaply at a McDonald's or a pizza house, where the children are happy, than at a restaurant where they have to sit still and find it difficult to wait twenty minutes for the arrival of more nutritious food. How you sneered at that Happy Eater before you had children. How you long for their baby-changing facilities now that the baby is screaming and the three-year-old is hurling cartons of Ribena at the windscreen out of boredom. 'Not long now before we stop for fish fingers and chips, *and* you can have a go on their Mr Blobby Swing,' you chortle enthusiastically as you slam another nursery-rhyme CD into the player.

Gradually, for an easier life we find ourselves being sucked into another world where children are welcome. Occasionally I resist this slide into banality and stand resolved to take my children into the wider world I know and love. I convince myself that I'm a groovy get-out-and-go type of mother, who eats out, explores and visits cultural centres with her small children on her shoulders. But actually I spend most of my spare time pushing them in buggies to playgrounds, or carrying home their bikes when they are bored with riding them. I remember being adamant one summer that my children should see the 'Landscapes of France' exhibition at the Hayward Gallery because I wanted to. It would do them good to look at beautiful paintings rather than television, I reasoned, and it wouldn't be an expensive day out as the children would be given free admission. Then I discovered why. After a long argument with the cloakroom attendant who stood at a desk in charge of square footage larger than my sitting room but refused to take the buggy due to lack of storage space, I wheeled the buggy, bags and children into the gallery packed full of adults. I tried hard to interest them in the pictures but all the eldest one wanted to do was go to the shop. I tried hard to stop the younger one from getting lost or annoying the other adults as she ran about the vast hall screaming at the top of her voice, but it was no use. I spent more time looking at my children than I did at the pictures.

We have to navigate our children through life as we find it rather than through the idyllic child-friendly place we would like it to be. But often the effort to integrate children into the adult world takes such immense powers of distraction and negotiation in order to spend our leisure time in the way that we would like, that it seems easier to stay at home or to let them lead the way to playgrounds and video rentals. Our social and cultural needs get consumed by theirs as we search for new playgrounds, stand thigh-deep in swimming pools holding children rather than swimming ourselves, develop intricate criticisms of the latest Disney film, organize our own children's birthday parties and socialize there with our children's friends' parents because we never see our own friends. Parents go out for fun during the day, often first thing in the morning, leaving the night-time free for the childless.

Parents inevitably get sucked into the joys of theme parks, fairgrounds, zoos and museums, packed with the rest of the world's children, where they find every other parent struggling with exactly the same issues – coaxing whining children out of their misery, rationing sweets and drinks, queuing for the lavatory and delaying the trip to the shop for as long as possible. I found myself singing Legoland's praises to a friend one day, holding forth on its tasteful layout and the surprising quality of the food in the restaurant, when my pre-parent self would have run like a gibbering lunatic from its mayhem. Standards drop because you haven't been anywhere else and you find yourself captivated by the bright lights just like a child.

There are bureaucratic, institutionalized hell-holes called 'indoor soft play' or 'indoor adventure playgrounds' springing up all over Britain, which children clamour to be taken to. As you enter a large, windowless, fluorescent-lit, noisy hall you have to exchange your buggy for one of their regulation buggies, take off your shoes and get them numbered and have your child tagged so that you can't leave with anybody else's. Claustrophobic adults feel as if they are entering the torture chamber of the world's worst prison, while their children cannot wait to be let loose into a fantastic, multicoloured, inflatable concourse with hundreds of other screaming, flushed-faced children.

Clearly it is fun for the children, but why is their idea of fun so different from ours? And why do parents so often have to feel excluded or peripheral to a child-centred environment? How did we sink so quickly from the idyllic, quiet childhood of *Watch with Mother* and *Winnie the Pooh* to this? According to the historian

Philippe Aries,[3] children used to play the same games as adults, such as bowls, card games, gambling and tennis, from the sixteenth century onwards. Festivals were far more important than they are today and people of all ages took part. There wasn't such a distinction between the childless world and that of families as there is today. Yet, in these modern children's playgrounds, you can't even interact with your child and join in the fun because the whole point is for the child to be in a self-contained, comparatively safe environment without you. You can't leave them to it either because there is nothing else for you to do. So you strain to catch sight of your child as he leaps around and jumps into great vats of multicoloured balls with hundreds of other children, hoping they don't hurt themselves and standing around like a giant purse.

I watch more children's television now than programmes meant for adults. *Blue Peter* educates me and *Sesame Street* makes me cry. I have rediscovered my love for making papier-mâché bowls or models out of salt dough and nothing beats singing *all* of the songs from *The Sound of Music* in the bath at the top of our voices.

It gives me immeasurable pleasure to watch the glow and sparkle of circus lights reflect off my children's mesmerized faces as they stare up at lithe, enviable bodies somersaulting from trapeze to outstretched hands, or laughing at the antics of the clowns as they scream, 'He's right behind you!' Fireworks night thrills me so much more when I am hugging their chilly, excited cheeks close to mine and Christmas would now seem pointless without them. The rustle of the stocking as they scream '*He came! He came!*' hurtling down the stairs. Christmas carols and the religiousness of Christmas move me now as a mother in a way that they never moved me before because its significance now seems so much more relevant – celebrating the birth of a baby, a special baby, as mine are.

Often, parents find that their values and sense of priorities change radically after the arrival of their precious firstborn. Many feel increased sensitivity towards issues which will affect the future wellbeing of their child, such as education or road safety. Sometimes, new parents find themselves enraged about local issues which directly affect their wellbeing. One woman I interviewed found herself sending off angry letters to her local authority when she became incensed about the fact that women at home with children who were not on benefits were not entitled to a leisure card. 'I'd never have bothered before,' she told me.

Others turn inwards to consolidate and nurture their own family and cease to be interested in wider concerns of equality or the injustices of the troubled world, unless those issues have a direct impact on the welfare of their child. Penny, who works for an ecological charity, found that her convictions shifted dramatically after the birth of her baby. She feels that she has become less political. 'Now, when I hear about poor air quality, I don't think, Bloody government and bloody cars. I find myself saying, "What should I do? Keep her in? Shut the windows?" I'm not interested in long-term or even short-term political solutions, but what do I have to do to protect Rebecca from this threat?'

Focus on the future welfare of our precious children is far more intense. We worry about their education and how they will manage in such a fast-changing world, and the money we earn gets spent on their welfare not ours. The burgeoning industry of baby- and childcare products in the past twenty years means that there is now so much more that a loved child should have. Peer pressure from other parents, their children and intensive television advertising, means that we now consider it essential for a child to have plenty of toys, CDs and DVDs, as well as all of the latest childcare equipment, books and a bulging wardrobe. The poor children captured in Maud Pember Reeves's classic account of working-class childhood before the First World War, *Round About a Pound a Week*, had none of these things: 'There are no books and no games, nor any place to play the games should they exist. Wet holidays mean quarrelling and mischief, and a distracted mother.'[4]

As children get older the peer pressure and the expense increases, with mobile phones, electronic toys, Game Boys, computers, roller blades and iPods on the average Christmas list. Shopping may be 'a feeling' and essential retail therapy for the childless, but when it's for yet another pair of school shoes or trainers, or for the third coat that winter because the first two have been lost in the playground, then parting with such vast wads of money really hurts.

Holidays change dramatically as soon as a child is old enough to be able to tell the difference between a city sightseeing tour and a beach. Flying seems seductively cheap at first because children under two travel free so we easily fall into the trap of believing that we can holiday in much the same way as we always have. Then when you fly off on your first holiday you realize why they travel free – they don't get a seat. Childless people on planes read newspapers, books, sleep and eat bits of cold meat off their plastic trays. Parents with small children jiggle them up and down on their laps and try to keep them happy in a space no bigger than eighteen inches square. They shove dummies and bottles into their babies' mouths to stop them from screaming at the discomfort of take-off and landing, walk with them up and down the aisles behind the duty-free trolley and change their nappies with difficulty because there is never enough room in an aeroplane lavatory to lay a baby down. Pressure change in the aircraft tends to draw out the excrement in small children and so you see new parents surging towards the back of the aircraft soon after take-off. Children who travel free are not automatically guaranteed a free meal on most airlines because they don't have a seat, but that doesn't much matter. Parents of small children have no space to put their table down for their tray of food, so they feed their own lunch to the baby, nibbling bits in between.

Then, when children pay almost the full fare at the age of two, parents reassess their holiday needs and settle for the British seaside, punctuated by the occasional package holiday abroad when the children are old enough to appreciate it and provide their own entertainment on the plane. Holidays with small children are often not very peaceful for the grown-ups. They find themselves guiltily looking forward to going back to work for a rest. I have gazed longingly at the brochures for Center Parcs and Club Med when my children were very small, simply because their child-centred activities and round-the-clock childcare might give us bedraggled grown-ups some time off to recuperate.

But as my children have got older and I have got used to being their mother, the prospect of a holiday without them seems less and less appealing. Sandcastles, beach games, kite flying and hunting for shells; splashing through puddles on wet afternoons or travelling in a downpour to the nearest town cinema for the matinée performance of anything, are magical moments between parents and their children. It is the holidays that children remember, times when their family is entirely together as a unit, when nobody is distracted by telephone calls, household chores or invitations to tea. We have walked along wet lanes rescuing snails from oncoming cars. We have chased across fields after a runaway kite. We have ridden horses together across a beach and eaten fish and chips by the side of a quiet country road as the sun set over the hills of Dorset.

Children make holidays what they are, entirely different from the holidays we enjoy without them but precious and irreplaceable all the same. On holiday we have time and space just to be with each other and follow a child's slower timescale, and there is relief from the rigid structure of daily life with no need to coax, nag or cajole children to school, nursery or bed. And while I still do hanker occasionally for romantic weekends in Paris, lie-ins and siestas in the hot Tuscan hills, I also find it hard to imagine choosing to spend so much of our rare free time without my beloved daughters when in just a few years they may not want to go on holiday with us at all.

Occasionally we need a window on the world of the childless to remind us of how life was and of how rich and sublime life now is. 'I really miss it when I don't have a little one with me now,' says Maggie, who has a son and a daughter aged three and two. 'I went to Derby yesterday on the train and normally when I'm on a train I have the children with me. It was really strange because I was complelely anonymous. With kids, they sit and stare at people, or throw things at them and suddenly you have people talking to you, you have to connect.'

When our two-year-old spent her first night away from home with her grandmother and we spent our first night and day alone at home, we wandered out to a local pub and then to a restaurant and sat dazed at the prospect of twenty-four hours of freedom, of being able to stay in bed for as long as we wanted, make love before breakfast, linger over the newspapers and then decide how to spend the rest of the day. Then when we looked at the other people in the restaurant and it dawned on us that most of these people probably didn'thave small children and had the prospect of a whole weekend to themselves, *every five days*. We laughed and admitted our envy at the luxury of so much freedom and spare time and tried to remember how we spent our weekends before we became parents. But as we went to collect our adored first child, I was hankering for her presence as if I was missing a crucial part of my anatomy. When I hugged her, I felt blissfully complete and marvelled at the way she seemed to have changed in just twenty-four hours. I couldn't imagine ever wanting to be parted from her again.

Our perspective on the world and our friendships can alter radically after the birth of a child. We join a club that we barely knew existed, form new friendships with other parents and sometimes find that the common ground between us and old childless friends evaporates. At first, it seems as if our social lives are severely restricted by being parents, but as we grow used to having a small child almost permanently by our side, a liberating new view of the world begins to emerge. Children give us licence to look at things afresh from their point of view. We can revisit childhood pleasures and enjoy them again with our own children. We look at the smallness of things, at the simple miracles of life, at rainbows, full moons and spiders' webs and can rediscover a sense of wonder.

'I get a perverse pleasure from the daytime life,' says Sue. 'I'm certainly noticing my immediate environment more. I've lived here for twelve years, but never really noticed it before I had my son because I was always rushing out into the wider world of work in journalism. I never knew my neighbourhood, I didn't know the local shopkeepers. Now I know them all. I go to a playgroup and have met all sorts of different types of women, and I walk. I've rediscovered looking and I'm finding pleasure in things which I used to think were boring. With Joe, going on a bus is fun.'

As Hannah says, 'Grown-ups are constantly telling children what they can't do. We limit the world for them when it's unlimited. They say, "You can fly on a broomstick to the moon," and we say, "No, you can't." She reminds me that I can ask questions like "How do we know everyone else's 'now' is the same as ours?" Children don't limit possibilities. When you watch children grow you realize that they can do everything – they can change, adapt and develop so quickly and I have learnt so much from watching my daughter. It never occurs to me now that I can't do anything any more.'

10

Family Life

'Family, whatever its form, however shaky, however disappointing, however many false hopes and illusions it must carry . . . remains the common way to root ourselves into the earth, to protect ourselves against too terrifying isolation,' writes Anne Roiphe.[1] We reject family when we leave home as young adults and presume to forge our own path. But as soon as we become parents, we discover that this was just a brief period of respite. For we get tugged firmly back into family line as our own childhood resurfaces vividly. We become more aware of the generational influences which preceded us and are now being passed on to our child. We become more dependent on family ties for emotional, practical and sometimes financial support. Relationships with our own mother and father change as we become parents and there are now in-laws to deal with, who are also grandparents to our child. We feel it important to heal old feuds so that our child has an extended family and relationships with aunts and uncles and grandparents. But perhaps most important of all, mortality in older people is easier to deal with. Anne's father died soon after the birth of her second child. 'To see my mother grow frail and gradually fading away is much easier to deal with because while that's your childhood disappearing, the childhood of one's own children is very much there and that pattern is very important.'

Cultural, scientific and technological change has been so swift since the 1950s that there have been more differences between generations than at any other time in history. For centuries, the experience of mothering was largely the same. 'Throughout history, Jonathan Gathorne Hardy writes in *The Rise and Fall of the British Nanny*, 'the one area of human life that has changed least and changes slowest is the bringing-up of children.[2] We bring up very small children as we were brought up ourselves.'

Most mothers were present while their daughters gave birth until the mass move to hospitals took place after the Second World War and they were involved in passing on a collective knowledge about pregnancy, labour and motherhood, which many new mothers lack today. A mother passed on all of her skills to her children, and knew that she had to inculcate strong notions of gender and place in her daughters in order to maximize their marriage prospects.

Mothers and daughters were intimately linked and rarely separated in middle- and working-class families, while the sons left for school, apprenticeship or work. The relationship between mother and daughter used to be the strongest of family ties in Western culture, with the daughter turning first to her mother for advice and support. Until the outbreak of the Second World War, when massive evacuation broke up close communal bonds by moving people into the suburbs, young couples in working-class neighbourhoods often lived with the wife's mother after childbirth. Intermarriage between families living close by was common, which strengthened ties and meant that there was always somebody around to help if need be.

The urban poor lived much the same way as their parents and grandparents had done until the outbreak of the Second World War, handing down attitudes to family life and child-rearing. The status of the 'married mother' was high in such communities. They were the linchpins, acting as unofficial and unpaid midwives; washing and dressing dead bodies; controlling the finances of all of the working members of the family, and setting rules of discipline which people were expected to obey. Granny usually played a key role and lived nearby. Her grandchildren would regularly eat and sleep at her house and sometimes, in large families, one or more of the children would live permanently at Granny's because there was no room for them at home. Illegitimate children were often raised by their grandmother, whom they would believe to be their mother.

Small pockets of this type of relationship between mother and daughter remained after the Second World War. A study of mothers and daughters, conducted in Bethnal Green, London, during the 1950s found that many mothers continued to live nearby, often in the same street after their daughters got married. At least half of these mothers and daughters saw each other every day, many would go shopping together, do favours and generally be far more supportive of one another.[3] But, these days, few new mothers have their own mothers living nearby to depend on in the early days. A study of social change amongst new mothers in Aberdeen comparing 1951 with 1985, shows a marked decline in reliance on the extended family. In 1951, 39 per cent of new mothers were living with relatives and nearly 50 per cent of all new mothers were being helped by their own mothers. But in 1985, only 25 per cent of new mothers were receiving help from their mothers and nearly two-thirds cited their husband as their main source of support.[4]

We have lost some of the many obvious advantages of having a large extended family living nearby or actually within the home. Many of the difficulties of early motherhood, and certainly those feelings of being trapped alone at home, would be alleviated through having a mother and other family members close by. In other cultures, where new mothers live very close to their own mothers, much of the hard work of adjusting to motherhood is shared. The Navajo of northern Arizona share responsibility for each other's children, and the Comanche and Hopi Indians – and also many African communities – call all maternal aunts 'mother'. There is always someone to mind the baby.

But there are also great advantages to our newer, smaller 'nuclear' families. Without a close-knit extended family living on our doorstep we have greater freedom to bring up our children as we think best, rejecting the negative influences of our past and encouraging the positive. We may feel less supported during the early days of motherhood because there is no one nearby to hold the baby, but as our children grow older we have more privacy as a unit. No one outside your immediate family, including your own parents, can understand how you operate. We have more time, not less, to enjoy our children and build up our own unique family culture. 'In pre-industrial England, children had to be sent away – into domestic service or as child labour on another farm,' writes Ferdinand Mount in *The Subversive Family*. 'Now families can stay together until the children wish to move away. Shorter working hours and longer holidays mean more time spent together.'

In the past forty years, changes in childcare theory and in the development of childcare products have been so swift that most new mothers now turn first to childcare books, health visitors or friends with children of a similar age for advice, rather than to their mothers. More childcare handbooks have been published in the past thirty years than at any other time and Hugh Jolly even discourages mothers from consulting their own mothers in his bestselling *Book of Child Care* because their ideas are likely to be out of date.

Never before has there been such a discrepancy between the experiences and expectations of parents from different generations. Our fathers tended to leave childcare to the women; now, increasingly, we expect the fathers of our children to be as involved as we are. The growing number of women having their first babies in their thirties means older grandmothers.

When our mothers are old enough to have raised us without the benefits of disposable nappies or bottle sterilizers, they are as ignorant of the practicalities of modern babycare as we are. And theories of good child-rearing have changed so radically that our mothers are bound to have done things differently, which inevitably exacerbates conflict between us. My mother insists that I was put on the pot regularly from the age of twelve months, because mothers at that time were desperate to reduce the amount of nappy washing. Newer theories of child development maintain that toddlers are unable to control their bowels effectively until they are at least two, so I see no point in putting my child on the pot until she is ready.

Good relations between parents and children are now considered to be more important than ever, at a time when, paradoxically, the differences between generations have never been so great. Often, when we have our first child we become childlike again. Difficulties with parents resurface and become more acute. A woman who always felt distanced from a remote, or over-critical father finds herself feeling even more distanced as her focus inevitably shifts away from him to her child. Some women find they feel embarrassed about breastfeeding in front of their fathers. If a woman experienced emotional difficulties with her mother then, inevitably, those conflicts resurface during pregnancy, labour and new motherhood.

At a time of such acute vulnerability and emotional sensitivity, we find ourselves needing our mothers or in need of mothering if they are not there for us, in exactly the way that we would like them to be. 'When I was pregnant, I remember longing for an ideal mummy and not getting it,' says Ann a single mother. 'Then, when my son was born, there was a bit of a power struggle over caring. She took three or four days to come and see him, partly because I pushed her away, but soon they clicked and adore each other now. Suddenly your relationship with your mother becomes more important. You think of your mother as a fellow mother rather than your own mother.'

Some women, who have particularly good relationships with their mothers, find that they are immediately closer than ever and that their mothers are exactly what they need when they have a child. 'My mother has come into her own and is just the most useful person in the whole world.' Natasha's partner had to go away on business when her son was three weeks old so she went to stay with her mother for a week. 'It was just such bliss because my mother wasn't working so she was around to help all day long and was tremendously calm and reassuring. If he was crying all afternoon she would look at it as just an interesting problem. She was totally there for me. All she was concerned about was that I got some rest.'

Emily's mother is a teacher who comes to stay with her in the holidays and appears to like nothing better than to help out with household chores so that Emily can look after her baby, now aged seven months. 'She knows there are jobs that have to be done and she'd rather do them than have me do them. We're closer than ever now – how we can talk for half an hour about Catherine standing and holding on to the sofa I'll never know.'

But many other women cannot help but admit to feeling a deep sense of disappointment, of being let down by their mothers at their time of greatest need, a time when they feel that their mothers, of all people, should understand. We want our mothers to step into the breach and pamper us so that we can cosset our new babies. We need to feel love from every quarter so that we can recover and give the energy and emotion required of motherhood. But our mothers may not be able to offer that level of support. They may be finding it difficult to come to terms with being a grandmother, or 'losing' a daughter to motherhood. They may feel jealous of the things that we have that they lacked – a child they wished they'd had, a better relationship, a nicer more helpful partner; more money, disposable nappies, as well as a career to go back to. Or, they may be more childish themselves and feel unable to offer the love that we need because they lacked it themselves as children or as young mothers. Women who have more complex, unstable relationships with their mothers often find them suddenly more demanding, more needy, more prone to sickness or ridiculous family scenes than usual.

Suddenly all of the good and bad aspects of our own experience of being mothered resurface as we contemplate mothering our own child. Research shows that a woman whose mother died before she reached puberty is likely to feel that loss and sadness recur when she has her own child and has no one to turn to for help or guidance.[5] We have been brought up to believe that 'good' motherhood encompasses entirely positive attributes. Mothers are expected to be unconditionally giving, understanding, tolerant, loving, non-judgemental, encouraging, supportive and loyal all of the time. Clearly this is an unreasonable request of even the most devoted parent, but it is in the nature of every child to want all of this and more and then to feel rejected because a child's demands are limitless.

We feel childlike and vulnerable when we have just given birth. We present our babies to our mothers, attempting to divert attention from our neediness to their new status as grandmother and then find that we have to manage their visits carefully in order to limit the demands on our depleted resources of energy. 'Good' mothers always have to be giving and loving, but 'good' daughters always have to do more it seems and be ever dutiful even as new mothers.

Many of the women I interviewed for this book expressed disappointment or resentment. Even when their children are grown up mothers can never get it quite right it seems. Women often complained that their mothers never offered to babysit but had to be asked, and then they only helped when they could squeeze the time in rather than when their daughters actually needed the help. Grandmothers nowadays are often reluctant to interfere and have lives of their own to lead, with work and social commitments limiting time for their own families. Whatever the reason, their unavailability increases the conflict between them, because the daughters resent the fact that their mothers were not there for them and the grandmothers complain about not seeing their grand-children enough.

'We're very unlucky in some ways in that both sets of parents live nearby in London.' Clare has two children aged six and three, works full-time and therefore feels that she has limited time alone with her own family. 'So both say "Are we going to see you this weekend?" But they don't get more involved with the children by themselves. I'd love them to ring up and suggest that they pick up Jamie from school and take him home for tea but they never do that. My parents aren't frightfully good with small children so it's only increased my irritation with my mum. She doesn't seem to realize that if she rings up at 6.30 we can't have a long chat on the phone.'

Other women feel demoralized or over-anxious about their ability to mother well because their mothers constantly interfere questioning their capabilities. Questions such as 'Shouldn't she be wrapped up more before she goes outside?' or warnings against picking her up too often for fear of 'spoiling' her, are uncom-fortable reminders that her own mother still considers her a child. 'My mum had her chance to bring me up her way, now I want my chance to bring him up my way.' Martha is a young single mother who still lives at home. 'I can't do it my way while I'm living here because she's constantly interfering. People seem to think that because I'm sixteen I can't have that chance.' Her baby wants to be held all of the time and her mother blames Martha for not encouraging him to go to sleep on his own by putting him down from the beginning. 'She keeps saying, "I told you to put him down but you didn't and now look what's happened," and I say, "I know but it doesn't bother me so why should it bother you?"' Her mother also has a five-year-old daughter and says that her partner has to stop her from getting out of bed when she hears her grandson crying at night with the gentle reminder that he is not her baby.

Many working-class women find that they have no choice but to get closer to their own mothers because they lack the financial means to be self-sufficient. Often, they cannot afford childcare and become dependent on their mothers and other family members in order to be able to work. Martha's mother has offered to look after her son when Martha goes back to college to do a course in hairdressing, which she is deeply grateful for. 'I love my mum, she means the world to me but it would probably be better for both of us if there could be a bit more distance between us, but what can you do?'

Keelie had her first child at the age of twenty when she was still living at home. Her son was the first grandchild and she found herself heavily dependent on her mother for help, because her relationship with her boyfriend broke down. 'I used to wake up at six in the morning and the baby was gone. My mum had already taken him downstairs and fed him and that used to drive me mad even though I know she was just trying to help me out, because he was mine, not hers.' When her son was ten months old, Keelie moved into bed-and-breakfast accommodation and missed the support. 'It's not really far away, but then to me it seemed so very far away. All of a sudden I had to do everything for him.'

Even though both mother and daughter have gone through what is essentially the same experience, many of the qualms and conundrums of motherhood are still taboo. 'I had hoped that during my pregnancy we would have this amazing mother-daughter bonding thing when all of the unspoken things between us would be spoken, and that she would tell me at great length what it was like to be in labour and to look after small children, given that she has had four,' says Penny. 'Maybe I wasn't explicit enough but whenever I asked she just said that she couldn't remember. I don't know why I expected twenty-eight years of a relationship to change but I did.'

Josie had her first child in her late thirties and considers her parents' upbringing to have been quite narrow and sheltered.

'When I was pregnant, my mother asked me if I wanted a maternity nurse when I came out of hospital and I was completely shocked. Until I got pregnant I'd never had a conversation with her about babies and small children and until I was in my twenties, I'd never even held a small baby.'

Some women with difficult relationships with their mothers live in deep fear of becoming like them. Boys manage to differentiate themselves from their mother as soon as they become aware of gender, but girls have to invest huge amounts of energy in order to mark out the differences between them. Then when we become mothers we hear her voice, her words, her mannerisms, passing through our bodies as if we are possessed by them. 'I say the things my mother used to say.' Charlotte has three children. '"You treat this place like a hotel"; "I'll read the riot act", and I talk to people in shops totally irrelevantly. My mother used to go into the greengrocer's and chat away and I'd be thinking, Why is she doing this? and now I do it, in exactly the same way.'

Trudi also has three children. 'When I was a teenager my mother was always bossing me around and I thought I'd never ever speak to my own children like that. I thought I'd give them what they want, I'd be with it, a trendy parent, not a dinosaur. I'm going to be really laid back. But it's not until you have children that you realize that our mothers were right and I now hear myself saying all the same things that my mother used to say.'

We may hope to free ourselves from the intensity of the bond wth our own mother by having a child, but as soon as we have given birth we feel ourselves being sucked back into it, far more dependent on her now for childcare, babysitting, financial support and forced to see her more often. We are forced to face up to the fact that many of the more 'witch-like' aspects of her personality, which we hated as a child, lie dormant in ourselves, just waiting for the trigger of motherhood to set them going. When I hear myself nagging my children to get dressed, to eat breakfast and get themselves ready in the morning I hear my mother. When I deny my children fancy shoes or frivolous things that we cannot afford, I hear my mother, the mother who denied me. When I see aspects of my grandmother's personality in my own mother as she gets older, I wonder whether the same may be in store for me. Is it that years of mothering, of clearing up the mess and coaxing good food into growing children drives us all into replicas of one another?

We may be a product of their genes and their upbringing but we are also influenced by a whole range of other circumstances beyond our mothers' control. The political, economic and social environment that shaped our upbringing is very different from that which shaped our mothers'. Radical change in society since the end of the Second World War has brought about massive improvements in our education and health, and it has influenced our expectations and attitudes far more than our mothers ever could, and such change has left many women of our mothers' generation far behind.

Inevitably, we will bring up our children in a different way from the way we were brought up and find ourselves being challenged to change again as our children bring the world that they encounter home. All of a sudden your five-year-old lectures you on the greenhouse effect and insists that you separate your newspapers for recycling and the next time you go shopping you find yourself reaching for the ecologically friendly washing-up liquid.

We don't repeat the patterns set by our parents willy-nilly. Of course there are similarities, but mothers and daughters are not replicas of one another like painted Russian wooden dolls. Our children are individual and different from us, not extensions of ourselves, just as we are different from our parents, and that difference adds richness to the average family life as well as a whole range of new conflicts.

Caroline dislikes the sarcasm her mother uses. 'She'll say things like "If she doesn't go to sleep just thump her." I know it's just a

joke, but I really don't like it. Isabel is going to be weaned vege-
tarian and I've been trying to express milk so that I can leave her,
but my mother thinks that I should just water down cow's milk.
I know that part of what she is saying is just "be a bit more
relaxed and don't worry", but actually giving her cow's milk is
probably a really bad idea. Too much of her advice conflicts with
the advice that I've been getting from the health visitor. I don't
ask her any more because I find it quite difficult to thank her and
then ignore her. Instead it becomes an issue between us. It's far
more difficult to ignore bad advice from her than it is from a
stranger.'

Our parents' generation maintain that we are spineless and
easily romanticize the past. Trudi's mum 'says things like, "When
you were young there were never any temper tantrums, you were
just shoved into another room".' But her children must have had
tantrums, she just wasn't prepared to listen to them, while the
modern mother with only the most basic reading of modern
childcare manuals knows that a toddler having a tantrum needs to
know that you understand his anger rather than feel isolated
because of it. Child psychologists now maintain that if a baby is
only fed when the carer maintains it is hungry, or only picked up
when it suits the carer, then that baby finds it harder to develop
a small sense of self and is more likely to feel undervalued and
powerless in later life. People lacking in a stable identity can find
it harder to form lasting, trusting relationships, which can lead to
narcissism, solipsism or even megalomania as the unrequited
child struggles to make himself heard as an adult. And that raises
uncomfortable questions about our emotional relationship with
our own mothers. For if our mothers were only ever fed at four-
hourly intervals and left to cry when they needed to be hugged
and loved, how could they have found enough love and sense of
self-worth in their hearts to give us the love that we needed as
children?

'I need to make sure that my children know that I love them,
with lots of hugging and kissing because I didn't have that.'

Charlotte is in her early forties and has three school-age children. Her mother died just before her third child was born. 'During my very early childhood she was in hospital for a lot of the time and I was brought up by my grandmother so I was very close to her. I don't ever remember being hugged by my mother and I remember once I said, "You never hug me," and she said that that was the way that she was treated as a child. She was perpetuating it, whereas I am making a conscious effort to try and stop it from happening.'

I too feel that I want to give my children so much more emotionally than I ever had. A happier, more outgoing and positive mother and a father who will not leave them as wounded and defenceless as I was by my parents' divorce. My mother once said to me, 'You put so much into motherhood.' The unspoken implication was that I put so much more into it than she had done. But what does that statement say about her and me? That she could have given me more and didn't want to, or that we are simply different mothers, different products of different times?

If our mothers gave up work when they had children then conflict and misunderstanding can develop if they find it hard to understand why we may need to work, or the difficulties we encounter juggling the two. Many women know that their mothers sacrificed a great deal personally when they gave up work in order to look after their children and are resolved to do things differently. Hannah's mother was 'very, very angry that I went back to work. She was a nurse who gave up work when she was pregnant with me and hasn't worked since. I think that when she sees that Jill is a fine child and that both John and I go out to work and that John takes care of her when I'm out late and does the washing-up, it makes her question the choices that she made, which makes her angry. I think that was why there was a lot of, "You're not doing it right" stuff, when Jill was first born, which I deeply resented. She wanted to be the unconditional, all-loving mother and what she then finds hard is that I'm not the unconditional mother and yet it seems to be working all right and that makes her question everything that she did with me.'

'I want my daughters to see me as a person with my own life as well as being their mother,' says Irene. 'My mother never went out and had no friends. She'd do everything for us. We'd come home and she'd cook the tea and ring a bell so that my dad knew that it was ready, and I despised her. I go out now in the evenings. That's one change I've made on purpose because I don't want my children to see me as some sort of housewife drudge. Most of my childhood memories are negative, lots of rowing. When I sit back and think about it I know there must have been good times but I can't remember them. I want that to be different with my kids, I want them to remember good times.'

Most women do eventually reach reconciliation with their mothers as mothers, even if that bond is forged solely by their shared love for the new child. 'We weren't united,' writes Margaret Forster of her mother in her family memoir *Hidden Lives*. 'We were miles and miles apart in thought and feeling while caring deeply for each other. We needed the children to bind us together. So long as they were demanding our attention real communication was avoided.'[6] When our mothers become grandmothers they may be too old to change. If we feel enraged or entrapped by them then perhaps we have to let them go and accept them for who they are, fallible human beings who have inevitably made mistakes.

The birth of a child marks the marriage of two families as well as two people. Four sets of mainline genes descend down the family tree into a tiny baby and suddenly the entire status quo of wider family relationships changes as you have to cope with in-laws as well as your own parents. You find yourself on a completely different footing with the in-laws as soon as you have a baby. Suddenly you're closer than you were before, exposed to all of the intimacies and irritations of another family network which were previously hidden from view. You are no longer an outsider because you have given birth to their new grandchild, but you are not entirely accepted as an insider either. And there are two more parents to come into conflict with as you struggle to raise your own child in the way that you see fit.

'My mother-in-law has different ideas about how to do it,' Kate says. 'She won't tell you what to do, but she'll tell me what she did and when I disagree, it's best to keep my mouth shut, so I sit there fuming.'

'She didn't like some of the dangerous habits I had brought with me from London,' writes Maureen Freely about her mother-in-law in *What About Us?*

> . . . like taking the baby into bed for feeds, and picking him up every time he cried. And she was appalled at some of the safety measures I was unwilling to adopt – like bed clamps to keep him from kicking off his blankets when he cried in his cot, washing the entire house down in disinfectant, wearing a surgical mask while breastfeeding. In her opinion, I was just not up to the job. The first thing she would do in the morning was stand at the doorway to the bedroom, look at me and the nursing baby, shake her head, and say 'He's not going to make it.'

Sometimes mothers-in-law feel at greater liberty to trespass on your new mothering territory and assess your competency because you are not their flesh and blood. Sharon's in-laws never much liked her and she found them deeply unsympathetic to her pregnancy difficulties. They used her problems to take sides with their son and sympathized with him, rather than her, making worse the difficulties in her relationship. But when her son was born, Sharon found that a loving, strong relationship with her baby more than compensated for the tensions with her in-laws. 'He is mine not theirs. They can have their son.'

Emily produced the first grandchild for both sides of the family and found her mother-in-law beginning to lecture her on the importance of breastfeeding when she was just three months pregnant. 'She was already going into areas where she shouldn't go. She wasn't waiting for our relationship to become more established, but decided to make it more intimate.' Emily was so furious about the intrusion that she decided never to let her mother-in-law see her breastfeeding just to spite her. Emily feels that her parents-in-law are trying to compensate for a rather distant relationship with their son by forging a closer relationship with her. 'They have this fixed idea of what a daughter-in-law is and they try to see me in that role. They're not willing to help by doing what I think is right, only what they think is right. They don't try to find out why I do things my way because that challenges the way that they brought up their own children. When you have a grandchild for people you are letting yourself in for a lot more hassle than you realized. It's not just that they come to visit and then go away again. They want to be in there and if you don't have a really close relationship then it's very difficult to let them.'

As our children grow older, our relationship with our in-laws can improve immensely when they see that their concerns over the way that we were raising their grandchildren have been proved wrong. Clara's mother-in-law did not approve of the way that her granddaughter Lily was being brought up. 'She thought I wasn't strict enough on her. I was too tolerant. I wouldn't put her in a room and let her scream and I breastfed her much too long. But now that Lily is four and she can have a direct relationship with her without me, my mother-in-law thinks that she is absolutely wonderful. She even said, "She's a credit to the way that she was raised," which is a great step down for her.'

We are forced back into our own family if we want our children to have their own relationships with their grandparents, however much we may disapprove of their attitudes or priorities. Ruth had her first child by IVF at the age of forty and has a difficult relationship with her mother, and found it particularly hard after her daughter was born. 'But my in-laws have welcomed me in more and my attitude towards my family has changed now. I feel that I ought to have better relations with my family. I could do without it, but if something happened to me, the only person that I could trust at the moment with my child is my sister. I want her to have cousins that she knows.'

The omnipotence of our parents dwindles slowly as they get called 'Granny' or 'Granddad' more often than 'Mum' or 'Dad' and our focus shifts away from the family we came from to the family that we now create. The conflicts may still be there, but they come second to the needs of our children and are often reinterpreted as characterful idiosyncrasies rather than damaging deficiencies. They now have a newer, more important function as grandparents and we have a new role brokering between the oldest and youngest generations. My mother is always pleased to see my children when she comes to lunch, but then usually within half an hour of her arrival she complains of a headache, asks for paracetamol and has to lie down. 'You're such a noisy family,' she complains, failing to realize how much she contributes to the noise and my stress level by telling me her news at the same time as the children are clamouring for attention. Eagerly I attempt to bridge the gap by getting them to play with the toys that Granny has given them or by showing off their new creative accomplishments or skills as if they were performing dogs, so that she can leave content and entertained by their antics.

Again and again, our children force us to face aspects of our own childhoods, and heal old wounds. As our children start school the terror of playground thuggery returns to haunt us. When my eldest daughter started school my greatest fear for her was that she wouldn't have any friends. I remember vividly sitting alone on the playground bench every playtime when I first started school because I didn't know what else to do. Her social life is rich and my fears groundless and her greater social confidence has helped to bury memories of my own shakier start.

When my father forgot her seventh birthday I became preoccupied and hurt by his absence just as I had been as a child. My daughter was surrounded by far too many presents and people who loved her to notice that a card from Grandpa had failed to plop on to the mat. But I was hurt on her behalf, reminded of the forgotten promises of my own childhood and the hours spent pressing my nose against the windowpane, waiting for him to come, late again. I have long forgiven him the emotional crimes of divorce, concentrating my energy on my children instead. But the forgotten card makes me realize that some part of me hoped that he would make amends as a grandfather. I remember how his mother sent me a card with a five-pound note in it every birthday until I was eighteen, even though I hardly saw her, and I want more than that from him for my own children. Several days later a card and a present arrive and my daughter is even more focused on her grandfather and step-grandmother, because the present is isolated from the rest. She stood on a chair so that she could reach the phone and tapped out the number without prompting to thank him and talk to him. As I listened to their conversation I realized that their relationship is healthy, far more relaxed than mine ever was with my own grandparents, and that my emotional problems with my father are specific to me, private and not her concern.

I sit sobbing so hard that I can barely see the screen at the end of *The Railway Children* when Bobby runs through the smoke on the railway platform screaming '*Daddy, my daddy!*' because my own daddy never did come back to the family home. But my eldest daughter sits dry-eyed on her father's lap and somehow her emotional security makes me feel better. Other mothers discover that some of the emotional scars of their own upbringing become less painful as they become mothers to their own children.

Imogen, one of two sisters, was always labelled the 'clever

one' while her sister was the 'pretty one'. When she then had two daughters in her late thirties many of the insecurities surrounding her own looks resurfaced. 'When Beatrice was born, her face was squashed up and I thought, Oh God, she looks just like me. But when I was feeding her five days later, I realized she looked like Peter and that was such a relief for me. There was so much self-loathing of me as a child that I had to construct her as not like me. Then when Laura was born, the minute I looked at her I saw that she looked like me. I wrestled with that for weeks and Peter thought I was mad. He'd say, "She's only three days old, how can you know what she's going to look like?" I got out all the pictures of me as a baby and I looked really pretty and sweet. I thought, This is my script, my story because my mother loved us madly but was not good about making me feel good about the way I looked. We get the babies we need and it's been very healing. I got out the pictures and thought I was a lovely baby and I can see that Laura's different from her sister and she doesn't look a bit like me really. She's lovely.'

Sue and her siblings were seriously hot-housed educationally as children because their parents considered it very important. 'It had good results in many ways in that we were bright and passed exams but it had drawbacks emotionally. Now we take all that need for learning for granted and what we care about passionately is the emotional quality of things, the ability to express things and feel things. Then our own children will probably take all that for granted and have some other obsession, but for me it's part of growing up again which I really like.'

Our children force us to face our own childhoods by making us tell stories from our past, stories which allow them to feel even closer to us and to understand how common the problems of childhood are. Modern principles of 'good' parenting require us to get down on the floor and play with our children, rediscovering a meditative love for colouring-in, the intellectual challenge of Lego or the images evoked by our favourite stories. We only inherit genetically a percentage of our parents' faults.

Studies of twins show that intelligence, personality traits, attitudes and beliefs are more influenced by environmental than hereditary factors. While much of this environment is determined by the family in childhood, we have the power to change that and do things differently within the family structure that we create and control, healing our own wounds and hoping, foolishly perhaps, to create fewer emotional problems for our own children.

Inevitably we feel more conscious about the need to pass on accurate information about family backgrounds, to fill in the gaps when our children ask unanswerable questions. It is only when we become parents that we realize how much the linear imperative of family life forces love and attention down rather than up and how 'the great love that holds the mother to the child does not necessarily travel in the other direction', as Elizabeth Jolley writes in her short story 'Three Miles to One Inch'. All too often it then feels as if it is too late to make amends

> It was not until she was a grandrnother herself that she, because of her own love for her grandsons, realized how much she, as a small child, had been loved. And the pity was that it was too late now to acknowledge this to anyone. It was no longer possible to offer, unsolicited, a kiss, a caress, or a tender phrase backwards, as it were, over the shoulder.

Gaps in knowledge about one's own family history suddenly become pertinent gigantic holes because we are like lightning conductors between the past and the future and feel responsible for accurate transmission. The sense of slipping up a generation means that there is even less time left to ask all of those questions of our parents that we never dared or thought to ask. 'It makes you more tolerant and more interested in what's happened before. I now have a stronger sense of shared family history and I'm more conscious of not knowing who someone is when I look at family photographs,' says Anne. 'I realize I must ask my mother before she dies because if I don't then no one's ever going to know the answer and those people, those stories will disappear for ever.'

'I haven't yet been able to ask my parents about my childhood although there are a lot of things that I want to know.' Gemma's sister died of leukaemia at the age of two. Gemma now has two children under five and knows that eventually she will have to talk to them adult-to-adult about what happened for her own peace of mind. 'I've held back for fear of hurting them. My memories of the event are as a ten-year-old and I was told what they felt was appropriate at the time, but now that I'm in my thirties I have a lot of questions. I need to know what happened, but my parents don't raise the subject and I don't yet know how to ask them. You can't stop dragging the past into the present and yet you have to remind yourself that that is what you're doing, and that they aren't the same.'

Belinda was taken into care when she was twelve. She is a lesbian who had her baby through artificial insemination and has no idea where her mother is now. 'She's alive and I'd like to find her I want her to see Saskia and to hold her in her arms. My mother was brutalized by her father, so I can comfortably and with love forgive her for what she did. I forgave her a long time ago but I love her more now. When you're changing the thousandth nappy at three in the morning or cleaning up the vomit or doing the beautiful, beautiful breastfeeding – I think of her conditions in 1955, unmarried with one child, living in hovels and on the game to make ends meet.'

Isis has never met her father, who was a lawyer in Trinidad. Her mother married her father's brother and her father died when Isis was seven. She has a distant and difficult relationship with her mother, but goes to see her regularly so that her mother can have a relationship with her granddaughter, who is sixteen months old. 'When I was younger I used to despise my father and refused to have any contact with him, even though he wanted to meet me. But now I don't feel resentment, I feel that half of me is missing. When I got pregnant I realized how important it is to know your parents. They ask you questions about family medical history and I just wouldn't know on my father's side. There may be horrible abnormalities and I wouldn't know.'

We cannot avoid the fact that our past has an important and at times overbearing presence when we have children, as we seek to preserve family tradition and religious values and yet feel determined to do things our own way. Rachel is a lesbian and the mother of a mixed-race son aged seven months; she is also the daughter of upright, synagogue-going Jewish parents. Her parents were shocked at the idea of her becoming pregnant by artificial insemination but came round to it when they thought that she might use a Jewish donor after her brother diluted their Jewish heritage by marrying out. When she told them that the sperm donor of her child was black, her mother went 'berserk' and said that her grandchild would commit suicide when he was old enough to understand. 'My mother said something about never having Jewish grandchildren and I pointed out that I'm Jewish so they'll be Jewish but she felt that the genes wouldn't be strong enough. I then said that they had a responsibility to love the child and that if he did have problems it would be down to them dumping all this stuff on him. That threw them for a bit.'

Rachel had a difficult labour which mellowed her mother somewhat, and then decided to have her son circumcised, not just to please her parents, but because she felt strong enough about her identity as a Jew to pass it on 'We went to the Moyah surgery with just my parents and a friend of both of ours. My dad held him and had to make a covenant to the Moyah, accepting him as a Jew. The fact that the Moyah didn't say this baby can't be a Jew because he's black, and they held him, has made them bond with him and made it a lot better. I'm obsessed with my son but when I'm with my mum I'm deliberately offhand with him so that Mum can end up advocating for him – I'll go, "Stop moaning" and she'll pick him up and say, "Poor baby". I want him to know that he's Jewish and have an awareness of Jewish culture and an affection for Jews, but I don't want to burden him with it. Maybe watching *The Fiddler on the Roof* a hundred times will be enough.'

Numerous different sets of genes are handed down from generations with the birth of each child. What is extraordinary about family life and family lineage is how quickly each generation moves on to forge its own way of being, rather than repeating the patterns of their forebears. My children's great-grandparents include two German Jews who just managed to escape from Berlin in 1939, and a window cleaner and his wife who lived for years in slum accommodation behind the Tate Gallery in London. As my beloved grandparents, their spirits live on with cherished memories even though they are all dead. But to my children they are just names on the family tree, hazy stories from my own childhood.

Family life in the post-Freudian, Western world means accepting that much of the script of family drama is written down long before you become a mother or a father. If you were yet another girl when your mother hoped for a son; if your father subjected you to daily criticism because he was constantly criticized as a child; if you were branded the wicked sister as opposed to the angel as a child, if you were sexually or physically abused, then these discriminatory and damaging patterns of behaviour can be repeated with your own children, but only if we let them. We can draw a line between our past and their future.

Previous generations of parents often resorted to a strait-jacketed life full of rules and routines for an easier life. Now we know that if we relax that structure enough to let children feel recognized, but not so much as to make them feel insecure, we give them greater room for their difference. 'Almost from the start the new baby has his own ideas,' writes D. W. Winnicott, 'and if you have ten children you will not find two alike although they all grow up in the same house – your household. Ten children will see ten different mothers in you.'[7] If we see our children as unique and random then we find it easier to accept that we are not complete clones of our own parents. Patterns of behaviour can be severed as well as recreated, for, as Erik Erikson writes in *Childhood and Society*, 'This weak and changing little being moves the whole family along. Babies control and bring up their families as much as they are controlled by them; in fact, we may say that the family brings up a baby by being brought up by him.'[8]

The progress of time suddenly becomes terribly poignant through the growth of a child. Photographs capture our children's images but not their entire essence. Their smell, the sound of their voices, the way they feel in your arms and their particular way of saying things or of shuffling across the floor gets easily forgotten as they change and develop. 'Having children forces upon you a different relationship with memory and time,' writes David Flusfeder about the birth of his own son. 'As you watch your child grow, each stage of development feels absolute, sucks time into itself. He can focus now. He makes these little cooing noises. The previous stage is almost forgotten. And then comes along a different time. A new perpetual present.'[9]

'Love set you going like a fat gold watch,' begins Sylvia Plath's poem 'Morning Song', and as the minutes tick away, we get pulled back into the maelstrom of family life – the family we came from and the family that we now create. Emotional difficulties with parents can resurface and the childhood we thought we'd left behind returns to haunt us as we watch our children grow. We move up a generation, we put down roots through our children and have to accept, sooner or later, that we are being dragged into maturity because of the responsibilities of parenthood, just as our parents once were. It is only when we become mothers and fathers that we realize that we have joined a vast procession of mothers and fathers which stretches way back into history.

The 'Squire' looks down at her five children in Enid Bagnold's novel . . .

> They did not know yet that they were part of her flesh, her past, her heredity, her mother and her father, they did not know till they grew older that they could barely escape her and what she brought down to them. Yet each had a chance of escape, each had a chance of being, not a grandchild, but a grandfather. In every family there is the seed of a new start, something transcending the family mixture, an explosion, a creation, and the Phoenix is born.[10]

At the beginning of the twentieth century many women were still ignorant of the most basic aspects of pregnancy and reproduction. 'I didn't know how a baby was born, and when the labour pains started, I didn't know what they were,' was one working-class woman's description.[11]

> My dad said, 'I think you've got the flu.' So they put me to bed. But I felt uncomfortable and I was in pain. I got no sympathy from my husband. He went to sleep and that was that. In those days you used to have a bucket, a zinc pail to use if you needed it in the night. Well, I felt ill, so I sat on this bucket and I didn't know what was happening to me. The baby started to be born and even then I didn't know. I said to my husband, 'Wake up, there's something wrong, I've got a bladder coming out down here.' I thought my insides was all coming out. Then I put my hand down and I felt the profile of the child, the nose and the eyes. I said, 'It's the child, the child's being born.' My husband said, 'Well, put it back till morning.' That was how I learnt about childbirth. And that was when I stopped being a child.

Nowadays women are a lot better informed, but there are still acres of silence surrounding motherhood. We have unprecedented knowledge and control over our fertility. We can decide when to have a child, beat sterility with IVF or reject the experience altogether through contraception, abortion or sterilization. We can read handbooks describing every stage of pregnancy and childbirth, yet new motherhood is still riddled with taboo. In this book, I have tried to describe the radical change of motherhood so that women might be a little better prepared for the negative aspects as well as the positive. A woman's physical, emotional and psychological state of being can be thrown into complete turmoil for a while by pregnancy and labour. The presence of a small baby alters a woman's relationship with her friends, family and her partner and it can mean that her priorities and attitudes to work and the outside world shift dramatically.

It takes most women far longer to accept and settle into motherhood than they anticipated and adequate preparation with enough information builds our capacity to cope with the stress of such change. They used to say that women should not know about the pain of labour until it is upon them in case it should put them off. But knowing that labour hurts hasn't turned huge numbers of women away from childbirth. Women need adequate information so that they can cope with one of the most important and powerful experiences of their lives. There is now a large body of literature on psychological preparation for surgery which shows that when patients are told what to expect and given pre-operative counselling, they show less anxiety before and after the operation, they request fewer analgesics, they stay in hospital for shorter periods and they report increased feelings of control and ability to cope. Studies of women in childbirth have come to similar conclusions.[12]

But these are principles which apply to life in general and not just to the medical imperative. Reading about every aspect of new motherhood can only help the expectant and new mother to cope with the more stressful aspects if she encounters them. 'It needs to be part of our cultural knowledge, so that everyone knows that it is likely to be hard for a bit,' says Imogen, 'but that it does get better and then it's just the best thing that has ever happened.'

When the fog of those early months and years lifts, parents can rarely remember what life was like before and find it impossible to imagine how they would have lived had they not had children. 'Some days it certainly seems to me that I might have remembered to put lotion on my face, exercised daily, put money away in the bank if I had not had children,' writes Anne Roiphe. 'Other days I have no interest in those things and I think that without my children, whatever I might be, I would be less, diminished, reduced, imprisoned inside my own skin, a person who will not leave a forward trace, the trail would only wind back.'[13]

The good bits of motherhood are better than I ever imagined possible. We swim through oceans of intimacy and pleasure with our children. Wrapping your children in bath towels at the end of each day as they sit tired on your lap wanting nothing more than to be held, brings fathomless contentment. The smallest ladybird crawling across a leaf suddenly comes into focus with a child, time stands still and races too fast as children romp and grow with flesh so radiant and youthful that you can almost watch a scratch heal. I have never known such pride, such satisfaction, such joy, pleasure and love. I never knew that there could be so much laughter daily, that children are naturally funny. But the bad bits of motherhood were also so much worse than I ever imagined possible. If I had known that every mother lives with these bad times as well as the good when I first had a baby then it would undoubtedly have been easier. How trapped in silence women are when things get rough, because of the fear of being labelled 'selfish', 'immature' or 'not fit to be a mother'.

I think occasionally of how these two small girls of mine may one day have children of their own and relish the thought of grandmotherhood. I think too of how they will undoubtedly experience the rich extremities of emotion, the pleasures and the pain of motherhood and I envy them already. But if their experience could be lightened by knowledge rather than by shrouded taboo, if they could go into motherhood with their eyes wide open, then perhaps there would be more room for pleasure between shorter periods of pain.

Common Health Problems After Childbirth

Caesarean

For the one in four British women and one in three American women who give birth by Caesarean section there is the added complication of recovering from major abdominal surgery as well as from having a baby. When men and women have major surgery they are told that it may take months for them to recover fully and that they must rest for several weeks before they go back to work. When women give birth by Caesarean, they are not given guidelines on rest and convalescence and are encouraged to look after their babies in the same way as all new mothers. The psychologists have been so successful in impressing the (as yet inconclusively proved) need for continuous care by the mother for improved early bonding, that the mother is rarely allowed to hand over her baby to a midwife for even a few hours so that she can begin to recuperate.

The pain of a Caesarean can be considerable and for women who have never experienced surgery before, that deep agonizing pain as well as the psychological shock of having been cut almost in half can be very distressing. It takes a Herculean effort to heave yourself up on to your elbows, twist yourself around and then lift your baby from its cot when it cries, and that sense of impotence and inability to care properly for one's baby can cause subsequent psychological problems for the mother. Breastfeeding often hurts more because the accompanying uterine contractions pull on the internal wound. So many layers of muscle are cut that it often takes months for the discomfort to subside. A survey of 588 women three months after giving birth by Caesarean in 1986 found that 35 per cent had still not recovered and 28 per cent felt less healthy than before pregnancy, with 18 per cent still experiencing wound pain.[1]

Women who have had Caesareans suffer greater blood loss than those who have had a vaginal delivery and are therefore in greater danger of developing anaemia. It feels as if your lower half has been stitched to the bed after a Caesarean and it is hard to contemplate ever walking again, but any attempt to shuffle just a few yards will greatly aid the healing process and should be attempted bravely. When women have a second Caesarean they know what to expect, they are less frightened of opening the scar, less shocked by what has happened and move around earlier which aids their recovery.

You do recover from a Caesarean but you need to look after yourself. Heavy weights mustn't be lifted for at least six weeks and stomach exercises should be avoided until the scar feels as if it has fully healed. A common side-effect of all abdominal surgery is wind, so that's another symptom to contend with for a while. Holding your hand over the wound when you move, cough, sneeze or fart will ease the discomfort and make you feel more secure. Gradually the red scar will fade to pink and then eventually it will whiten, although that can take years.

Sore Perineum

Roughly two-thirds of all women in Britain require stitching after giving birth because of an episiotomy or tears. The genitals and lower abdomen are also likely to be bruised and sore and most women find that they have pain or discomfort in the days after childbirth. A large number of new mothers still feel uncomfortable weeks later. Twenty per cent of new mothers have long-term problems such as pain during intercourse and 10 per cent are still having trouble some 12–18 months after giving birth. Research shows that those women who have been stitched by an experienced midwife or doctor suffer less perineal pain afterwards, as do those who have been stitched with a continuous running stitch rather than with interrupted transcutaneous stitches.

The perineum tends to heal quickly because the area is packed with blood vessels. Midwives recommend that you pour a jug of warm water over the perineum as you urinate in order to ease stinging, and keep the area clean and thus free of infection. Women are often afraid of emptying their bowels after childbirth and fear putting pressure on their stitches. The digestive system will have been suppressed by stress during labour and lack of food, and many women do not open their bowels until at least three days after giving birth. Drinking plenty of water and holding a sanitary towel against the stitches helps to ease the strain, but if you're worried about this, or if the midwives are putting you under pressure before they discharge you then the odd suppository can really help.

Women with a deeper or longer episiotomy, or with a third- or fourth-degree tear, will find that the wound will take longer to heal. Ice packs and local anaesthetic sprays or gels containing lignocaine can help as can oral pain relief such as paracetamol and mefenamic acid.

Infection

Women are particularly prone to catching a urinary, uterine or perineal infection immediately after giving birth because a mother's resistance is lowered through the stress of labour and she has open wounds. Roughly 20 per cent of women who have had a

Caesarean develop a wound infection. A urinary infection is usually accompanied by a rise in temperature and pain when passing urine and can be treated quickly with antibiotics. The first sign of a uterine infection is usually heavier, brighter bleeding after the lochia has begun to show signs of drying up. The uterus may be slightly tender or there may be more discomfort on one side than on the other. One of the most common causes of a uterine infection is the presence of a small part of the placenta and once again antibiotics such as penicillin are prescribed.

Infection of the Breast

Infection should not be confused with engorgement, which occurs naturally on the third or fourth day after childbirth. For the first two or three days, the baby suckles colostrum, which contains antibodies to help build the baby's immunity; then the breasts swell with milk and often become hard and painful. This is engorgement and may be accompanied by a slight rise in temperature. The discomfort will pass quickly provided that the baby feeds well by being latched on properly with the nipple and the end of the breast thrust right to the back of the baby's mouth. If the baby is allowed to chew on the nipple itself, or the nipple passes too often across the baby's gumline, the nipple may become grazed or sore and then if it becomes cracked, an infection can enter the breast. Breastfeeding is an acquired skill and it seems like chronic masochism thrusting an agonizingly swollen breast into your baby's mouth for yet more pain as the baby latches on and the let-down reflex begins. Some women experience no discomfort from day one of breastfeeding. Others find that their breast glands ache at first as the baby draws off the milk. Once breastfeeding has become established most of the discomfort disappears.

Rubbing breast milk into the nipples and exposing them to the air to dry after feeding will help prevent and alleviate the symptoms of sore nipples. Research seems to suggest that the nipple creams currently on the market are of little use and are probably a waste of money. If a reddish tender patch appears on the breast then you have a blocked duct and feeding the baby normally should clear the blockage. Massaging the breast with gentle strokes towards the nipple with a hot flannel will also help relieve the pain and clear the blockage. If you develop a sore breast and have a high temperature, and feel as if you have flu, then you are likely to have mastitis and should call the doctor who will prescribe antibiotics. It is important to treat mastitis adequately in order to prevent the development of a breast abscess which is far more painful and may require lancing and the cessation of feeding.

Haemorrhage

It is not unusual for women to bleed for up to six weeks after giving birth and this is normal provided that the blood flow gets progressively lighter and paler. Women often pass small clots in the first day or so and the cleansing of the uterus is aided by afterpains. The contractions are stimulated by breastfeeding, which can be painful. It is normal for a woman to feel more blood loss on standing after she has been resting, but if you experience a gush of very heavy bleeding after the first twenty-four hours and soak more than three sanitary towels in an hour then you should consult your midwife. Consistent bright-red bleeding, which may or may not be accompanied by an unpleasant smell and a temperature, may mean that part of the placenta has been retained. This is usually removed by D and C.

Anaemia

Anaemia can extend into the first few months of motherhood, and can be exacerbated by heavy blood loss during labour or by poor diet. Often anaemia is well disguised by the tiredness many new mothers feel from sleepless nights and breastfeeding. It is a common complication of the puerperium, which is often left untreated and can make women feel far more tired than they need be. The symptoms of anaemia are a pale, pasty complexion; excessive tiredness; impatience; shortness of breath; irritability and a general feeling that everything is too much trouble. Women who have been prescribed iron during pregnancy should continue taking the pills for two to three months after childbirth and all new mothers should eat an iron-rich diet, for iron deficiency can lead to impaired resistance to infection up to six months after giving birth.

Thrombosis

Varicose veins and indeed haemorrhoids can become swollen and more painful in the days after childbirth. The condition is known as superficial phlebitis or superficial thrombosis. The good news is that there is nothing serious to worry about even though it has the terrifying word 'thrombosis' attached to it, but the bad news is that it cannot be cured other than with rest and bandages until the swelling subsides. Deep vein thrombosis is unlikely to occur if the mother gets up and moves around soon after giving birth, but usually starts on or around the fifth day after delivery. There is a tightness in the middle of the calf in one leg, there may be pain on walking or there may be swelling in the ankle, foot or leg. This is considered a serious medical condition because the blood clot could become dislodged and travel up through the pelvis and become lodged in the heart or lungs so if you do have symptoms of thrombosis tell your midwife or doctor immediately.

Incontinence

Since the beginning of recorded medical history childbirth has been known to damage the pelvic floor, causing such ghastly and now mercifully rare upheavals in the West as fistulae (long narrow gashes with ulcers), incontinence of faeces, and prolapse of the uterus. Prolonged labour with the baby's head bashing repeatedly against the pelvic floor increases the likelihood of damage to the intricate system of interconnected muscles, nerves, ligaments and viscera which control continence. Medical insistence on reducing the length of time a woman spends in labour has undoubtedly spared many women these unpleasant after-effects However, even without prolonged labour and excessive obstetric intervention, studies show that the power of the pelvic floor to contract can be impaired by vaginal delivery and a substantial number of women suffer nerve damage. While most women will not notice any change, their pelvic floor may have been weakened, and subsequent deliveries and the effects of ageing may weaken a mother and take her further along the road to incontinence.

Approximately one in four women experience stress incontinence after the birth of their first child, defined as 'hard to hold urine when jumping or sneezing' and a further 5 per cent experience urinary frequency which means that they have to pass urine often. The bladder is an acutely sensitive organ which takes quite a battering through labour. Older women having large babies with a second stage over two hours are particularly at risk of developing stress incontinence after the birth, and it doesn't appear to clear up quickly. Seventy-five per cent of women questioned in the largest study on health after childbirth accomplished in Britain[2] still had symptoms a year after the birth of their baby, with few women seeking medical advice for their condition even though it inevitably modified their lifestyle.

Abdul Sultan, a Senior Registrar in Obstetrics, has undertaken research on postpartum health. 'Not a single woman in all of my studies actually volunteered the information. They are too embarrassed to talk about it, but they shouldn't have these problems. It becomes more and more difficult for women to talk about it as time goes by because you say, "Oh well, it's getting better," and you accept it. Then you adjust your lifestyle by either changing your diet, or you empty your bladder more frequendy or you don't drink as much as you used to and you don't do certain sports. Subconsciously, you make all these changes to your life and believe there's nothing wrong with you.'

Mild urinary incontinence after childbirth doesn't have to be put up with as one of those things that just happen to you when you have a child. Old ladies develop full urinary incontinence far more often than old men because they have had babies, and tackling the problem in its early stages after birth may well prevent future problems. Any woman who finds that she has to hurry to reach the toilet in time, that she leaks before she gets there and that she goes to the toilet more than six times a day, or has to get up more than three times a night in order to pass urine, ought to see her doctor.

Pelvic-floor exercises are not just meant for getting through labour, they are more important than ever after the birth and any form of regular exercise will help strengthen perineal muscle function. Like any other muscle, the pelvic floor will become more flaccid if it is not exercised and daily squeezing can help strengthen the pelvic floor against future incontinence. Vaginal cones can also be used to help strengthen the pelvic floor. These are a graduated series of small weights which are held in the vagina for a short period each day. They have a similar success rate to pelvic-floor exercises and are good for women who are either not keen on surgery or who are planning to have more children. However, if the incontinence is restricting a woman's lifestyle and she doesn't plan to have any more children then bladder-neck surgery is the most effective solution, with a 90 per cent success rate. It is a harder operation to perform successfully in older women so it is well worth considering for the future.

Faecal incontinence is rarer than urinary incontinence, with approximately 5 per cent of women suffering short-term effects, but when it occurs, the effects can be devastating.

Sandra is a GP and mother of two who experienced faecal

incontinence just days after the birth of her first baby in hospital. 'As I sat trying to clean up the mess, I realized that like a child I had to relearn a few basic bodily functions. I cried. Later that day the senior house officer looked in, smiled and said that I could go home the following day. My pain was still not adequately controlled, I couldn't control my bowels and we had no one at home to help. To my relief the consultant suggested staying in hospital a little longer. At home people remarked on our beautiful baby. So new, so perfect. But I felt dirty and ashamed. My body had not just given birth; it had been used and spoilt in the process.'

While it is fairly common for mothers to remark on how their bladder is not what it once was, incontinence of faeces is still a taboo subject and many find that their complaints are not taken seriously by their GPs in the rare instances when they pluck up the courage to visit them. While vaginal delivery inevitably puts the anal sphincter under great stress, the use of forceps and episiotomy appear to play a significant part in disrupting the anal sphincter. 'The work on faecal incontinence was shelved in the mid-1980s,' says Abdul Sultan, 'because they thought that it was due to nerve damage and you cannot really prevent that. Then with ultrasound and the use of sonograph technology, we discovered that we were actually tearing the sphincter and not realizing it.'

Full faecal incontinence can only be cured with surgery, with an 80 per cent success rate. It can be controlled by changing the diet, or through the use of constipating agents but that can lead to additional problems. Incontinence of flatus (farting) can cause some women as much embarrassment as incontinence of faeces and can be controlled by reducing the intake of gas-producing foods. 'It's a spectrum starting off with flatal incontinence,' says Abdul Sultan, 'and it's something that may get worse, leading to soiling and then frank faecal incontinence. Women with, say, irritable bowel syndrome before pregnancy, and then a noticeable disruption of the anal sphincter, are at higher risk of developing incontinence in later life because they have higher colonic pressures.' Sultan has also found that the use of the ventouse cap may be less damaging to the mother's sphincter than forceps.

Backache

Research has found a link between the use of epidurals during labour and subsequent backache, headaches and aches in the limbs and tingling in the hands and feet.[3] Backache can be caused by direct trauma from the needle, or by a reaction to the drugs, but it could also be caused by the postural alterations of pregnancy and the loosening of ligaments, which then become exacerbated by the exertions of labour, particularly if the mother is desensitized by an epidural and adopts an uncomfortable position for too long. Many osteopaths believe that epidurals damage spine tissue and that the ensuing scar rubs against the spine causing pain. Whatever the cause, 14 per cent of women in Christine MacArthur's study of more than 11,000 mothers in Birmingham had long-term backache after the birth of their babies and a higher proportion of these symptoms were found in the women who had had epidurals.[4]

Joanna Trevelyan was deputy editor of *Nursing Times* for five years before she had her first baby and therefore thought she knew most of what there was to know about having a baby, 'but I did not, as I imagine many other women do not, anticipate the long-term effects of epidurals and episiotomies. Once the effects of the epidural wore off, I suffered from acute back pain (something I have never suffered before) in the area where the epidural had been sited.' Four visits to a cranial osteopath sorted out the problem but she says that she still gets acute backache when she is tired. 'Six months on, I still suffer from neuralgia in both feet. When I get up after sitting for more than ten minutes my feet are so painful that I sometimes find myself hobbling like an old woman. My GP was not remotely surprised; apparently neuralgia, especially in the legs, is common among women who have had an epidural. I an told that the pain usually goes after a year but may last up to three years. Joanna also had to have a long episiotomy because her son's head was 12 centimetres in diameter and for two weeks she was unable to carry her baby without the scar hurting. She blames midwives and authors of pregnancy and childbirth books for not warning women about the potential health risks of having babies, fearing that the truth might frighten or put them off. 'The fact is,' writes Joanna in *Nursing Times*, 'that if I had known about potential problems in advance, I would not have worried so much, and would have sought help earlier.'

Postnatal Depression

Chapter 3 explores postnatal depression in detail because I believe that aspects of new motherhood such as the physical drain of pregnancy and labour, the shock and hard work of full-time responsibility for a newborn, and exhaustion are major contributory factors. The symptoms of postnatal depression are all-encompassing: tearfulness, irritability, feelings of despondency and inadequacy, self-reproach, excessive anxiety and sleep disturbance. These feelings are common and experienced by the vast majority of new mothers to some degree. But if you feel overwhelmed by them, consult your GP. Postnatal depression is treated with anti-depressants and/or psychotherapy and counselling. Some women find such treatment helps, others suffer side-effects or feel that their problem hasn't really been resolved, merely placed on hold. Postnatal depression is a very real and often debilitating reaction to new motherhood and should be treated seriously by family and friends. Emotional support, particularly from the father of the baby, is crucial, as well as practical help and relief from some of the burdens of motherhood in order to recover. There are many organizations, listed under 'Adjusting' in Appendix II, that will be able to help.

Organizations

Health

www.birthchoice.com for information on what's available in your area.

www.caesarean.org.uk for information and support.

National Childbirth Trust
For advice and contacts for local Caesarean, breastfeeding and post-natal support groups.
Breastfeeding line 0870 444 8708
Pregnancy and birth line 0870 444 8709
www.nct.org.uk

NHS Direct
0845 46 47
www.nhsdirect.nhs.uk

National Institute for Health and Clinical Evidence
Midcity Place, 17 High Holborn, London WC1V 6NA
020 7067 5800
www.nice.org.uk

Association of Breastfeeding Mothers
Publications, extensive list of local counsellors and phone and email
support.
Counselling hotline 0870 401 7711
www.abm.me.uk

La Leche League of Great Britain
Advice and support for breastfeeding mothers.
0845 456 1855
www.laleche.org.uk

British Acupuncture Council
Contact for free list of local practitioners.
63 Jeddo Road, London W12 9HQ
020 8735 0404
www.acupuncture.org.uk

British Homeopathic Association
Hahnemann House, 29 Park Street West, Luton LU1 3BE
0870 444 3950
www.trusthomeopathy.org

Action for Victims of Medical Accidents
Provides advice and support to patients injured during the course of
medical treatment.
44 High Street, Croydon CR0 1YB
020 8688 9555
www.thepatientsforum.org.uk
www.patient.co.uk

Adjusting

www.mumsnet.com
www.netmums.com
www.pni-uk.com for postnatal illness.

Association for Postnatal Illness
Offers advice, leaflets with an sae, and a network of volunteers who were past sufferers offering support.
145 Dawes Road, London SW6 7EB
020 7386 0868
www.apni.org

Cry-sis
Phone counselling with local volunteers for parents with babies who cry excessively or won't sleep.
08451 228 669
www.cry-sis.org.uk

Parentline Plus
Organization for stressed parents of children aged from 0 to 18 plus.
0808 800 2222
www.parentlineplus.org.uk

Women's Therapy Centre
10 Manor Gardens, London N7 6JS
Advice line 020 7263 7860
www.womenstherapycentre.co.uk

Multiple Births Foundation
Hammersmith House, Queen Charlotte's & Chelsea Hospital, Du Cane Road, London W12 0HS
020 8383 3519
www.multiplebirths.org.uk

Twins and Multiple Births Association (TAMBA)
0800 138 0509
www.tamba.org.uk

Careline
Confidential telephone crisis counselling service.
0845 122 8622
www.carelineuk.org

Home Start
0800 068 6368
www.home-start.org.uk

New Parent and Infant Network (NEWPIN)
Sutherland House, 35 Sutherland Square, London SE17 3EE
020 7358 5900
www.newpin.org.uk

Work

Working Families
1–3 Berry Street, London EC1V 0AA
www.workingfamilies.org.uk

Your local authority is obliged to keep a list of local registered child-minders. Local children's shops, playgroups and newspapers also advertise childcare.

Emotions

The Foundation for the Study of Infant Deaths
Helpline 020 7233 2090
www.sids.org.uk

Baby Life Support Systems (BLISS)
Support for parents with premature babies and for those who have lost a baby.
Helpline 0500 618 140
www.bliss.org.uk

Cruse
Bereavement care.
0844 477 9400
www.crusebereavementcare.org.uk

Disabled Living Foundation
Independent advice on specialists in children's equipment.
0845 130 9177
www.dlf.org.uk

National Society for the Prevention of Cruelty to Children (NSPCC)
Helpline 0808 800 5000
www.nspcc.org.uk

Stillbirth and Neonatal Death Society (SANDS)
020 7436 5881
www.uk-sands.org

Exhaustion

Cry-sis
08451 228 669
www.cry-sis.org.uk

Relationships

Relate
0845 456 1310
www.relate.org.uk

Gingerbread
Advice and local self-help groups for one-parent families.
0800 018 5026
www.gingerbread.org.uk

National Council for One-Parent Families
Helpline 0800 018 5026
www.oneparentfamilies.org.uk

Rape Crisis Centre
www.rapecrisis.org.uk

Meet-A-Mum Association
0845 120 3746
www.mama.co.uk

Contact A Family
Support for families with special needs children. Has a parent line that offers a listening ear and can link you with support groups in your local area.
0808 808 3555
www.cafamily.org.uk

Women's Aid
Twenty-four-hour domestic violence helpline.
0808 200 0247
www.womensaid.org.uk

Mother and baby magazines often organize letter swaps between new mothers.

Notes

1. Childbirth: Just the Beginning

1 *The Squire*, by Enid Bagnold (Virago, 1987)
2 *Torn in Two: The Experience of Maternal Ambivalence*, by Rozsika Parker (Virago, 1995)
3 Mortality in pregnant and non-pregnant women in England and Wales 1997–2002
4 *The Female Brain* by Dr Louann Brizendine (Bantam, 2007) www.cemach.org.uk

2. Health After Birth

1 *Operating Instructions: A Journal of my Son's First Year* by Anne Lamott, (Bloomsbury, 1994)
2 *Scientific Foundations of Obstetrics and Gynaecology*, edited by Elliot E. Philipp, Josephine Barnes, Michael Newton (Third Edition, Heinemann, 1986)
3 Quoted in *The Captured Womb: A History of the Medical Care of Pregnant Women*, by Ann Oakley (Blackwell, 1984)
4 Ibid.
5 *A History of Women's Bodies*, by Edward Shorter (Penguin Books, 1984)
6 *Maternity: Letters from Working Women*, edited by Margaret Llewelyn Davies (Virago, 1978)

7 *Working Class Wives*, by Margery Spring Rice (Virago, 1982)

8 *The Woman's Hour*, by Jenni Murray (BBC Books, 1996)

9 *Working Class Wives*

10 *A History of Women's Bodies*

11 *The Captured Womb*

12 *Health After Childbirth*, by Christine MacArthur, Margo Lewis and George Knox (HMSO, 1991)

13 *Postnatal morbidity after childbirth and severe obstetric morbidity*, Waterstone M., Wolfe C., Hooper R., Bewleys British Journal of Obstetrics and Gynaecology, 2003 Feb.

14 *Fundamentals of Obstetrics and Gynaecology*, by Derek Llewellyn Jones (6th Edition, Mosby, 1994)

15 *A History of Women's Bodies.* See also *The Art of Midwfery: Early Modern Midwives in Europe*, edited by Hilary Marland (Routledge, 1993)

16 *The Crying Baby*, by Sheila Kitzinger (Viking, 1989)

17 *Anthropology of Human Birth*, by Margarita Artschwager Kay (Davis Co., 1981)

18 Ibid.

19 Ibid.

20 Ibid.

21 *Scientific Foundations of Obstetrics and Gynaecology*

22 *The Female Brain*, by Dr Louann Brizendine (Bantam, 2007)

3. Adjusting to Motherhood

1 'Transition to Parenthood: Risk Factors for Parents and Infants', by Howard J. Osofsky in *Journal of Psychosomatic Obstetrics and Gynaecology* (1985, Number 4)

2 Ibid.

3 *Depression After Childbirth*, by Katharina Dalton (2nd Edition, Oxford University Press, 1989)

4 Quoted in *A Lasting Relationship: Parents and Children over Three Centuries*, by Linda Pollock (Fourth Estate, 1987)

5 Quoted in *Childbirth in Seventeenth- and Eighteenth-Century England*, by Adrian Wilson (PhD thesis, 1984)

6 *Pregnancy, Birth and Parenthood*, by Frances Kaplan Grossman,

Lois S. Eicher and Susan A. Winickoff (Jossey-Bass Publishers, 1980)

7 *Reactions to Motherhood*, by Jean Ball (Cambridge University Press, 1987)

8 *Psychological Processes of Childbearing*, by Joan Raphael Leff (Chapman and Hall, 1991)

9 'Caesarean Blues', by Sarah Clement in *New Generation* (1989)

10 'Post-Traumatic Stress Disorder in Women Who Have Undergone Obstetric and/or Gynaecological Procedures', by Janet Menage in *Journal of Reproductive and Infant Psychology* (Vol. II, 1993)

11 Debra K. Creedy, Ian M. Shochet and Jan Hasfall, 'Childbirth and the Development of Acute Trauma Symptoms' *Birth* Vol. 27 2 2000

12 'Post-traumatic Stress Disorder', Jean Robinson, *Aims* Vol. 14, No. 4

13 Quoted in *Forgotten Children*, by Linda Pollock (Cambridge University Press, 1983)

14 *Out of Me*, by Fiona Shaw (Viking, 1997)

15 *The 'Highs' and 'Lows' of Maternal Mood*, by Ann Shelagh Robertson (MSc thesis University of Surrey, 1995)

16 'New Mothers Have Increased Depression Risk', by W. F. Nash and L. Phillips in *Nursing Times* (July 7, 1993)

17 NCT Evidence-based Briefing, *New Digest*, December 2002

18 *The Blue Jay's Dance*, by Louise Erdrich (Flamingo, 1996)

19 *The Scent of Dried Roses*, by Tim Lott (Penguin, 1997)

20 *Midwives, Research and Childbirth*, Vol. 3, edited by Sarah Robinson and Ann M. Thomson (Chapman and Hall, 1993)

21 *The Transition to Parenthood: Current Theory and Research*, edited by Gerald Y. Michaels and Wendy A. Goldberg (Cambridge University Press, 1988)

22 *Out of Me*

23 *The Mother Knot*, by Jane Lazarre (Beacon Books, 1986)

4. Working and the 'Good' Mother

1 *The Prospect Before Her: A History of Women in Western Europe*, Vol. I, by Olwen Hufton (HarperCollins, 1996)

2 *For Her Own Good*, by Barbara Ehrenreich and Deirdre English (Pluto Press, 1979)

3 *The Myth of Motherhood*, by Elizabeth Badinter (Souvenir Press, 1981)

4 *Perfect Parents: Baby-care Advice Past and Present*, by Christina Hardyment (Oxford University Press, 1995)

5 Quoted in *Round About a Pound a Week*, by Maud Pember Reeves (Virago, 1979)

6 Quoted in *A Labour of Love: The Experience of Parenthood in Britain 1900–1950*, by Steve Humphries and Pamela Gordon (Sidgwick and Jackson, 1993)

7 *For Her Own Good*

8 *The Mother Knot*

9 *Perfect Parents*

10 *The Continuum Concept*, by Jean Liedloff (Penguin Arkana, 1986)

11 *What About Us?*, by Maureen Freely (Bloomsbury, 1995)

12 Quoted in *Childcare and the Psychology of Development*, by Elly Singer (Routledge, 1992)

13 *A History of Women's Bodies*

14 *The Captured Womb*

15 *A History of Women's Bodies*

16 *Wives and Mothers in Victorian Industry*, by Margaret Hewitt (Rocklift, (1958)

17 *They Worked All Their Lives: Women of the Urban Poor in England 1880–1939*, by Carl Chinn (Manchester University Press, 1988)

18 Ibid.

19 *Inventing Motherhood*, by Ann Dally (Burnett Books, 1982)

20 Both Lily Felstead's and Esther Peel's accounts from *A Labour of Love*

21 *They Worked All Their Lives*

22 *Wives and Mothers in Victorian Industry*

23 *The Making of the Modern Family*, by Edward Shorter (Collins, 1976)

24 *Round About a Pound a Week*

25 *The Woman Who Works, The Parent Who Cares*, by Dr Sirgay Sanger and John Kelly (Transworld, 1988)

26 *The Blue Jay's Dance*

27 *The Woman Who Works, The Parent Who Cares*

28 Ibid.

29 *Fruitful*, by Anne Roiphe (Houghton Mifflin, 1996)

5. Emotions

1 *Psychological Processes of Childbearing*

2 *Nisa: The Life and Words of a !Kung Woman*, by Marjorie Shostak (Penguin, 1981)

3 *The Blue Jay's Dance*

4 Quoted in *A Lasting Relationship*

5 *Perfect Parents*

6 *The Mother Knot*

7 *Perfect Parents*

8 Quoted in *Life on a Low Income*, by Elaine Kempson (Joseph Rowntree Foundation, 1996)

9 *The Transition to Parenthood: Current Theory and Research*

10 *Motherhood and Modernity*, by Christine Everingham (Open University Press, 1994)

11 *The European Experience of Declining Fertility: A Quiet Revolution 1850–1970*, edited by John R. Gillis, Louise A. Tilly and David Levine (Blackwell, 1992)

12 *Forgotten Children*

13 *Social Trends* 22 (HMSO, 1992)

14 *Foetal Attraction* text adapted from the BBC *Horizon* programme transmitted 3 April 1995

15 *Operating Instructions*

16 *The Child, the Family and the Outside World*, by D. W. Winnicott (Penguin, 1964)

17 Quoted in *For Her Own Good*

18 *Foetal Attraction*

6. Exhaustion

1 *A Study on the Post-natal Sleep Patterns of Scottish Primagravid Women*, by Heather Shaw (MSc thesis, University of Surrey, 1994)

2 'Sleep Disturbances, Vitality and Fatigue Among a Select Group

of Employed Childbearing Women', by Kathryn A. Lee and Jeanne F. DeJoseph in *Birth* (19:4, December 1992)

3 'Fatigue in Early Pregnancy', by Nedra Reeves et al. in *Journal of Nurse Midwifery* (Vol. 36, Number 5 Sept./Oct.)

4 *Sleep Thieves*, by Stanley Coren (Simon & Schuster, 1996)

5 Ibid.

6 *Health After Childbirth*

7 *Teach Your Baby to Sleep Through the Night*, by Charles E. Schaefer and Michael R. Petronko (Thorsons, 1989)

8 *Three in a Bed*, by Deborah Jackson (Bloomsbury, 1989)

9 Cochrane Database in *British Medical Journal*, (1995, Issue 2)

10 *Working Class Wives*

11 *Life on a Low Income*

12 *The Squire*

13 *Forgotten Children*

14 *Maternity: Letters from Working Women*

15 Quoted in *A Labour of Love*

16 Quoted in *Maternity: Letters from Working Women*

17 *Working Class Wives*

7. Relations with the Father

1 *The Transition to Parenthood*, by Jay Belsky and John Kelly (Vermilion, 1994)

2 'Fathers: Recent Research Perspectives', by Charlie Lewis in *Journal of Reproductive and Infant Psychology* (Vol. 8, 1990)

3 *The Female Brain*, Dr Louann Brizendine (Bantam, 2007)

4 'Pregnancy Symptoms in the Expectant Man', by L. Y. Bogren in *Journal of Psychosometric Obstetrics and Gynaecology* (Suppl. 10, 1989)

5 'Labour Support by First-time Fathers: Direct Observations with a Comparison to Experienced Doulas', by T. D. Bertsch in *Journal of Psychosometric Obstetrics and Gynaecology* (Vol. II, 1990)

6 *Father's Presence at Childbirth*, by Mary Gleeson (MSc thesis, University of Surrey, 1995)

7 *Father's Presence at Birth: The Expectation and Reality as Experienced by the Father*, by Christin Roostan (MSc thesis, University of Surrey, 1995)

8 'Social Support in Labour: A Selective Review', by B. Chalmers and W. Wolman in *Journal of Psychosometric Obstetrics and Gynaecology* (Vol. 14, 1993)

9 'The Influence of Birth Setting on the Father's Behaviour Towards his Partner and Infant', by Ruta Westreich in *Birth* (18:4, December 1991)

10 *The Second Child: Family Transition at the Second Birth*, by Robert B. Steward (Sage, 1991)

11 *Effective Care in Pregnancy and Childbirth*, edited by Iain Chalmers, Murray Enkin and Marc J. N. C. Keirse (Oxford University Press, 1989)

12 Office of National Statistics

13 *Reassessing Fatherhood*, by Charlie Lewis and Margaret O'Brien (Sage, 1987)

14 *The Transition to Parenthood*

15 *Families and How to Survive Them*, by Robin Skynner and John Cleese (Mandarin, 1983)

16 *Fatherhood Reclaimed*, by Adrienne Burgess (Vermilion, 1996)

17 *The Secret Life of the Unborn Child*, by Dr Thomas Verny with John Kelly (Warner Books, 1981)

18 *The Woman Who Works, The Parent Who Cares*

19 *The Transition to Parenthood: Current Theory and Research*

8. Sex and Sensuality

1 'Maternal Sexuality During First Pregnancy and After Childbirth', by K. M. Robson et al., in *British Journal of Obstetrics and Gynaecology* (September 1981)

2 *Prima* Baby Magazine 2002

3 *The Experience of Childbirth*, by Sheila Kitzinger (Penguin, 1984)

4 'Labour and Sexuality', by Meg Southern in *ARM Midwifery Matters* (Summer 1994)

5 *Maternity: Letters from Working Women*

6 *A Lasting Relationship: Parents and Children Over Three Centuries*

7 *Health After Childbirth*

8 Barrett G., Victor C. R., Postnatal Sexual Health, *BMJ* 1994;309

9 *Is There Sex After Childbirth?*, by Juliet Rix (Thorsons, 1995)

10 'Sexual Behaviour of Lactating Women', by Elizabeth Alder and John Bancroft in *Journal of Reproductive and Infant Psychology* (1983: 1)

11 'Sexuality and Lactation', by T. Hakansson in *International Journal of Prenatal and Perinatal Studies* (Vol. 4, 1992)

12 *The Prospect Before Her*

13 Quoted in *A Labour of Love*

14 'Maternal Sexuality During First Pregnancy and After Childbirth'

15 'Heavy Weather', from *Dear George and other Stories*, by Helen Simpson (Heinemann, 1995)

16 *Women Who Sexually Abuse Children*, by Jacqui Saradjian (John Wiley and Sons, 1996)

17 *Women as Mothers*, by Sheila Kitzinger (Fontana, 1978)

18 *The Sexual Relationship: An Object Relations View of Sex and the Family*, by David E. Scharff (Routledge, 1982)

9. Friends and the Outside World

1 *Life on a Low Income*

2 *A Labour of Love*

3 *Centuries of Childhood*, by Philippe Aries (Pimlico, 1996)

4 *Round About a Pound a Week*

10. Family Life

1 *Fruitful*

2 *The Rise and Fall of the British Nanny*, by Jonathan Gathorne Hardy (Hodder & Stoughton, 1972)

3 *Beyond the Myths: Mother–Daughter Relationships in Psychology, History, Literature and Everyday Life*, by Shelley Phillips (Penguin, 1991)

4 *Having a First Baby: Experiences in 1951 and 1985 Compared*, by Barbara Thompson, C. Fraser, A. Hewitt and D. Skipper (Aberdeen University Press, 1989)

5 *Torn in Two*

6 *Hidden Lives*, by Margaret Forster (Penguin, 1996)

7 *The Child, the Family and the Outside World*

8 *Childhood and Society*, by Erik Erikson (Vintage, 1995)

9 *Fatherhood*, edited by Peter Howarth (Gollancz, 1997)

10 *The Squire*
11 *Working Class Childhood: An Oral History,* by Jeremy Seabrook (Gollancz, 1982)
12 *Effective Care in Pregnancy and Childbirth*
13 *Fruitful*

Appendix I: Common Health Problems After Childbirth

1 From *Birth* (Vol. 19, no. 4, December 1992)
2 *Health After Childbirth*
3 Ibid.
4 Ibid.

Further Reading

(Books listed under Notes are not duplicated here)

Health

A Guide to Effective Care in Pregnancy and Childbirth, by Murray Enkin, Marc J. N. C. Keirse, Mary Renfrew and James Neilson (Oxford University Press, 1995)

Losing Weight After a Pregnancy, by Elizabeth Bing and Libby Colman (Piatkus, 1995)

Teaching Physical Skills for the Childbearing Year, by Eileen Brayshaw and Pauline Wright (Books for Midwives, 1994)

Caring for Your Pelvic Floor (National Childbirth Trust, 1988)

Pain and its Relief in Childbirth

The results of a national survey conducted by the National Childbirth Trust, edited by Geoffrey Chamberlain, Ann Wraight and Philip Steer (Churchill Livingstone, 1993)

Rebounding from Childbirth, by Lynn Madsen (Bergin and Garvey, 1994)

Post-Natal Care

A research-based approach, edited by Jo Alexander, Valerie Levy, Sarah Roch (Macmillan, 1990)

The Perineum in Childbirth

A survey conducted by the National Childbirth Trust, edited by Sandy Oliver (1993)

Midwives, Research and Childbirth, edited by Sarah Robinson and Ann M. Thomson (Chapman and Hall, 1991)

Childbirth Unmasked, by Margaret Jowitt (Peter Wooller, 1993)

The Year After Childbirth, by Sheila Kitzinger (Oxford University Press, 1994)

Myles Textbook for Midwives (Churchill Livingstone, 1981)

Endocrinology and Physiology of Reproduction, edited by P. C. K. Leung (Plenum Press, 1987)

Physiology of Childbirth, by Linda K. Brown (Distance Learning Centre, South Bank Polytechnic, 1990)

Raging Hormones, by Gail Vines (Virago, 1993)

The Physiology of Human Pregnancy, by Frank E. Hytten and Isabella Leitch (Blackwell, 1971)

The Caesarean Experience, by Sarah Clement (Pandora Press, 1995)

Women Writing Childbirth: Modern Discourses of Motherhood, by Tess Cosslett (Manchester University Press, 1994)

The New Pregnancy and Childbirth, by Sheila Kitzinger (Penguin, 1989)

Pregnancy for Older Women: Assessing the Medical Risks, by Phyllis Kernoff Mansfield (Praegar, 1986)

What Every Pregnant Woman Should Know: The Truth about Diet and Drugs in Pregnancy, by Gail Sforza Brewer (Penguin, 1985)

While You Are Pregnant: Safe Eating and How to Avoid Infection from Food and Animals (Department of Health, 1991)

Nutrition in Mother and Child Health, by G. J. Ebrahim (Macmillan, 1983)

The Better Pregnancy Diet, by Liz and Patrick Holford (Ebury Press, 1987)

Nutrition and Metabolism in Pregnancy – Mothers and Foetus, by Pedro Rosso (Oxford University Press, 1990)

Regaining Bladder Control, by Eileen Montgomery (Clinical Press, 1989)

Incontinence: A Critical Review of the Literature and Current Initiatives, by Patricia M. Rivers (thesis, University of Surrey, 1986)

What Every Woman Needs to Know: Facts and Fears about Pregnancy, Childbirth and Womanhood, edited by Penny Junor (Century, 1988)

Health and Society in Twentieth Century Britain, by Helen Jones (Longman, 1994)

Adjusting

Crying for Help: How to Cure your Baby of Colic, by Carol Young (Thorsons, 1986)

Cry Baby: How to Cope, by Pat Gray (Wisebury, 1987)

Crying and Babies: Helping Families Cope, by John Kirkland (Croom Helm, 1984)

Life After Birth: Everywoman's Guide to the First Year of Motherhood, by Wendy Blumfield (Element Books, 1992)

On Being a Mother, by M. G. Boulton (Tavistock, 1993)

The Captive Wife, by Helen Gavron (Routledge and Kegan Paul, 1984)

Balancing Acts: On Being a Mother, by Katherine Gieve (Virago, 1989)

Mad to be a Mother: Is There Life After Birth for Women Today?, by Brigid McConville (Century, 1987)

From Here to Maternity, by Ann Oakley (Penguin, 1970)

Motherhood: What it Does to Your Mind, by Jane Price (Pandora Press, 1988)

How Not to be a Perfect Mother, by Libby Purves (Fontana, 1987)

From Here to Maternity: Confessions of a First-time Mother, by Carol Weston (Little, Brown, 1991)

Birth and Beyond, by Betty Williams (Boxtree, 1994)

Psychological Aspects of Pregnancy, Birthing and Bonding, by Barbara L. Blum (Human Sciences Press, 1980)

Talking with Mothers, by Dana Breen (Jill Norman, 1981)

Motherhood and Mental Illness, 2nd Edition, by R. Kuma and I. F. Brockington (Wright, 1988)

Motherhood and Personality: Psychosomatic Aspects of Childbirth, by L. Chertkok (Tavistock, 1969)

The Psychology of Birth, by L. Feher (Souvenir Press, 1980)

Coping With Postnatal Depression, by Fiona Marshall (Sheldon Press, 1993)

On Birth and Madness, by Eric Rhode (Duckworth, 1987)

Banish Post-Baby Blues, by Anne-Marie Sapstead (Thorsons, 1990)

Mother Courage: Letters from Mothers Living in Poverty at the End of the Century, edited by Christine Gowdridge, A. Susan Williams and Margaret Wynn (Penguin, 1997)

Parenting in the 1990s, by Elsa Ferri and Kate Smith (Joseph Rowntree Foundation, 1996)

Becoming a Family, by Anna McGrail (National Childbirth Trust, 1996)

Mothering Psychoanalysis, by Janet Sayers (Penguin, 1995)

The Stress Factor, by Dr H. E. Stanton (Optima, 1983)

Women and Children First, edited by Valerie Fildes, Lara Marks and Hilary Marland (Routledge, 1992)

Realities in Childbearing (2nd edition), by Mary Lou Moore (W. B. Saunders Company, 1983)

Birth Tides, by Marie O'Connor (Pandora Press, 1995)

The Science of Women: Gynaecology and Gender in England 1800–1929, by Ornella Moscucci (Cambridge University Press, 1990)

Eve Since Eve: Personal Reflections on Childbirth, by Nancy Caldwell Sorel (Oxford University Press, 1984)

Work

Managing Mothers: Dual Earner Households after Maternity Leave, by Julia Brannen and Peter Moss (Unwin, 1991)

Working Mothers: You, Your Career and Your Child, by Carol Dix (Unwin, 1989)

Women in Britain Since 1945: Women, Family, Work and the State in the Post-War Years, by Jane Lewis (Blackwell, 1992)

Women, the Law and the Workplace (Labour Research Department, 1993)

Work and Home: Finding the Balance, by Teresa Wilson (National Childbirth Trust, 1996)

Mothers at Work – How Real Women Successfully Combine a Career and Family, by Melanie Hart (Michael O'Mara Books, 1997)

Children and Day Care: Lessons From Research, by Ellis Hennessy, Sue Martin, Peter Moss and Edward Melhuish (Paul Chapman Publishing, 1992)

Emotions

Attachment and Loss, Vol. 1, by John Bowlby (Penguin, 1984)

The Making and Breaking of Affectional Bonds, by John Bowlby (Tavistock, 1979)

Childcare and the Growth of Love, by John Bowlby (Penguin, 1979)

Parent-Infant Attachment in Premature Infants, by J. A. Davis, M. P. M. Richards and N. R. C. Robertson (Croom Helm, 1983)

Mother-Infant Bonding: Scientific Fiction, by Diane E. Eyer (Yale University Press, 1993)

Babies, Breasfeeding and Bonding, by Ina May Gaskin (Bergin and Garvey, 1987)

Bonding: The Beginnings of Parent-Infant Attachment, by M. H. Klaus and J. H. Kennell (C. V. Mosby, 1983)

The First Six Months, by Penelope Leach (Fontana, 1986)

Of Human Bonding, by Alice S. Rossi and Peter H. Rossi (Aldine de Grayter, 1990)

Breaking Down the Wall of Silence to Join the Waiting Child, by Alice Miller (Virago, 1991)

The Drama of Being a Child, by Alice Miller (Virago, 1987)

For Your Own Good: The Roots of Violence in Childrearing, by Alice Miller (Virago, 1987)

Gender, Sex and Subordination in England 1500–1800, by Anthony Fletcher (Yale University Press, 1995)

Sibling Without Rivalry: How to Help Your Chiidren Live Together, by Adele Faber and Elaine Mazlaish (Sidgwick and Jackson, 1988)

The Developing Relationship Between a Mother and Her Unborn Child, by Helen Crafter (MSc thesis, University of London, 1991)

The Heart of Parenting, by John Gottman with Joan Declare (Bloomsbury, 1997)

He Hit Me First: When Brothers and Sisters Fight, by Louise Bates Ames (Alington, 1988)

When a Baby Dies: The Experience of Late Miscarriage, Stillbirth and Neonatal Death, by Nancy Kohner (Grafton, 1991)

Exhaustion

Solve Your Child's Sleep Problems, by Richard Ferber (Dorling Kindersley, 1986)

Sleepless Children, by David Haslam (Futura, 1985)

Silent Nights for You and Your Baby, by Jane Asher (Pelham, 1984)

Sex

Sexuality and Motherhood, by Irene Walton (Books for Midwives Press, 1994)

Sex During Pregnancy and After Childbirth, by Sylvia Close (Thorsons, 1984)

Women's Experience of Sex, by Sheila Kitzinger (Penguin, 1983)

Human Sexuality, by Z. Luria (Wiley, 1986)

Sex in Pregnancy and After Childbirth (National Childbirth Trust, 1988)

Water and Sexuality, by Michel Odent (Arkana, 1990)

Fatherhood

How Fathers Care for the Next Generation: A Four-Decade Study, by J. Snarey (Harvard University Press, 1993)

Parenthood Preparation for Men: Some Experiences and Expectations, by E. O. Paden (MSc thesis, University of Surrey, 1994)

Marriage: The Definitive Guide to What Makes a Marriage Work, by Jack Dominion (Heinemann, 1995)

Journey Through Single Parenting, by Jill Worth with Christine Tufnell (Hodder & Stoughton, 1997)

Beginner's Guide to Fatherhood: How to Cope with Life Before, During and After Birth, by Colin Bowles (Fontana, 1992)

The Essential Father, by Tony Bradman (Unwin, 1985)

Fatherhood: Men Writing About Fatherhood, by Sean French (Virago, 1992)

The Expectant Father, by Betty Parsons (Elliot Right Way Books, 1994)

Family Life

Family Life in Western Societies: A Historical Sociology of Family Relationships in Britain and North America, by J. E. Goldthorpe (Cambridge University Press, 1987)

Inside the Family: Changing Roles of Men and Women, by M. Henwood, L. Rimmer and M. Wicks (Family Policy Studies Centre, 1987)

Transition to Parenthood: How Infants Change Families, by R. Larossa and M. M. Larossa (Sage, 1987)

Families: What Makes Them Work?, by D. H. Olsen et al. (Sage, 1983)

Explorations With Families: Group Analysis and Family Therapy, by Robin Skynner (Methuen, 1987)

Index